Mayfield Publishing Company

ISSUES IN PHYSICAL EDUCATION AND SPORTS

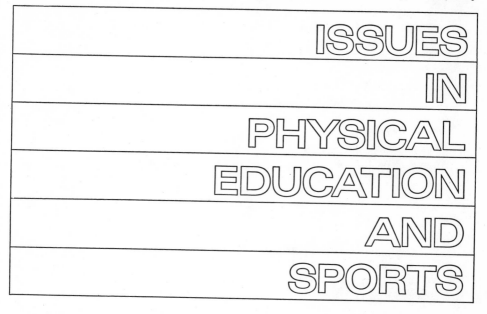

Compiled and edited by *George H. McGlynn*

UNIVERSITY OF SAN FRANCISCO

Library of Congress Catalog Card Number: 73-91388
International Standard Book Numbers: 0-87484-238-7 (paper)
0-87484-239-5 (cloth)

Manufactured in the United States of America
Mayfield Publishing Company, 285 Hamilton Avenue, Palo Alto, California 94301

This book was set in Elegante by Applied Typographic Systems and was printed and bound
by George Banta Company. Sponsoring editor was Richard W. Bare. The production editor
was Linda Brubaker and Michelle Hogan supervised production. The book and cover were
designed by Nancy Sears.

Contents

iii

Contents

4 CULTURAL

Preface

This anthology presents a diverse selection of original essays that reflect the complex problems confronting physical education programs today. Also included are a number of articles which present new and innovative ideas, along with suggestions for future change in physical education.

The book is organized in four main sections: psychological bases, physiological bases, curriculum, and cultural aspects. The editor has attempted to bring together contributions from authorities in these fields who discuss the issues or problems that they feel are paramount. The reader will find that some articles utilize a scholarly approach, while others may be considered polemic in nature. Many of the ideas presented in the book may conflict with those of the reader, others may be completely acceptable to him. While these essays do *not* attempt to provide complete answers to current problems, nor to vilify or condone present methods, I trust they will contribute new insights and lead to productive thought.

Our contemporary age has to its credit a sense of possibility and openness to experiment. Hopefully, this attitude will be stimulated by the essays in this book. It is essential that we continually re-evaluate, criticize, reflect on, and justify our methods and objectives; otherwise our physical education programs will be doomed to apathy, passive resistance, and eventually complete disregard.

I would like to express my appreciation to the authors who so graciously contributed to this book. Appreciation is also extended to Vivienne Rowe, whose assistance in the correspondence and the organization of the manuscripts has been invaluable.

George H. McGlynn
University of San Francisco

Issues in physical education and sports

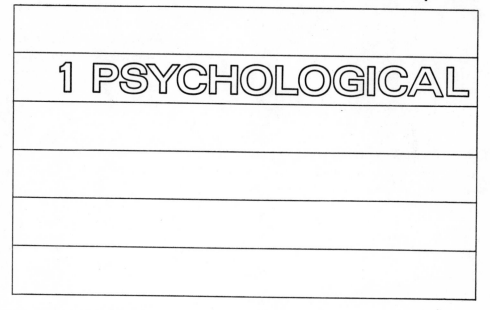

1 PSYCHOLOGICAL

The humanistic education movement: some questions

*Daryl L. Siedentop**

The Ohio State University

Several years ago, during a break between sessions at a motor learning symposium, a fellow participant and I were getting acquainted over a cup of coffee. In the course of the conversation, she asked about the nature of my work. I replied that my approach was Skinnerian; when I asked about her interests, she declared that her orientation was humanistic. We chatted on quite amiably until the next session began, but later I began to ponder what exactly my new friend had meant by the humanistic approach. I had heard, read, and used the term frequently and knew the territory so to speak, having had an intellectual affair with Rollo May,

*I would like to express my appreciation to my colleague Barbara Nelson for lending me her humanistic expertise in preparing this paper.

Abraham Maslow, and Carl Rogers during my graduate school days, but I could not delineate clearly what it meant to be an advocate of humanistic education.

During recent years, the humanistic movement in education has generated a great deal of activity and developed a considerable literature. It is also clearly making inroads into the theory and practice of physical education. Warren Fraleigh's (1969) basic instruction experiment at San Jose State College seems clearly within the parameters of the movement. Numerous investigations using self-concept and body image measures have appeared in the research literature. Other hints of the movement can be found in calls for enhancing the "physical-me" of children (Varnes, 1970), "physical self-awareness" (Schmidt, 1970), and the "open gym" (Millan, 1972). Barry Pelton (1972), in a recent examination of graduate education, called for a commitment to sharing "selfhood," and Stratton Caldwell (1972) has sounded the humanistic trumpet loud and clear:

> The emergence of a physical education in accord with the direction of third force psychology, humanistic in orientation and design, would be characterized by a thrust toward the ultimate goal of educational experiences, the human goal, the "self-actualization" of humanness and human fulfillment in the here and now.

It seems probable that the humanistic influence will increase in the immediate future, and it therefore seems an appropriate time to examine some of the assumptions of the movement, to bring out some of the key concepts, and to discuss the implications of a humanistic physical education.

The humanistic movement in education has its roots in the "third force" psychology that has emerged in recent years as an alternative to and reaction against the Freudian and behavioristic models. Among the more prominent groups under the humanist umbrella are Adlerians, Rankians, Jungians, organismic psychologists, personality psychologists, gestaltists, and phenomenological psychologists. Many subgroups are subsumed under the labels of growth psychologies or humanistic psychologies. Prominent figures in this movement include Kurt Goldstein, Kurt Lewin, Gordon Allport, H. A. Murray, Fritz Perls and Rollo May. The two men who have given the movement its strongest leadership are Carl Rogers and the late Abraham Maslow. Among the many who have supported the extension of this movement to education are Jonathan Kozol, Harold Lyon, Gerald Weinstein, Mario Fantini, Terry Borton, George Leonard, Masha Rudman and George Brown.

The goals of humanistic education are not always easy to uncover. Maslow (1971) describes it as the self-actualization of the individual, that is, helping

The humanistic education
movement: some questions
Daryl L. Siedentop

a person to reach his own highest level of development. Rogers (1969, 1971) talks about psychological maturity and inner freedom, and aims for a fully functioning person. Weinstein and Fantini (1970) postulate educational objectives resting on a personal and interpersonal base and dealing with students' concerns. Lyon (1971) says quite simply that humanistic education is the integration of cognitive learning with affective learning. Although much emphasis is given to the affective aspects of experience, these tend to blur as one attempts to define them. McMurrin (1967) characterizes affective education as dealing with the emotions, passions, dispositions, motives, and concerns of students as well as to their moral and esthetic sensibilities, sympathies, and appreciations. Bloom (1956) describes the affective domain as including interests, attitudes, values, appreciations, and adjustments.

The techniques of third force psychology and humanistic education are many and varied. From actualism and *aikido* to *yoga* and *zen*, with stops along the way for some movement exploration, *I Ching*, natural foods, parapsychology, and SUBUD. In educational contexts, one is more likely to find sensitivity training, encounter groups, guided fantasy, creativity training, role playing, psychodrama, various kinds of homemade games, and many different movement-oriented tasks.

During its infancy there was a tendency to ridicule much of what the human potential movement was doing, but many of the laughs have faded away. Humanistic psychology is now Division 32 of the American Psychological Association, and is on its way to becoming what most of its pioneer workers always intended it to be, a discipline. The less serious aberrations have tended to fall by the wayside: while nude marathon groups have not yet gained general acceptance, T-groups are as common as the weekly Lions Club meeting.

THE CONCEPT OF SELF

Central to the humanistic approach is the concept of self. A brief examination of this concept is crucial because much of what follows hinges upon how the concept is defined. For example, when Pelton (1972) talks about physical education graduate students developing their "unique potential" and sharing their "selfhood," it becomes important to have some clear idea of what "self" means. Likewise, when Caldwell (1972) suggests that physical education can facilitate the development of "self-identity, self-acceptance,

5

self-direction, self-esteem, and self-actualization," one can evaluate such sloganeering only when one has some firm idea of what the too often elusive self is intended to mean.

An analysis of what the humanist means when he uses the term "self" reveals quickly the lack of any substantive conceptual commonalities within third force psychology. In an educational context it is perhaps most profitable to examine this issue in terms of the degree to which the self is learned. From this point of view several representative positions can be identified and placed on a continuum from a self that is unlearned or given to a self that is learned and can, therefore, be taught, including: 1) A given self that is unmodifiable, different from, and in opposition to the conditioned mind; 2) A biologically determined self that is mostly unmodifiable, fragile, and capable of being submerged under learned patterns of behavior; 3) An inner, cognitive-perceptual self that is modifiable and innately strives toward congruence with the experienced world; 4) An inner self that is primarily learned, affective in nature, modifiable, and is a primary determinant of overt behavior.

The first of these positions is basically that described by Kent and Nicholls (1972), although it is representative of those in the humanistic movement who start from a spiritual view of man. The self is by definition good, somewhat mystically conceived, and not necessarily genetically transferred. It is unmodifiable and can be discovered ("uncovered" is the more proper term) by breaking through the conditioned mind. Since the mind is environmentally determined, this position posits a new dualism, that between mind and self.

> The mind is a function of the brain. All it does is to fulfill a program imposed on it very early in life but capable of modification by sufficiently decisive intervention from outside. Not, however, from inside, it appears (Kent and Nicholls, 1972, p. 50).

The self is the "real" person, and the person in each of us is not separate but one with other persons, implying a common humanity and a source of meaning and values. There is much to suggest that this position represents a modern version of the concept of the soul.

The second position is that proposed by Abraham Maslow (1962-1971), generally considered to be the spokesman for third force psychology. From Maslow's point of view the self is biological in nature (therefore genetically transferable and somewhat unmodifiable), inherently good, yet delicate and easily overcome by environmentally imposed processes. Maslow says that the self is not intrinsically evil, but is either neutral or intrinsically good.

6

**The humanistic education
movement: some questions**

Daryl L. Siedentop

However, his entire psychological system is understandable only when an intrinsically good self is assumed. Despite his statements, self-actualization makes no sense when starting from a biologically neutral self. Self-actualization is gaining full knowledge of and acceptance of this intrinsic nature and overcoming the environmentally imposed patterns. As in the first position, gaining selfhood is seen as a "bringing out" or "uncovering" of the intrinsic self. Maslow sees this intrinsic self as having a positive growth function and interprets concepts such as illness, conscience, and guilt in terms of patterns which compromise the intrinsic growth tendencies of the self.

The third approach, representative of the Rogerian influence, defines the self as the pattern of perceptions that a person holds about himself. The basic division here seems to be between an outer self, the behavior of a person as viewed by others, and an inner self, the self as viewed by the person. This particular point on the continuum is perhaps the most difficult to sort out. Rogers (Rogers and Stevens, 1971) plainly subscribes to a deterministic position in what he calls the "psychological universe of cause and effect." The inner self is formed primarily on the basis of interaction with the environment (Rogers, 1961), and is capable of growth and modification. Although there is not an open postulation of basic goodness, there is a construct (the "actualizing tendency") which suggests an innate drive toward congruence between the inner self and experience. Rogers talks about "psychological maturity" in which the inner self is set free, but the relationship between this freedom and overt behavior (which is determined) is not entirely clear.

> In the first place, the freedom which I have been trying to describe is essentially an inner thing, something which exists in the living person, quite aside from any of the outward choice of alternatives which we so often think of as constituting freedom. . . . Freedom, rightly understood, is a fulfillment, by the person, of the ordered sequence of his life (Rogers and Stevens, 1971, pp. 45,46).

There is more than a little mysticism in such a position, and, at best, it provides only a fuzzy basis from which to develop strategies for achieving the goals of a humanistic education.

The fourth position is farthest from any given or biologically determined self and closest to a self that is primarily learned on the basis of interaction with the environment, thus approaching a behavioristic position. Here the

7

self is a cognitive-affective mixture with primary emphasis on the affective. The self is an affective internalization of the person's interaction with the environment and it is modifiable. The affective self directs and controls overt behavior (Weinstein and Fantini, 1971). There is some implication in this position of intrinsic needs and drives, such as the need for a positive self-concept, but the primary emphasis is on an affective self that is learned. The degree to which the view approaches a behavioristic position is suggested when Weinstein and Fantini (1971), in their objectives for identity education, say that each child should "realize that his personality is a composite of many kinds of behavior, and that these behaviors are determined" (Weinstein and Fantini, 1970, p. 69). Whereas in the first position discussed the emphasis was on an "uncovering" of the self, here the emphasis has shifted decidedly to a learned self.

There is another position that could be included within the general humanistic field, that of the European existentialists, such as Sartre. These thinkers do not assume any given self, biologically determined self, or learned self. They stress the willing or self-making of the self, and, therefore, do not fit on the above continuum. Moreover, they have not had a significant influence on the humanistic education movement.

SOME BASIC CRITICISMS

The obvious shortcomings of the humanistic movement can be briefly reviewed by citing some of the healthy self-criticism within the movement. Reaction against the misuse and potentially dangerous side effects of certain human potential methods has been quick to arise.

> There is no reason to doubt that the most skilled practitioners in the movement can bring about such results (peak experiences) for many people. But there is considerable doubt as to whether such effects bring about any lasting change in those who experience them. More seriously, the groups have many potentially dangerous side-effects, and it is questionable whether the value of their claimed results is sufficient to justify taking these risks (Kent and Nicholls, 1972, p.13).

One easily conjures up a vision of well intended, but inadequately trained "humanists" fooling around with the psychological lives of week-end adventurers who may be seeking only to expand their awareness, when they may really be in need of professional help. The major objections to the misuse of some of these methods takes three forms (Kent and Nicholls, 1972). First, there are ethical objections to the failure of group leaders to assume the kind

**The humanistic education
movement: some questions**

Daryl L. Siedentop

of professional responsibility for participants that a psychiatrist or psychologist assumes for the patient. A second objection is to the lack of a research
base of any kind, which is reflected in the scarcity of usable data and the
lack of machinery for its validation. A third objection is to the lack of standards for group leaders, who may be unqualified to deal with psychiatric
emergencies. Indeed, some people seem to have felt that attending one sensitivity training workshop qualifies them to conduct another one. There is
also the question of the relationships between the participants in humanistic
group work. Traditionally, in psychiatrically oriented groups, members have
not become involved with one another outside the group and have maintained a confidential attitude about the entire situation. Such is not always
the case within the human potential movement.

Self-criticism has also been generated within the educational wings of
the movement. Jonathan Kozol (1972) has recently declared that many "free
schools" fail simply because they do not teach fundamental skills. Free
school leaders may choose self-actualization as an educational objective
for children who may want or need something else.

> Leather and wheat germ may do the trick on somebody's radical estate
> 10 miles east of Santa Barbara or 16 miles south of Santa Fe but it does
> very little good on Blue Hill Avenue in Boston on a Sunday night when
> a man's pocket is empty and his child has a fever and the buses have
> stopped running (Kozol, 1972, p. 114).

But those aspects of the movement toward which these criticisms are directed are already being remedied, thereby strengthening the movement and
making it all the more important to ask some probing questions about its
theories and practices.

SOME QUESTIONS AND ALTERNATIVE POSITIONS

From an examination of the concept of self, it is clear that the basic question
is whether the self is given—either in a quasi-mystical or biological sense—
or learned. This is the important distinction and all that follows is dependent
upon it. Many of the most serious writers in humanistic psychology assume
a unitary, intrinsically good self that is given in the sense that it exists as a
potentiality within the person, regardless of the culturally and socially determined patterns of behavior that may overlie it. The first two positions on our

9

continuum clearly emanate from this view and the Rogerian position borders on it. The primary goal of education, then, becomes the emergence of the self, but one must be careful to recognize the implications of the use of the verb "emerge."

> While self-realization sounds impressive in a statement of educational theory, it is very difficult for the teacher in the classroom to decide what sort of "self" John in the first row or Jane in the second row is supposed to be realizing, and there is always danger that some preconceived notion of "self" will inhibit or retard development of the very quality that is embodied in the aim (Siedentop, 1972, p. 168).

The concept of a unitary self, whether given or learned, is basic not only to the humanistic movement, but indeed to psychology in general. However, an alternative position is gaining credibility rapidly. Learning theory argues quite persuasively that man can be better characterized as many learned selves rather than as a distinct and coherent self. In the sense that man behaves differently in different situations, he is many selves. One acts somewhat differently as a teacher in the gymnasium in the morning, as a colleague in the faculty lunchroom at noon, as a coach with an athletic team after school, and as a parent with the family in the evening. Each of the roles played reveals a different self and each is adopted for effective functioning within a particular environment. This suggestion of multiple identity (Gergen, 1972) has always been considered harmful. However, it may be desirable for an individual to wear many masks, and to be open to the possibilities for new roles and identities.

The above analysis reveals a dichotomy between the view of self as an intrinsic potentiality which needs to be realized or uncovered and the view of self as a learned set of experiences that can be modified. These views have different implications for education and at many points are irreconcilable.

The emphasis on *realizing* the self can be characterized as a therapeutic view of education.* Only in the fourth position on the continuum does one find a view of Self that would result in planned learning experiences to *develop* the Self. The first positions are very clearly therapeutic in nature and the third, while less clear conceptually, is much closer to therapy than to

---

*I recognize the potential difficulty of differentiating between a therapeutic (uncovering) and educational (learning) role for the schools. There are important therapeutic techniques based entirely on learning theory, while many in the humanistic movement would suggest that the uncovering process is a learning of self. Nevertheless, the differentiation is useful here in that it helps clarify some basic differences.

**The humanistic education
movement: some questions**

Daryl L. Siedentop

education (in the sense of a set of planned learning experiences designed to develop behaviors that do not now exist). Since the third position is representative of the Rogerian influence its application would obviously be non-directive and student-centered. Rogers has said that the " 'best' of education would produce a person very similar to the one produced by the 'best' of therapy" (Rogers, 1969, p. 279). Rogers (Rogers and Stevens, 1971) cites A. S. Neill's Summerhill as the prototype for a humanistic education, and, as Neill and many others have pointed out, the Summerhillian model developed from the assumption that it would primarily serve emotionally disturbed children. It is meant to be a therapeutic environment.

This tension between a therapeutic and educational role for the schools deserves serious consideration. Its reflection can be seen in Kozol's previously cited statement about free schools that do not teach fundamental skills. It can be seen in the inordinate use of "rap sessions" to share experiences. If based on a Summerhillian model it no doubt will achieve some of its objectives, for example, certain kinds of affective stability and self control. However, one should also recognize the possibility that it might produce what Skidelsky (1969) has so appropriately labeled "well-adjusted mediocrity." Skidelsky's analysis of Summerhill is well taken at this point:

> In practice, of course, no parents send their children to a school like Summerhill to get a good education in the conventional sense. They send them there to be "sorted out" emotionally, and then whisk them off to "proper" schools where they may learn something (Skidelsky, 1969, p. 29).

Corresponding to the therapeutic-educational issue is the question of the degree to which one views the child as intrinsically self-educating. Those advocating the view of an intrinsic self tend to see the child as self-educating. That is, he learns best if left alone to pursue his own interests, with the teacher neither pushing nor pulling, but standing as a resource person (therapist?), on the sidelines. The opposite view, of course, results in a set of planned learning experiences that may be rigid, as in traditional forms of education, or may appear unplanned, as in the British "open classroom" or in many "behavior analysis" classrooms. The point is not whether the planning is visible, but whether it does or does not exist.

The self-educating view can be seen clearly in the free school movement and particularly well in George Leonard's (1968) advocacy of free learning, **11** that a child should be able to go anywhere in the school and do anything, as long as he does no harm to himself or others. Maslow (1971) describes the ideal school as having no grades, no credits, no degrees, no required courses; students are instead free to pursue whatever they choose to pursue in their own ways. The implication seems to be that any controls, overt or covert, are improper. Rogers (1969) suggests that students must be permitted the opportunity to choose their own path in learning. It is important to understand that these methodological suggestions are consistent with their view of self, that the actualizing tendency, if left free to operate, will through trial and error create a responsible, creative, vigorous individual who will achieve inner freedom, psychological maturity, and self-actualization. The alternative to voluntarism is a progression of planned learning experiences to *develop* the self (or selves) and to *teach* the student to be self-educating. From the behaviorist point of view voluntarism is at best a dubious proposition totally dependent upon the behaviors brought to the situation by the learner, or by contingencies imposed from outside the immediate educational environment. For example, when children at Summerhill suddenly begin to learn at rapid rates it is due more to the pressure imposed by the 0-level exams than to an emerging self. Likewise, when it is assumed that children will learn to read when they want or need to, it may be that that time never does come (Powers, 1971).

The next step is to inquire about the skills necessary for a humanistic educator. Should the emphasis be greater on therapeutic skills than on educational skills in the traditional sense? The objectives for humanistic teacher education would appear to be different than those normally postulated, that is, good command of subject matter and methodology. Rogers (Rogers and Stevens, 1971) has suggested that the important characteristics of the humanistic teacher are trust in organism, realness, acceptance, empathy, and resource provision. It is instructive that the first four of these are identical to his characterization of the skills necessary for successful therapy. The emphasis would seem to be on relaxed, informal relationships in which teachers—a term which begins to seem an improper label for this function—avoid an authority role. Teachers would be selected more for their social and therapeutic qualities rather than what they know or how they can teach. The implications for teacher training programs are considerable.

As mentioned earlier humanistic movement in education places great emphasis on the affective domain. Sometimes this is taken to mean emotional development and maturity, while at other times "affective" is seen more as interests and attitudes. Most of the humanistic movement pays its

**The humanistic education
movement: some questions**

Daryl L. Siedentop

due to what is generally referred to as the cognitive aspects of education, but the emphasis on these skills lessens considerably once one scratches its rhetorical surface. In the first view of self on our continuum, the attack on acquisition of knowledge borders on serious anti-intellectualism. In the third view, lip service is paid to cognitive skills, but Weinstein and Fantini (1970, p. 26) maintain that "cognition makes scant contribution to the broader behavioral goals of education."

One might suspect that an analogous situation will develop in humanistic efforts in physical education. The development of skill in sport and dance will remain an objective, but less and less attention will be paid to it as physical educators shift their focus to the affective aspects of activity. Less time will be spent in actually practicing the skills and more time will be spent in introspection, discussion, and other group-oriented techniques associated with humanistic educational methodology.

Certain aspects of the humanistic education movement have been examined in order to raise some questions of basic importance. Needless to say, the major positions within the movement are considerably more complex than presented here. However, this degree of simplification does show that the field comprises different views of the self, and that these views imply methodologies that, although they appear to be similar, are working toward dissimilar ends. Awareness groups, for example, could be used to uncover the real self, to learn a new perception of self, or simply to learn some new behaviors that allow more satisfactory participation in groups.

In summary, let me reiterate some of the questions that should be considered in new efforts to create a humanistic physical education:

Is the self given or learned?

Is the self intrinsically good?

Is there a unitary self or is man better characterized as a group of selves?

Is humanistic education an uncovering process or a building-up process?

Is the child intrinsically self-educating, or does he need a set of planned experiences in order to learn to be self-educating?

Should the emphasis in the selection and preparation of humanistic educators be on therapeutic or educational skills?

Are major objectives and efforts primarily in the affective or the motor domain?

13

When humanistically oriented physical educators take a position on these issues, we will all have a much clearer view of their basic assumptions and goals.

REFERENCES

Bloom, Benjamin S., ed. *Taxonomy of Educational Objectives*. New York: David McKay, 1956.

Caldwell, Stratton. "Toward a Humanistic Physical Education." *JOPHER* 43(1972):31–32.

Fraleigh, Warren. "An Instructional Experiment in Actualizing the Meaning of Man as a Moving Being." *JOPHER* 40(1969):53–58.

Gergen, Kenneth. "Multiple Identity." *Psychology Today* 5(1972):31–35. May, 1972.

Kent, Ian, and Nicholls, William. *I AMness: The Discovery of Self Beyond Ego*. Indianapolis: Bobbs-Merrill, 1972.

Kozol, Jonathan. "Free Schools Fail because They Don't Teach." *Psychology Today* 5(1972):30.

Lyon, Harold. *Learning to Feel—Feeling to Learn*. Columbus: Charles E. Merrill, 1971.

Leonard, George. *Education and Ecstasy*. New York: Delacorte Press, 1968.

Maslow, Abraham. *Toward a Psychology of Being*. Princeton: Van Nostrand, 1962.

Maslow, Abraham. *The Farther Reaches of Human Nature*. New York: Viking Press, 1971.

McMurrin, Sterling. "What Tasks for the Schools." *Saturday Review*, 14 January 1971.

Millan, Anne. "An Open Gym." *JOPHER*, May 1972.

Pelton, Barry. "The Right Questions to Ask about Graduate Education." *JOPHER*, May 1972.

Powers, Thomas. *The Making of a Terrorist*. New York: Houghton Mifflin, 1971.

Rogers, Carl. *On Becoming a Person*. Boston: Houghton Mifflin, 1961.

Rogers, Carl. *Freedom to Learn*, Columbus: Charles E. Merrill, 1969.

Rogers, Carl, and Stevens, Barry, *Person to Person*. New York: Pocket Books, 1971.

Schmidt, Charles. "A Personal Philosophy of Physical Education." *JOPHER* 41(1970):24–30.

Siedentop, Daryl. *Physical Education: Introductory Analysis*. Dubuque: Wm. C. Brown, 1972.

Skidelsky, Robert. *English Progressive Schools*. Baltimore: Penguin Books, 1969.

Varnes, Paul. "A Personal Philosophy of Physical Education." *JOPHER* 41(1970):24–30.

Weinstein, Gerald, and Fantini, Mario. *Toward Humanistic Education: A Curriculum of Affect*. New York: Praeger, 1971.

Reassessment of the value of competition

Hollis F. Fait
University of Connecticut

John E. Billing
University of Connecticut

If traditional physical education and athletic programs have one vital element, it is certainly competition. Competition is used to motivate the learning of motor skills and to increase physical fitness; it is used to create learning situations purportedly conducive to the development of desirable behavior. The values that accrue to participants in competitive sports have been described and, in some instances, documented by numerous writers. However, the subjects of these studies and articles were almost exclusively successful competitors. Although some writers have criticized the detrimental effects of competition on inter-personal relationships and the disproportionate physical injury that results from some forms of competitive play, few have analyzed and recorded the effects of competitive sports on those who are *not*

15

successful. Now that a growing number of young people are challenging the competitive ethic, it seems appropriate for the profession to examine the effects of competition upon the losers and to determine possible new directions for physical education.

Competition has been defined by Slusher (1967) as a "contention of interests," that is, it is a rivalry between opposing forces (man, animal or nature) in which the interests of both are not mutually obtainable. In sports and games, the contenders are, of course, individual players or teams who seek the same goal, to win the contest. Contention of this kind has been labeled direct competition. In contrast, competition against a record or one's own past achievements is indirect competition.

Direct competition by its very nature requires at least one competitor to fail for every one who is successful. Game theorists call this situation a "zero sum game," i.e., the sum of winners and losers is zero. In fact, most sport situations produce a negative sum game, in which the number of losers exceeds the number of winners. A zero or negative sum game is the inevitable outcome of any direct competition, but we in physical education and coaching make our own unique contribution to the creation of even larger numbers of losers. We construct elimination tournaments and plan championships at the conference, regional, sectional and finally national levels, always increasing the percentage of losers in comparison to winners. In classes we hold races, play competitive games, and conduct skill contests—all creating only one or a few winners and many losers.

Inevitably, direct competition in sports and games focuses strongly upon winning. In recent years winning has come to receive such heavy emphasis that it has obscured all other objectives. The "winning is everything" philosophy is reflected in the practice of judging all results by one criterion and in directing all effort, funds and talent to the one goal of victory. As a consequence, we are forced into, at best, a zero sum game.

Indirect competition, on the other hand, allows positive sum results. If a performance is measured against past performances, then success does not hinge upon another's failure: it is not necessary to beat someone else to be successful. It is within the realm of possibility for all to succeed, to reap the benefits of achieving. Obviously, positive sum conditions are highly desirable in an educational context.

Indirect competition should not be confused with cooperation. Competition denotes a struggle among a number of individuals to obtain values which are scarce, while cooperation can be defined as achievement of a goal that is only possible if another is also successful. In direct competition one individual or group opposes another, whereas in cooperation individuals are mutually reinforcing. Although cooperation is often cited as the antithesis of competition, this is not entirely true. In both cooperation and competition the ultimate outcome is affected by the participation of others. The success or failure of an individual in both cooperative and competitive situations relies heavily on the actions of others; their performance either enhances or detracts from the individual's success. Although indirect competition could involve cooperative effort, it is generally a self-directed endeavor that is not dependent upon the actions of others for success.

It should be noted here that competition is neither inherently good nor bad; it is simply one type of human behavior. With respect to education, it is good if it maximizes the acquisition of knowledge and skills; it is bad if it detracts from learning. If maximum development of *all* students is desired, direct competition, by its very nature, negates this goal.

Using direct competition in teaching sports and games is based on the assumption that competitive relationships are more stimulating and interesting and thus create higher motivation in students. This increased motivation, it is contended, produces rapid learning and good performances. But is this true for the habitual loser, or only for the continual winner? Have we not for too many years directed our sole attention to the winners and ignored the effects of competition upon the losers who, as we have seen, constitute at least half the participants? All physical education teachers have seen individuals who actively avoid competitive situations, who are frightened and withdraw from the challenge. Most of these are students who are not highly skilled and who have had a poor record of success. But might not the same person view his competition on the football field quite differently from competition in a mathematics class, where he has achieved success? Might his differing reactions be related to his relative competency in the two areas? Even casual observation leads to the conclusion that the effect of competition on motivation is situationally specific and reflects individual expectations of success or failure.

Rosenthal (1966) demonstrates that people make prophecies about many events and consciously or unconsciously operate to fulfill their prophecy. The concept of the self-fulfilling prophecy is well documented in psychological literature (Aronson, 1962; Lowin, 1965). Common athletic parlance reflects this phenomenon: "You must think like a winner to be a winner;" the team "was beaten mentally;" "the game was lost before the players ever went out on the field." Coaches and players are well aware of the value 17 of positive thinking and the necessity to prepare mentally for the competition.

When individuals expect to fail because of a history of past failures or because they know that only a small minority is allowed to succeed, a self-fulfilling prophecy of failure results, and in all but the rarest of instances is realized. If teachers are to help students develop the very necessary expectations of success, we must provide experiences which support a success prophecy. We must work against any situation which produces large numbers of failures and thus expectations of failure. Possibly then we can stop our unintentional, but nevertheless detrimental, division of students into winners and losers.

Another facet of the assumption that competition serves as a stimulant to the learning process is that increased motivation or anxiety increases learning and performance. The fact that heightened arousal increases strength and endurance in the performance of simple motor tasks has been well established (Oxendine, 1970). Evidence concerning complex tasks, however, appears to indicate that anxiety is detrimental to maximum performance (Oxendine, 1970; Milne, 1972). This is especially true in tasks requiring intellect (Hussman, 1969). Here we must distinguish between learning and performance. Performance is short-term in nature, fluctuating from time to time, subject to many variables. Learning is a more permanent change in behavior resulting from practice or experience, furthering the development of current capacities.

In education the major concern is learning. Since anxiety correlates negatively with superior learning performances (Martens, 1969; Oxendine, 1970), the conclusion must be that competition, with its concomitant anxiety produced by inherent success and failure, is not a useful adjunct to learning. We need instead a situation with the least possible amount of anxiety, in order to produce students who are free to question, try, experiment and gamble with little fear of failure. But such situations do not seem to exist in our schools today. Holt (1964) claims that most children are scared most of the time in school. He is convinced they fail because they are afraid, bored, and confused. They are afraid, above all else, of failing. When physical educators use direct competition, in which significant numbers must inevitably fail, we induce many students to avoid failure rather than to seek success. For many students this is a reasonable tactic, since their chances of avoiding failure are better than their chances of succeeding. Although it might seem that a student would work hard to avoid failure, just as he does to ensure success, this is not the case. The student seeking to avoid failure never attempts anything of his own volition: he never volunteers, takes an extra trial, or ventures an idea or response to a question. In fact he may actively avoid participation, for he cannot fail if he does not attempt. Every teacher has observed many such students in both classroom and gymnasium. In the classroom they simply refuse to answer. In the gymnasium they may refuse to participate, become ill, complain of an injury, or hide in line to avoid their turn. When pressured into making an attempt, they respond with a half-hearted effort that shows the others they aren't trying, for it's not so bad to fail if you don't really try.

The effect of competition on learning, then, is to force many into behavior strategies directed at avoiding failure rather than achieving success. This is obviously detrimental to learning. As Holt (1964) further notes, "A scared fighter may be the best fighter but a scared learner is always a poor learner." By ensuring a large percentage of failures, direct competition creates the fear of failure in many students which, in turn, destroys their ability to learn effectively.

The tendency to approach or avoid an activity appears to be the result of several variables. Willis and Bethe (1970) have discussed the complexity of these variables: approach is affected by the desire to achieve, the perceived probability of success, and the incentive value of success; avoidance is determined by the desire to avoid failure, the perceived probability of failure and the incentive value of failure. As pointed out previously, for many students the probability of success in direct competition is so low and the desire to avoid failure so great that the result is often a desire to avoid rather than to approach the activity.

It seems obvious that, if maximum learning for each individual is our goal, we must produce situations in which early experiences with any new task are met with a large percentage of success. Aspiration level appears to be directly related to successful experiences. Success results in a rise of aspiration level, failure in a lowering of this level. The results of past experience provide each individual with an expectancy of success or failure in a given area of endeavor. If we wish to reap the greatest gains in learning, our educational settings must provide for multiple winners, a positive sum game, which is impossible in direct competition.

Staunch defenders of competition maintain it is significant training for life in our competitive society. Certainly there is value in experiencing both success and failure when striving for a goal, but it is extremely doubtful if those students with a steady diet of failure learn better how to compete; 19

rather, they learn how to avoid failure through withdrawal, compensation, and rationalization. If one of our goals in physical education is to produce a populace which actively and enjoyably engages in sports and games throughout life, we must strive to prevent the development of these avoidance mechanisms by ensuring greater incidence of success for all students. This can be accomplished by structuring the learning environment to maximize success.

Many members of our profession have noted with alarm and despair the failure of students and adults to engage voluntarily in sports and fitness activities and, in response, continue to attempt to entice them into participation with prizes, awards, and so on. Some interesting findings are beginning to be reported concerning the influence of extrinsic and intrinsic motivators on voluntary participation. Although physical educators continue to use extrinsic rewards and punishments to motivate participation, many would concede the superiority of intrinsic motivation, recognizing it as less transitory and more conducive to permanent changes in behavior. To kindle a continuing interest in learning or activity, we must produce situations that are inherently interesting, challenging and gratifying. Surely motor activities meet these criteria for a large number of persons; yet these same persons do not engage regularly in or frequently select games and sports for leisure activities. Recent work by Deci (1972) points to some possible ways in which we operate to decrease the intrinsic motivation of activities by linking the activity with extrinsic rewards. When subjects in the Deci study were supplied with extrinsic reasons (rewards or the threat of punishment) for engaging in a basically interesting act, the construction of the soma puzzle, their desire to participate in the act decreased when the external reasons for doing so were removed. However, given the same challenge and no external motivation, the subjects consistently evidenced a stronger desire to continue. It appears, then, that when a person engages in some behavior without the influence of extrinsic rewards, he justifies his behavior as "doing it because I like it." As soon as an extrinsic reward is imposed on the participant, he tends to link his behavior to it, "doing it for the reward." This shift from internal to external rewards has important consequences for the probability of participation once the external motivator is removed. When winning becomes the primary reason for competing, and when it becomes obvious to a competitor either in a specific game or a broad category of experiences, that winning is no longer possible, he logically declines to continue. By way of illustration, consider how many intramural teams fail to complete their schedules after losing a significant number of games and how few students elect to take an additional course in an area in which they have received inferior grades. Is the decision to continue determined by the intrinsic values of personal improvement and joy of participation or by the extrinsic reward of winning, grades, etc.? Do extrinsic rewards decrease the perception of intrinsic value in an activity? It is likely that imposing external rewards shifts personal perception of the reason for participation toward the external and away from the internal. Later when extrinsic reasons are no longer present or potent, the individual is less disposed to find the intrinsic values sufficient to elicit participation. Thus, attempting to instill intrinsic values through extrinsic devices appears inherently contradictory. Should we not concentrate more in our teaching of motor activities on the pleasure of *doing* and less on the value of *winning* or the threat of *failing*?

If we wish to produce people who enjoy physical activity, we must redirect our emphasis from direct competition and winning to learning fostered by indirect competition. By judging performance and improvements in relation to past achievements, we raise self-development to the major criterion, allowing for multiple winners in a positive sum game. This will require a significant shift in our basic approach to and recognition of performance. We will need to reduce the number of direct competition situations, while we concentrate on producing intrinsic reward opportunities for all levels of performance. Success and gratification must be directed so as to emanate from continued participation and improvement, rather than from besting another. Some trends in our profession support these proposals, namely, the movement education approach and the problem-solving method. Their emphasis on individual development relegates winning to a minor role and elevates creative experiences and self-realization to paramount importance. To maximize the contribution that physical education can make to the development of all individuals, these trends must be accelerated. We will need to rephrase that old adage, "It's neither whether you win nor lose, it's how well *you* played *your* game."

REFERENCES

Aronson, E., and Carlsmith, J. "Performance Expectancy as a Determinant of Actual Performance." *J. Abnorm. Soc. Psych.* 65(1962):178.
Deci, Edward. "Work: Who Does Not Like It and Why." *Psychology Today* 6(1972):57.
Holt, John. *How Children Fail.* New York: Pitman, 1964.
Hussman, B. "Sport and Personality Dynamics." Proceedings N.C.P.E.A.M., 1969.

Lowin, A., and Epstein, G. "Does Expectancy Determine Performance?" *J. Exp. Soc. Psych.* 1(1965):248.

Martens, R. "Effect of an Audience on Learning and Performance of a Complex Motor Skill." *J. Person. Soc. Psych.* 12(1969):252.

Milne, Conrad. "The Relation Between Anxiety and Motor Performance in Young Children." *Abstracts AAHPER National Convention.* 1972.

Oxendine, Joseph. "Emotional Arousal and Motor Performance." *Quest* 13(1970)

Rosenthal, R., Jacobsen, Lenore. *Pygmalion in the Classroom.* New York: Holt, Rinehart and Winston, 1966.

Slusher, Howard. *Man, Sport and Existence.* Philadelphia: Lea & Febiger, 1967.

Willis, J., and Bethe, Don. "Achievement Motivation: Implications for Physical Activity." *Quest* 13(1970)

Psychological motivation in sport

Dorcas Susan Butt
University of British Columbia

What are the motivations of athletes? In sport, as in other forms of human activity, individuals may engage in similar behavior for quite different reasons. For example, members of a football team are involved in a similar activity, but their psychological motivations may vary. This is also true of athletes who are skiing or running the mile. Can we arrive at some basic categories of individual motivation?

Three theories of basic motivation which may be used to interpret sports behavior are those of aggression, neuroticism, and competence (Butt, 1971). Each theory hypothesizes in the individual a fund of energy which must find an outlet. This discharge of energy may combine with a reinforcement history, or the cumulation of reward and punishment effects in an individual's development, to produce the observed behaviors.

23

Konrad Lorenz's (1950, 1966) well-known theories on aggression may be applied to the interpretation of sports behavior. He sees aggression as stemming from an instinctive fund of energy which must be discharged in one way or another. The person with the greater fund of energy will have more motivation to channel and use it for athletic activity if there is no other outlet. Outright aggression no longer serves evolutionary functions in the human animal: Species-selective breeding and the development of weapons have rendered it a dysfunctional drive. Lorenz therefore suggests sports and competition as a major outlet for the potentially destructive impulses that plague mankind. Football player Charley Taylor of the Washington Redskins (Dowling, 1970, p. 86) represents this model when he says, "Well, when I was eight or nine, I had this energy built up and I had to find some way to get it off . . ." So does Althea Gibson, tennis champion, when she writes (Gibson, 1958, p. 26), "I had trouble as a competitor because I kept wanting to fight the other player every time I started to lose . . . after awhile, I began to understand that you could walk out like a lady, all dressed up, be polite to everybody, and still play like a tiger . . ." Incidentally, for those who would prefer to emphasize a social reinforcement explanation of aggressive behavior as supported by psychologists Bandura (1961, 1963) and Berkowitz (1969), many athletes with high aggression levels come from under-privileged homes, where physical punishment was common. Althea Gibson, for example, was uncontrollable and characteristically struck out at her environment. To young Althea, growing up in the streets of Harlem, fist fights and brawls with the boys in her neighborhood were an everyday occurrence. In fact, during her adolescence she identified with and emulated a champion boxer, Sugar Ray Robinson. Thus the innate versus learning controversy need not interfere with the observation of a high level of aggression in many athletes.

In Sigmund Freud's (1923) motivational model, all sports motivation results from personal conflict between opposing forces of the personality. Through sublimation the primitive drives of sex and aggression are expressed in socially condoned activities such as artistic expression, creativity and sports participation. Through maturation, the ego becomes educated to mediate between the demands of the instinctually motivated id and the demands of society as represented in the suppressing superego. Although the individual personality strives for equilibrium, at best only an uneasy balance is maintained, since the personality is always in conflict. The athlete has found a socially sanctioned method, in keeping with his personality development, of expressing impulses and dealing with neurotic conflict. As Beisser (1967, p. X), writes: "For some, the athletic field was a place where

24

they could act out certain desires that were unacceptable elsewhere. For them sports were a way of relating to people in what was otherwise a forbidding world. Sports were a way of pleasing or identifying with parents for some, whereas for others, they were a way of rebelling, in a socially acceptable way, against parents or the culture in which they lived."

In such circumstances, sports are a reflection of neuroticism, to the degree that primary instinct is redirected from its original object to another for satisfaction. Beisser (1967, p. 117), quotes a weightlifter as saying, "It's a crazy thing. I look at myself in the mirror and I can see that I am really tremendous, but I turn away and all of a sudden, I'm nothing again—I'm just a scared little kid . . . I can't afford to lose anything. If I get in a fight I might get hurt and lose a lot of ground. Girls can ruin a guy. I've seen it happen . . . they'll sap your strength until you are just nothing." A traumatic early upbringing by a well-meaning, but inadequate single mother led to an intense fear of women, impotence and overcompensation in sport.

An eminent female athlete abruptly ceased to compete in her sport due to psychological unrest, nervous symptoms and personal conflict. As a child she had spent long hours alone with her father practicing in a gymnasium close to her home, and her father always accompanied her to her competitions. When the father became ill and could not travel with her, the girl transferred her attachment to her coaches. She could not perform without the presence of her current coach, was intensely jealous of his attentions to other athletes, and had brief, unhappy and turbulent love affairs with two coaches. This girl's sports motivation resulted from an early fixation upon her father and an intense jealousy of her mother, acted out in her sports performance. Had the girl not had the psychosocial conflict precipitated by family dynamics, she would not have been motivated to perform in her sport.

There is much behavior from the everyday sports scene to give credence to this major form of sports motivation. Many athletes, most unfortunately, need therapy and not applause.

Robert White (1963) has presented a theory of motivation that is widely applicable to sport. He hypothesizes independent ego energies in terms of a drive to experience effect upon the environment. This experience then leads to feelings of confidence, well-being and mastery on the part of the individual involved. In the competence model, feelings about and confidence in the self are built up through interaction with the environment. Every

25

time an infant reaches out for an object and sees his effect upon the environment, it is presumed that a neurological or psychological change takes place within the structure of the organism. For example, the Swiss psychologist, Jean Piaget, in describing the behavior of his own son (1936, p. 185), says, "Laurent by chance strikes the chain while sucking his finger . . . he grasps it and slowly displaces it while looking at the rattles. He then begins to swing it very gently which produces a slight movement of the hanging rattles and an as yet faint sound inside them. Laurent then definitely increases by degrees his own movements: he shakes the chain more and more vigorously and laughs uproariously at the result obtained."

The theory of competence motivation has been supported in observations of animals, children and young adults. Areas in which competence motivation may be expressed include jobs, special skills, interpersonal relationships, sexual performance, and sports. Many athletes demonstrate the clearest form of competence motivation: the desire to witness and experience their effect upon the environment, to enjoy it, to react to it and to master it. Thus the mountain climber, thus the endless hours of sometimes solitary training for the athlete, thus the repetition and the slow and impossible struggle towards perfection.

Jim Bouton (1970, p. 340), pitcher, provides us with a clear example of the feelings of well-being as a result of competence motivation: "I could've cried. There wasn't a tear in me, though. Just joy, elation, satisfaction, vindication, a great sense of accomplishment. The knuckleball worked. In the National League. For ten innings. I struck out eleven, walked only four. A bounce, a bit of luck, I could have won. No matter. For the first time, for the first time in what seemed eons, I went all the way through a ballgame getting the hitters out on my stuff, my very own personal, natural stuff."

For the athlete motivated primarily by competence, the major purposes in engaging in sport are perfecting skill and ability, meeting challenge and enjoyment of performance. It may be predicted that such an athlete will tend to get along well with peers and fellow competitors, will have a history of leadership activities in school and adulthood, will take pleasure in assisting younger athletes and will continue to participate in sport for a longer time than those athletes in whom other forms of motivation are most central.

The three motivational models described above need systematic study and measurement. Such details have been discussed by Butt (1971) where variations across sport, sex, length of participation, and style of coaching have been suggested, in addition to the variations observed across individuals. The effect of winning or losing upon motivational orientations should also receive attention. Many champion athletes fit a competence model

**Psychological motivation
in sport**
Dorcas Susan Butt

(Warburton and Kane, 1966, pp. 77 ff.) and the study of their development usually reveals they have learned or been able to absorb defeat with minimum ill effect, hypothetically a by-product of competence orientation. In other words they have been relatively free from the fear of "losing," from the restrictions and manipulations of petty rivalry, and have been able to work and reach towards an ultimate performance level. It is important to note that two athletes appreciating a higher value to their sport and participating from a competence orientation need not be "competitive" towards each other except in the matching of athletic skill. In fact, the two might cooperate in accepting the given set of rules and actually appreciate the opponent's excellence in performance, regardless of the outcome of the game.

Closely related to the preceding motivational theories is the role of competition and cooperation as social motivations in sport. Logically, those athletes whose personal motivation stems primarily from aggression or neuroticism will tend to be competitively oriented towards others because they perceive others as obstacles to the satisfaction of their own drives, while those primarily motivated by competence will tend towards cooperation, because others usually facilitate their expression of their competence. The status of sports competition and the role it plays in character development and education is the center of much debate. Recently Ogilvie and Tutko (1971) bluntly stated: "Sport: if you want to build character, try something else." Several years ago the eminent philosopher Bertrand Russell (1961, pp. 55-57) came to a similar conclusion.* He wrote:

> . . . education has always attributed an enormous moral importance to school games . . . They are said to teach cooperation, but in fact they only teach it in its competitive form. This is the form required in war, not in industry or the right kind of social relations . . . it is more im-

---

*The conclusions are similar in that Ogilvie and Tutko and Russell doubt that constructive character change results from participation in competitive sports. However, Ogilvie and Tutko argue that sport probably has little effect upon character, either positive or negative, while Russell argues that competitive sports education is dysfunctional. It is difficult to find empirical support for the Ogilvie-Tutko stand, other than the psychoanalytic speculation that superego formation occurs during the Oedipal stage, after which few changes in moral development and character take place. Although their stand might relieve the consciences of coaches, most of the evidence from studies of imitative learning, conscience formation and situational determinants of moral behavior supports the Russell position.

portant . . . to cultivate the idea of cooperative enterprises in which the 'enemy' is physical nature, rather than of competitive enterprises in which there are human victors and vanquished . . . Brutality is pleasure in forcing one's will upon other people, courage is indifference to personal misfortunes . . . As far as possible, I would represent inanimate nature as the antagonist in the game; the will to power can find satisfaction in this contest just as well as in competing with other human beings (1961).

In fact sports, like other human activities, include both cooperative and competitive features. Deutsch (1960, p. 415) has defined cooperation as taking place when individual goals are promotively interdependent. For example, a baseball player on a team probably accepts the fact that it is not so important that he hit five home runs as that his team win the game. Competition takes place when individual goals are contriently interdependent, that is, the success of one person or group precludes the success of another. Thus the opposing baseball team and the home team cannot both win the game. Most sports include elements of both cooperation and competition, in that the participants must cooperate in conforming to a certain set of rules, usually at an agreed upon time and place. It is also difficult to find life situations which are exclusively cooperative or exclusively competitive. These opposing themes exist alongside each other in the study of international conflict, war, and education, as well as in sport. However, emphasis is most frequently placed upon competition and winning as opposed to cooperation, because competitive motives are so deeply ingrained in the predominant social values of the western world. To avoid competition or to refuse to win is often seen as due to deviance or illness rather than to differing values.

In sports and sports psychology the consideration of competition has been clouded by many problems, including inadequate definition of the term, an absence or low level of theory development, unwarranted assumptions regarding the morality of predominant social valuations, unsupported inferences about motivation, unspecified criteria for performance assessment, and a lack of systematic study.

Social psychology as a discipline has given considerable research time to studying the differential effects of cooperative and competitive motivation in groups and between individuals. This enterprise has been plagued with its own set of problems, namely, failure to account for variations in individual motivation, the oversimplification of the experimental models, and limitations regarding the generality of results. There are, however, consistencies in results across many studies, which are worth considering because they call into question the trends of much sports participation and

Psychological motivation
in sport
Dorcas Susan Butt

sports organization and should encourage much-needed systematic inquiry into their implications. The results of some key studies are therefore considered below.

Deutsch (1960) carried out one classic study in which groups of students plus an instructor were subjected to cooperative and competitive conditions while solving a variety of problems. The results showed cooperation to be more productive, that the subjects were group-centered, coordinated their efforts, were agreeable and accepting of other members, and showed more insight and understanding in their behavior, and as a group arrived at quicker solutions to problems. The competitive groups showed self-directed behavior, attempts to excel the performances of others, and group conflict. We might predict that long-term membership in such a group would result in neurotic symptoms and anxieties, in at least some group members. Deutsch's studies indicate that a cooperative atmosphere not only facilitates group organization but also raises performance level, as a result of increased attraction between group members, and a willingness to exchange roles with and to accept influence, advice, and help from other group members. Deutsch (p. 447) concludes that "To the extent that the results have any generality, greater group or organizational productivity may be expected when the members or subunits are cooperative rather than competitive in their interrelationships." Deutsch's results, however, refer to group productivity rather than to average individual productivity.

Mintz's results (1951) also demonstrated experimentally the greater productivity produced by a cooperative atmosphere. He used a simple individual performance problem in which his subjects stood holding strings attached to cones all of which were inside a large bottle with a narrow neck which was slowly filling with water. The subjects were first given competitive instructions, with monetary rewards promised to those individuals whose cones emerged least wet. In a second attempt, cooperation was encouraged by offering as an incentive "membership in a group of people who were going to show their ability to cooperate effectively with each other" (Mintz, 1951). In the first situation chaos resulted, as cones jammed up at the neck of the bottle and few could pass through. It was every man for himself and most failed. In the second condition calm and communication between subjects took the place of panic. Task achievement was considerably higher in the cooperative situation. This experimental result is directly parallel to real life panics such as the famous Iroquois Theatre Fire in

29

Chicago in 1903 (Brown, 1965, pp. 714ff). People were trampled, smothered, and knocked insensible in the struggle to reach the exits. The fire itself did little damage and was easily controlled, but 602 persons died. If the atmosphere had remained cooperative, perhaps none would have died.

The results of studies by Hartshorne and May (1928-1930) were a source of acute embarrassment to some (as reported by Cronbach, 1961, p. 556). They found that young subjects who had gone through a "character building program" and who had received most recognition from their adult leaders were actually the most likely to cheat on tests measuring dishonesty. Whether the same results would occur today is left to the reader's judgment. The message remains that when children are induced to work for prizes, with little guidance on how to obtain them, children are just like adults. A goal, if absolute in itself, will justify any means of obtaining it. If the ultimate object is to win, the individual will set about doing so.

That is why the confidence of some in endorsing such situations, without systematic study of the effects, is at the least alarming. A typical example is Ward (1967, pp. 313-314), who says:

> I am not a believer in the Little League philosophy that everyone who shows up should get to play, regardless of who wins . . . The Little League philosophy fosters security-seeking dependency, acceptance of weakness and goals of mediocrity. It does not breed superior athletes or even enterprising citizens. It has been said that the British Empire was won on the playing fields of Eton. There are many today who would therefore curse those playing fields for having nurtured imperialism and all of its much maligned concomitants. Perhaps too a similar hypothesis could account for the disdain with which intellectuals in general hold athletes and athletics. Perhaps the individual confidence, spirit of enterprise and independence nurtured on our playing fields constitute a threat to our current crop of social, economic and philosophical planners. If such has to be the case, let's get on with the game!

This statement is reminiscent of a similar statement by a notorious defeated military leader who said, "The victor will always be the judge, and the vanquished the accused." Such statements reveal a perception of life as a struggle, with no common ground or mediating values between the competitors. For a more realistic appraisal of socialization with regard to co-operation, competition, and human values, the reader is referred to Bronfenbrenner (1970, chapters 4, 5 and 6).

Kelly and Stahelski (1970) have reported the findings of an experimental game situation in which choices by the subject dictate his own reward and the reward of his opponent. A subject may choose a cooperative alternative

**Psychological motivation
in sport
Dorcas Susan Butt**

which might give him and his opponent three dollars each in payoff, or he might choose a competitive alternative which would reward him with five dollars and his opponent with one dollar. His opponent then has a chance to retaliate with the next choice and he also may make competitive or cooperative responses. Subjects who were basically cooperative in their approach on pretesting were paired with subjects who were competitive in their pregame philosophy. The researchers noted a number of trends in their data. It seemed that competitive players forced a competitive atmosphere on their trusting opponents as the game progressed. Thus a negative atmosphere dominated the games. Competitors seemed to have more influence than cooperators. Communication between players, however, increased trust and cooperation as did the presence of a third party and negotiations. Competitive responses tended to increase over trials and females tended to be less cooperative than males, at least in one study. The picture is a gloomy one. It seems that although competitive responses are dysfunctional and destructive, they tend to predominate at least in the interactions noted. Even more depressing is the possibility that because they predominate, competitive behaviors are viewed as morally more defensible.

How can cooperative behavior be induced? Extreme competition and conflict can be altered by the introduction of different reward systems or by the introduction of what Sherif and Sherif (1969, pp. 221–266) have called superordinate goals. The Sherifs carried out extensive studies in boys' camps in which they manipulated and studied the effects of competition between groups. When antagonistic feelings were at their highest and full-fledged warfare seemed the only solution, the subjects could be brought together by introducing a goal upon which all had to work and cooperate for common welfare. For example, the camp water supply might be cut off, or the food supply. These situations were set up so that they could only be corrected by the participation of all the boys. Superordinate goals, values, and ideals can thus unite conflicting groups, as has been demonstrated across many situations from dyadic relationships to international conflict.

How does the foregoing apply to the sports world and to sports activity? One must question Bertrand Russell when he states that school games only teach competition as required in war and not in desirable social relations. Sports can be as personally and socially constructive as other forms of human competence, providing the satisfaction lies in the perfecting of skill rather than in the defeating of others. The sports participant at any level   31 can do his or her best and at the same time appreciate and encourage the performances of others better than himself. Such athletes participate in sports primarily from a competence orientation, which unites them with other athletes in a common appreciation of the value of sports. They are not separated by the immediate pressure of winning or losing. Many champion athletes can compete with good feelings for and appreciation of their opponents, meeting with them after the game to discuss its high-lights. Such athletes are not competitive, are not contriently interdependent, because the success of one does not preclude the success of the other. On the other hand, extreme egocentric goals hamper the character development of many athletes as well as restricting their performance.

Some sports organizations and atmospheres parallel Deutsch's small groups experiment. That is, the performance of most of the participants is restricted, because of the narrow competitive values which predominate. On the other hand, some sports organizations facilitate individual performance by recognizing the values and ideals represented in the sport. Athletes train, develop together and help one another in a cooperative enterprise. Communications to the developing athlete in such a setting carry the message that individual goals should be centered around self fulfillment rather than the defeating of others.

If we conclude that competence motivation and cooperation in sports through adherence to superordinate goals is the most constructive, functional, and desired motivation for athletes and that it leads to later cooperation, the next step might be to develop a program in which competence motivation and cooperation would be encouraged, while dysfunctional aggression, neuroticism, and competition are discouraged. Such a program would reinforce the desired behavior with positive incentives and feedback while eliminating unwanted behavior with aversive incentives and feedback. Such principles are already in use or have been suggested, for example, in fertility control (Lipe, 1970) and in the control of socially undesirable behavior (Bandura, 1969). The wanted and unwanted behaviors must be carefully specified, as must be the positive and negative incentives. Monetary incentives, coach reaction, team support, and status are some of the reinforcements which might be used. Lest some be concerned by this sort of social engineering, it is important that the above factors inevitably influence athletes, but frequently in haphazard and dysfunctional ways. The sports world, more often than many care to admit, reinforces destructive behavior such as cheating, the use of ergogenic aids, and the belittling of the opponent's effort. Coaches are sometimes the worst offenders. Such behavior is self-destructive as well as socially destructive.

Psychological motivation
in sport
Dorcas Susan Butt

Much useful study on social learning and human development has accumulated. Bronfenbrenner (1970, chapter 5) has reviewed the effects of models, social reinforcement, intensive relationships, group forces, and superordinate goals on child development. Since participation in sports plays a major role in the socialization of many children, systematic study and application of the principles of social learning could contribute much to our understanding of this aspect of socialization.

But social learning principles cannot be applied immediately on a wide scale. Many research questions remain, such as those regarding the generality of the experimental results discussed. Experimental programs are needed to test these out. Even if the arguments presented in this chapter were to prove valid, there is still the question of whether we have reached a stage of civilization where individuals and groups would be willing to give up the dysfunctional values to which they have been committed. Foregoing discussion has not treated sports in which brutality and destruction are emphasized and in which pain, sadistic punishment, and even death are the lot of the defeated. If play and sports are meaningful preparation for adult behavior, as they appear to be in animals, children and young adults, then we may have as much to fear from boxing, bullfighting, and football as we have from war. I would predict that fighting to a real or symbolic death in fierce competition is a human activity which will in time either be replaced by cooperative activities or which will prevail so completely that no "winners" survive.

REFERENCES

Bandura, A. *Principles of Behavior Modification*. New York: Holt, Rinehart and Winston, 1969.

Bandura, A.; Ross, D.; and Ross, S. A. "Transmission of Aggression through Imitation of Aggressive Models." *Journal of Abnormal and Social Psychology* 63(1961):575–582.

Bandura, A.; Ross, D.; and Ross, S. A. "Vicarious Reinforcement and Imitative Learning." *Journal of Abnormal and Social Psychology* 67(1963):601–607.

Beisser, A. R. *The Madness in Sports*. New York: Appleton-Century-Crofts, 1967.

Berkowitz, L., ed. *The Roots of Aggression*. New York: Atherton, 1969.

Bouton, J. *Ball Four*. New York: World, 1970.

Bronfenbrenner, U. *Two Worlds of Childhood: U.S. and U.S.S.R.* New York: Russell Sage Foundation, 1970.

Brown, R. *Social Psychology*. Toronto: Collier-Macmillan, 1965.

Butt, D. S. "Aggression, Neuroticism and Competence: Theoretical Models for the Study of Sports Motivation." Paper read at 3rd Canadian Psychomotor Skills and Sports Psychology Symposium in Vancouver, 1971.

Cronbach, L. J. *Essentials of Psychological Testing.* New York: Harpers, 1960.

Deutsch, M. "The Effects of Cooperation and Competition upon Group Processes." In *Group Dynamics,* edited by Dorwin Cartwright and Alvin Zander, pp. 414-48. New York: Harper and Row. 1960.

Dowling, T. *Coach: A Season with Lombardi.* New York: Norton, 1970.

Freud, S. *The Ego and the Id.* In *The Standard Edition of the Complete Works of Sigmund Freud,* Vol. XIX edited by James Strachey. London: Hogarth Press, 1961 (originally published, 1923).

Gibson, A. *I Always Wanted to be Somebody.* New York: Perennial, 1958.

Hartshorne, H., and May, M. A. *Studies in the Nature of Character.* New York: Macmillan, 1928–1930.

Kelly, H. H., and Stahelski, A. J. "Social Interaction Basis of Cooperators' and Competitors' Beliefs about Others." *Journal Personality and Social Psychology* 16(1970):66–91.

Lipe, D. "Incentives, Fertility Control and Research." *American Psychologist* 26(1971):617–25.

Lorenz, K. "The Comparative Method in Studying Innate Behaviour Patterns." In *Symposia of the Society for Experimental Biology,* vol. 4, pp. 221–68. Cambridge: Cambridge University Press, 1950.

Lorenz, K. *On Aggression.* New York: Harcourt, Brace and World, 1966 (originally published in German, 1963).

Mintz, A. "Non-adaptive Group Behavior." *Journal of Abnormal and Social Psychology* 46(1951): 150–159.

Ogilvie, B. C., and Tutko, T. A. "Sport: If You Want to Build Character, Try Something Else." *Psychology Today,* October 1971, pp. 61-63.

Piaget, J. *The Origins of Intelligence in Children.* New York: International Universities Press, 1952 (originally published, 1936).

Russell, B. *Education and Character.* New York: Philosophical Library, 1961.

Sherif, M., and Sherif, C. W. *Social Psychology.* New York: Harper and Row, 1969.

Warburton, F. W., and Kane, J. E. "Personality Related to Sport and Physical Ability." In *Readings in Physical Education,* edited by J. E. Kane, pp. 61-89. Publ. by Physical Education Association at Great Britain, 1966.

Ward, S. D. "The Superior Athlete." In *Motivations in Play, Games and Sports.* edited by Ralph Slovenko and James A. Knight, pp. 307-14. Springfield: Charles C. Thomas, 1967.

White, Robert W. "Ego and Reality in Psychoanalytic Theory: A Proposal Regarding Independent Ego Energies." *Psychological Issues.* New York: International Universities Press, 1963.

The physical educator
and
the clumsy child

Bryant J. Cratty
University of California, Los Angeles

National and international attention is increasingly becoming focused upon the "clumsy child syndrome." These children, which some authorities contend make up from 15 to 18 percent of the population of children in the average school (Rappaport, 1969), exhibit movement problems which render them less likely to play well, less acceptable to their well-performing peers, and often unable to perform written work in the classroom within a reasonable time interval. For reasons not clearly understood, the problem under discussion seems at least twice as prevalent in boys as in girls. If sent to a pediatric neurologist, most would be diagnosed as having minimal neurological dysfunction, suggesting that moderate but subtle imperfections in their nervous systems render them less able to integrate body parts and to engage in coordinated tasks requiring either the larger or smaller muscles of their bodies.

The cause of their clumsiness is not easily diagnosed, nor in the final analysis are attempts to determine causation likely to be productive. They may have inherited their inability to move well; some have suffered moderate trauma during or near birth; others have had medical problems usually marked by high fevers during the early months of life; others may have suffered traumatic injuries during their formative years as the result of accidents, falls, and the like.

Their clumsiness may or may not be accompanied by learning difficulties; however, many evidence either too much physical activity when it is not called for (in the classroom, for example), or appear to be too passive for most of the situations they are in. Some have visual-perceptual problems which further confound their efforts to deal directly with their environment and may indirectly contribute to their clumsiness by preventing them from seeing and thus copying effective ways of performing motor skills from their more able peers. Needless to say, such youngsters bring a great deal of apprehension, negative emotion, and feelings of inferiority to situations calling for physical performance. These feelings may be heightened when the situation is a formal one presided over by a physical education teacher or coach.

In the following pages, we attempt to illuminate the problems such children have, and to describe how they see themselves and how they compensate for their movement difficulties. We also outline strategies, both constructive and destructive, which physical educators have taken or might take with reference to such children. Finally, we suggest what we believe are reasonable solutions to the problem of the clumsy child in the physical education class.

THE CLUMSY CHILD VIEWS HIMSELF

It may take some time for the parents and the child to discover that he does not move as well as other children. If the child has other well performing peers, the problem may become more readily apparent than if no adequately performing peers are present. As is the case with all problems in children, some parents may refuse to recognize that their child has some kind of imperfection. In the case of this type of physical problem, such repression seems more prevalent in fathers than in mothers.

As the child matures and enters school, his kindergarten or first grade teacher may bring to the attention of the parent that the child is slow to

The physical educator and
the clumsy child
Bryant J. Cratty

copy his letters and seems to sit alone in the sandbox when other children are forming small groups, indicating the presence of a physical problem. Soon, usually about age seven or eight, ridicule from his more able peers begins, and his problem is brought home to him in unkind but clear terms. His discovery of his physical ineptitude may result in several types of behavior, some of which are more desirable than others. He may, for example, remove himself from physical performance situations whenever possible, becoming a bookworm at a rather early age, retreating to the television set, the lounge, or preferring to remain in, helping the teacher during recess periods. On the other hand, he may approach performance situations as a kind of court jester, acting in outlandish ways when confronted by sports, in order to attract the attention of others in ways which are generally less acceptable than performing well, but which are apparently preferred to being ignored completely. We have also seen unusual cases in which boys have kept themselves within performance situations, but have not performed! That is, they line up, cheer, etc., but when it comes time for their turn they simply do not take it. Other clumsy boys retreat to the girls' games, in which they are likely to incur less social punishment. But of course in doing so, they are likely to increase the amount of ridicule they receive from their male classmates (Cratty and others, 1970). Statements from knowledgeable clinicians suggest that the early history of many (one estimation is over 70 percent) male homosexuals includes the rejection by male peers in physical activity, and the retreat to girls' games as a result. Some clumsy children retreat to fantasy bravery games.* The incidence of reports of playing "space man," "cops and robbers," and so forth is far more prevalent in statements collected from older boys with motor problems than is the case when similar reports are obtained from children who perform well (Cratty and others, 1970). Finally, some engage in hostile, anti-social acts. Increasing evidence suggests that many of the outbursts of violence are from individuals whose early history includes inability to per-

---

*We do not wish to imply that lack of coordination *causes* a child to evidence gender identification problems, or inevitably *causes* marked anti-social behavior in later life. The evidence, however, suggests that such behavior is often marked by clumsiness early in life, *in addition* to other social and psychological problems a child may evidence. Thus, it is suggested that such children, in addition to receiving help with their emotional problems, should also receive direct help in remediating their game skills when appropriate.

form coordinated skills well. This is true in the case of many who have hijacked airplanes and of several of the infamous mass-murderers. Moreover, a survey by a graduate student of mine revealed that about 40 percent of the adolescents arrested in Los Angeles evidence minor to moderate perceptual-motor problems, evaluated by exposing them to balance and drawing tests. While it may be true that many of these adolescents were suffering from problems engendered by drug abuse and by poor nutrition prior to their arrest, the implications of this statistic are ominous indeed.

REACTIONS OF PHYSICAL EDUCATORS

Physical educators may have several reactions to the appearance of a clumsy child in their class or even on their team. One, of course, is physical or emotional rejection. Such a child does not usually support the physical educator's self-image, nor fit his expectations of those whom he hopes to attract to his program. People often have a difficult time liking others who are different from themselves. This rejection may be direct or indirect. The teacher may admonish the child for being late to class, since such children usually have difficulty dressing, tying shoes, and working combination locks. When they get to class they are usually the last to be chosen, and it becomes painfully obvious to the youth that he is the least wanted child in the class. One classic case which came to my attention involved an elementary physical educator who permitted the team captains *each day* to discard the two less able players who then had to peddle themselves to another team!

But physical educators, sometimes termed perceptual-motor, or sensory-motor specialists, have also taken a different if only slightly more productive tack in recent years. In response to pronouncements that movement is the basis of all learning, they have seized upon the clumsy child with the aim not only of remediating his motor problems, but also of helping him to read via tasks which involve integrating body parts, walking balance beams, and similar exercises. Their efforts have often been less than effective, even in changing coordination, unless they offered a variety of movement experiences. The physical educator who claims to improve cognitive ability by exposing children with perceptual-motor problems to movement experiences is naive and is likely to produce a backlash from his more sophisticated colleagues. For centuries it has been apparent that the goals of educational programs are realistic to the extent to which the *content* of the program parallels the goals and outcomes which are sought (Cratty, 1972). Well-controlled research (Cratty, 1972; Cratty, 1970), has shown that

**The physical educator and
the clumsy child**
Bryant J. Cratty

the laudable goals of changing reading and other deficiencies are not likely to be realized while walking balance beams. However, well-constructed and comprehensive programs of remedial and basic motor activities may, if applied within an environment which is emotionally secure to the child, improve movement abilities. In addition, several researchers, including the present writer, have demonstrated that engaging the child in games into which academic content has been inserted can indeed change such abilities as letter recognition, spelling, and mathematical aptitude (Cratty, 1971; Cratty, 1972; Humphrey and Sullivan, 1970).

On the other hand, the physical educator may prove sensitive to the child's problem, providing him with special help and encouragement in the form of special classes. Too often such adaptive classes stress only posture exercises, or deal only with the child who has a cardiovascular or orthopedic condition. But such special classes are beginning to emphasize activities which improve function as well as strength, fitness, and posture.

CONSTRUCTIVE STRATEGIES

Enough data presently exists to suggest several positive steps physical educators might take when confronted, as they are daily, with the child who does not move well. Several studies, for example, have shown that children can improve in basic measures of motor function if exposed to sequentially arranged and comprehensive programs of activities. Younger as well as older children may change, if provided the opportunity to improve themselves in situations which are not accompanied by stress from the more able peers. Thus adequate programs of primary, elementary and secondary physical education should include special classes for the physically inept child. After all, if the government statistics are valid, they mean that within a class of sixty apparently normal youngsters, from seven to eleven children are likely to evidence the symptoms discussed above (Rappaport, 1969). Some of the guidelines which we have formulated through research and in our eleven-year clinical program for these youngsters are given below. We believe that further investigations might lead to even more viable and specific principles.

1. Initially, and as early in the school career as possible, children should be tested for motor skills, including balance, agility, ball handling, coordination, printing, and fine finger dexterity. Available tests include the Oseretsky

(Doll, 1946) and parts of the Denver Developmental Screening Test (1970). Such a test battery could be carried out by a committee composed of a school physician, psychologist, physical educator, and classroom teacher. Initial screening may be carried out by properly oriented classroom teachers, with a more thorough evaluation extended to suspected children by the physical educator or school psychologist. Extreme cases should be referred to a pediatric neurologist.

2. A program should be formulated based upon the test results as compared to *properly constituted averages*. The program should include a variety of motor activities designed to improve basic abilities such as balance and agility, as well as those which are directed toward the remediation of specific sports skills (Cratty, 1970). Generally, it is more productive to expose young children only to basic activities, adding instruction in sports skills to the program for older children.

3. Children evidencing handwriting deficiencies should be given specific help in this area. It should not be expected that practice of gross motor abilities will somehow transfer to writing skills, as some uninformed individuals fervently believe.

4. The remedial program should take place at least twice a week, but preferably three times a week or every day, and should last from thirty to forty minutes each session. The program should be conducted so that the children begin slightly above their skill level and work at this level until slightly more difficult tasks can be introduced and mastered. This principle has been termed the "stress-success" cluster method. That is, although the clumsy child is usually less secure in his self-concept than other children (Cratty and others, 1970), he should be given not only an abundance of tasks which he can accomplish, but must also be challenged to a slight degree each day, by exposing him to tasks which tax him to a limited degree. Without the opportunity for success he is not likely to persevere; on the other hand, if he is not pushed a little beyond his limits, he is unlikely to improve.

5. Finally, the program should be evaluated by retesting.

Physical educators well versed in evaluative methods and in program construction are being eagerly sought by school administrators around the country, to institute programs of remedial physical education as described on these pages. To serve in this capacity, physical educators may prepare themselves as undergraduates with classes in remedial techniques and in theories which pertain to the basics of motor development and motor learning. Moreover, the physical educator may serve as a valuable member of the educational community, not by exaggerating the role of movement in the

**The physical educator and
the clumsy child**
Bryant J. Cratty

education of the child, but by functioning as a knowledgeable member of a professional team, composed of educators, psychologists, and administrators, in dealing with the child with motor problems. As an individual, the physical educator might take a close look at himself when working with children and youth, and attempt to truly accommodate individual differences in the organization of his competitive teams and in the curriculum and conduct of his classes.

Helping the clumsy child takes maturity. It is not accompanied by the accolades of the spectators, which the athletically gifted youngster enjoys, but by the grateful response of parents and educators.

SUMMARY

Clumsy children constitute from 15 to 18 percent of the population of school children at all levels, from which the obviously physically and mentally handicapped have been removed. These children suffer from feelings of social inferiority and are often unable to write efficiently. They may or may not have reading or other learning problems.

Compensations for their problem may take forms which are neither pleasing to their peer group, nor to the educators who come in contact with them. At the same time, the strategies which have been used with (or against) them have at times been less than helpful.

Productive work with the clumsy child requires early identification through comprehensive tests and valid norms. Following this, remedial physical education stressing functional improvement by exposure to tasks of gradually increasing difficulty should be initiated. Such programs should stress basic skills, adding complex game situations for older children.

By working as part of a team of school personnel interested in the psychological and physical welfare of children and youth, and by formulating his methods, curriculum, and goals with reference to the readily available research findings, the physical educator can bring even better professional service to children and youth than he has in the past.

REFERENCES

Cratty, Bryant J. *Physical Expressions of Intelligence.* Englewood Cliffs, N.J.: Prentice-Hall, 1972.
Cratty, Bryant J. *Active Learning.* Englewood Cliffs, N.J.: Prentice-Hall, 1971.
Cratty, Bryant J. *Perceptual and Motor Development of Infants and Children.* New York: Macmillan, 1970.

Cratty, Bryant J., and Martin, M. M., *Perceptual-Motor Efficiency in Children*. Philadelphia, Pa.: Lea & Febiger, 1970.

Cratty, Bryant J., and Szczepanik, M. *The Effects of a Program of Learning Games Upon Selected Academic Abilities of Children with Learning Difficulties*. Washington, D.C.: U.S. Office of Education, Bureau of Education for the Handicapped, 1971.

Cratty, Bryant J., and others. *Movement Activities, Motor Ability and the Education of Children*. Springfield, Ill.: Charles C. Thomas, 1970.

Denver Developmental Screening Test, revised manual. Denver, Colo.: University of Colorado Medical Center, 1970.

Doll, Edgar, ed. *The Oseretsky Tests of Motor Proficiency*, Circle Pines, Minn.: American Guidance Service, 1946.

Humphrey, J. H., and Sullivan, D. D. *Teaching Slow Learners Through Active Games*. Springfield, Ill.: Charles C. Thomas, 1970.

Rappaport, Sheldon R. *Public Education for Children with Brain Dysfunction*. Syracuse, N.Y.: Syracuse University Press, 1969.

Personality traits
of competitors
and coaches*

Bruce C. Ogilvie

California State University, San Jose

The need for empirical data on personality and sport evolved from extensive clinical experience with athletes who had symptom patterns that either interfered with or blocked high-level motor achievement. The variety of somatic complaints and the severity of emotional reactions to high-level stress contributed to a growing doubt as to the value of such athletic participation. Exploration of the literature provided only a single reference to the personality of elite competitors (Heusner, 1952).

The Institute for the Study of Athletic Motivation was established at San Jose State College to gather data that would provide a

*Reprinted from *Modern Medicine,* June 26, 1972, pp. 61–68. Copyright 1972, by The New York Times Media Company, Inc.

basis for understanding the relationship between character formation and athletic participation. Early investigation involved Olympic, professional and university athletes in the anticipation that their characteristics would help in evaluating the somatic complaints and emotional reactions encountered in our clinic. Our studies emphasized the psychometric approach, using personality tests that had been found effective in industrial situations and containing variables that might be specifically related to athletic achievement.

Emphasis was placed upon the most successful athletes in such sports as football, basketball, baseball, and automobile racing. State college and university athletes provided our first data pool. Studies of professional and high school coaches followed. In our relationship with professional teams, we offered to provide service for data, the service being a promise on our part to create the most ideal psychologic environment for teaching and for anticipating where emotional factors might block acquisition of motor skills.

The pathologic reactions encountered in our studies have been described in our text, "Problem Athletes and How to Handle Them" (Ogilvie and Tutko, 1967). After lecturing throughout Western Europe and Canada, I can state unequivocally that the country or sport may change, but the problem athlete remains the same. When the diverse human motives that lead one to join what my colleague Dr. Thomas A. Tutko has labeled the "P.T.A." (pain, tears and agony club) are compounded by nationalistic motives, the stress often reaches a level beyond human tolerance. Miroslav Vanek, psychologic consultant to the Czechoslovak Olympic team, reported that half the team sought some psychologic counseling during preparation at Mexico City.

ATHLETIC MOTIVATION INVENTORY

There has been a significant increase in the publication of sports-relevant literature during the past decade, based on the use of a wide variety of psychologic instruments (Coffer and Johnson, 1960; Kane, 1966; Ogilvie, 1968; Ogilvie and Tutko, 1967). While designed to measure a wide variety of attitudes, the instruments generally failed to touch on the question of ego investment in sport, and it became increasingly apparent that what was needed was an instrument specifically designed to measure such attitudes. This realization contributed to our development and standardization of the Athletic Motivation Inventory (AMI), designed to measure a selection of personality traits found most consistently in successful competitors. Direct consultation experience plus empirical findings provided the basis for trait selections. Our essential goal was the provision of a new basis for effective communication between athlete and coach.

To date, we have compiled data on over 10,000 athletes aged 6 to 38 years. Reliable general statements can be made with regard to team sport and individual sport trends in terms of personality structure. It is also possible to make dependable statements about a "coaching personality," a "sports car racing personality," and a "football personality." Although there are significant trait differences among these, they share a highly consistent psychologic profile in being success-oriented, ambitious, highly organized individuals who tend to seek leadership roles, who have great psychologic endurance, and who find it easy to express self-assertion. They tend to have a very low need to express interest in the problems of others, and they expect others to show no special interest in, or concern for, them. They show low inclination to study the motivation of others and appear to be extremely self-contained individuals. The higher the criterion of excellence one establishes, the greater the probability that the athlete will be emotionally stable, tough-minded, conscientious, self-controlled, disciplined, self-assured, relaxed with low levels of resting tension, trusting, free of jealousy, and, for males, increasingly more outgoing in personality. The foregoing psychologic picture is certainly a most positive one.

THE SUCCESSFUL ATHLETE

Few areas of human commitment have the potential of reinforcing life's realities as have high-level competitive athletics; the very nature of sports demands the athlete place his achievements and his failures before the public eye. Unconscious denial of failure or unconscious fear of placing one's talent on the line can rarely be used as adequate defense against reality. The "moment of truth" is axiomatic in the life of a great competitor. Therefore, those who remain and those who excel have a higher-than-average potential for coming to grips with reality. To be a winner, it is essential that failure to achieve or failure to realize goals be accepted as a personal responsibility; this, of course, demands emotional strength.

Successful athletes are achievement-oriented people who derive personal satisfaction from striving. High achievement needs are based upon personal attitudes about the probability of success to failure associated with each investment of self or ego. All things considered, the outstanding athlete is

45

at his very best when the odds are slightly against him. Ambitious people derive slight joy, if any, when their ability remains uncontested. The great athletes I have interviewed do not dwell upon their losses but concentrate on that part of their performance that limits their excellence.

DESCRIPTION OF TRAITS

Pragmatic and clinical considerations interacted in our final selection of the 11 personality traits included in the AMI. In the professional setting where financial investment was a primary consideration, there was a willingness to permit extensive testing, usually between four and six hours. While a few universities made as much as four hours available, in general the coaching attitude was negative when the testing period extended much beyond an hour. The first pragmatic consideration was therefore to meet this time limit. The final AMI form included 190 questions that could be answered in slightly under one hour by 90 percent of the athletes. The selection of traits based on our clinical experience proved to be a most difficult decision since we were forced to exclude traits that had proved to be of value in the past, as, for example, the determination of extroversion or introversion.

Personality traits were found to fall into two broad categories: *drive traits* (athletic drive, aggressiveness, determination, guilt-proneness, leadership) and *emotional traits* (emotional control, self-confidence, mental toughness, coachability, conscientiousness, trust). Recent studies suggest that we might also have categorized them on the bases of overt and covert personality traits. The 48 personality aspects originally reported on were gradually reduced to the 11 traits that we felt were best suited, in terms of the reality of time and coaching, to supply useful psychologic insights.

The psychologic meaning of each of the 11 traits is summarized as follows:

Drive: Desires to win or be successful; aspires to accomplish difficult tasks; sets and maintains high goals for himself in athletics; responds positively to competition; desires to attain athletic excellence.

Aggressiveness: Believes one must be aggressive to win; releases aggression easily; enjoys confrontation and argument; sometimes uses force to get his way; does not allow others to push him around; may seek to "get even" with people whom he perceives as having harmed him.

Determination: Willing to practice long and hard; works on skills until exhausted; often works out willingly by himself; perseveres, even in the face of great difficulty; is patient and unrelenting in work habits; doesn't give up quickly on a problem.

**Personality traits of competitors
and coaches**

Bruce C. Ogilvie

Guilt-proneness: Accepts responsibility for his actions; accepts blame and criticism even when not deserved; tends to dwell on his mistakes and to punish himself for them; is willing to endure much physical and mental pain; plays when injured.

Leadership: Enjoys the role of leader and may assume it spontaneously; believes others see him as a leader; attempts to control his environment and to influence or direct other people; expresses opinions forcefully.

Emotional control: Tends to be emotionally stable and realistic about athletics; is not easily upset; rarely allows his feelings to show or to affect his performance; is not easily depressed or frustrated by bad breaks, calls or mistakes.

Self-confidence: Has unfaltering confidence in himself and his capacity to deal with things; is confident of his powers and abilities; handles unexpected situations well; makes decisions confidently; speaks up for his beliefs to coaches and players.

Mental toughness: Accepts strong criticism without feeling hurt; does not become easily upset when losing or playing badly; can bounce back quickly from adversity; can take rough coaching; does not need excessive encouragement from the coach.

Coachability: Respects coaches and the coaching process; is receptive to coaches' advice; considers coaching important in becoming a good athlete; accepts the leadership of the team captain; cooperates with authorities.

Conscientiousness: Likes to do things as correctly as possible; tends to be exacting in character, dominated by sense of duty; does not try to "con" his coach or fellow players; does not attempt to bend rules and regulations to his own needs; places the good of the team above his personal well-being.

Trust: Accepts people at face value; believes what his coach and teammates say and does not look for ulterior motives behind their words or actions; is free of jealous tendencies; tends to get along well with his teammates.

TRAIT ASSESSMENT BY COACHES

Coaches proved to be more aware of trait deficiencies in the drive area than in the emotional area of measurement; such traits as drive, determination, and aggressiveness are components of their own life-styles (Albaugh, 1970;

Hendry, 1968). Emotional traits were significantly more difficult for them to identify, particularly when the individual athlete possessed superior physical ability. There was a strong tendency for coaches to assume that physical giftedness and emotional qualities were directly related.

Recent research has forced us to consider the athlete-coach relationship in terms of the interaction of their unique personalities. We now request that every coach using the AMI take the inventory himself to improve his ability to apply the information received on his athletes as well as to experience in a personal way exactly what his athletes are admitting about themselves. We also hoped this firsthand experience would sensitize these men as to what the various traits actually mean in terms of behavioral expectancies. We felt further that coaches would benefit from any possible personal insight that might accrue from reviewing their own test profiles. This has proved to be fortunate, since we can now engage in more intelligent speculation about the areas where coach-athlete miscommunication can be expected.

The relationship of coaching personality to coaching perceptual objectivity is just beginning to receive the research interest it so richly deserves. This most promising area of investigation has been stimulated by active or former coaches who are seeking to alter the teaching environment in the direction of greater concern for possible individual differences among their competitors. Albaugh (1970), using the Athletic Motivation Inventory, examined basketball coaches' ability to perceive the degree to which these traits were present or absent in their athletes. He found that university coaches were able to assess reliably only the traits of leadership, drive and determination. It is interesting that these were also the traits in which they scored the highest. Conversely, they were much less accurate in their assessment of traits in which they personally scored low. The rank order of accuracy of assessment was as follows: (1) leadership, (2) drive, (3) determination, (4) conscientiousness, (5) coachability, (6) trust, (7) aggressiveness, (8) emotional control, (9) self-confidence, (10) mental toughness, and (11) guilt-proneness.

It is of considerable interest that there was no significant relationship between coaching experience and accuracy of assessing the 11 traits. Although the assessment ratings improved by the second year of experience, the ratings still remained unreliable statistically. Hendry (1968) offers some verification of this coaching trend using the Cattell 16 PF; he found that coaches were most accurate in rating those traits they themselves possessed to a greater degree and inaccurate for those in which they were low.

**Personality traits of competitors
and coaches**

Bruce C. Ogilvie

USES OF AMI PROFILES

It has been possible to explore a number of new avenues in our quest for improved communication. The profile of an entire team may be examined as a hypothetical model from which the coach may theorize as to which aspects of his athletic training program should receive positive reinforcement. Another extension would be to plot the coach's profile against the psychologic profile of the entire team and use the information as a basis for more objective speculation about problems of communication. This same technique can be applied in relation to the individual athlete and provide the basis for a collaborative effort by which coach and athlete determine the areas of personality that would best contribute to the achievement of his goals.

It is certainly obvious that 11 personality traits are not representative of the motivational system of an individual or team, but they can provide an objective basis for the exploration and determination of other contributing emotional factors. Every coach is requested to review the psychogram in a private session with each competitor in order that he might challenge the interpretation of the score on any of the dimensions included in the AMI. In almost every case reported to us, this has led to a more honest and deeper form of communication.

The following are examples of a variety of uses of the information provided by the AMI. Profile 1 is of an Olympic gold medalist, profile 2 is of a problem university athlete and his coach, profile 3 is of a problem university team and their coach, and profile 4 is of a professional team and their new coach. The profiles are presented in percentile form based upon the norms for the sport involved and the level of participation. Each coach is plotted on the basis of coaching norms.

Profile 1—Olympic gold medalist. The psychologic profile of this champion athlete was outstanding for the traits drive, aggressiveness, leadership, emotional control, self-confidence, and mental toughness. He was significantly below the university standard for guilt-proneness, coachability, conscientiousness and trust. Since it had been his wish to take the AMI immediately before his departure to Mexico City, it was possible to test the reliability of the inventory. His initial response was one of disbelief regarding the four low areas, but upon explanation and clarification of the meaning of each trait, he confirmed that the findings were in fact true. Since his freshman

49

year he had gradually lost his respect for coaches, had rejected conformity in almost every social form, had come to distrust those who represented authority in sport, and had felt betrayed by the fans. The opportunity to review in detail the social and athletic factors that contributed to these negative attitudes left me with the confidence to state that for this individual the findings were warranted on the basis of his personal experience. This same profile for a gifted freshman athlete would telegraph psychologic resistance and defensiveness that would seriously limit his capacity to use the skill and knowledge of even the most dedicated coach. It would be predicted that he would be in subtle rebellion against team conformity and remain emotionally distant in his relationship with his coach. The degree of reliability and perfection on the part of the coach necessary to reestablish a basis for trust and open communication would be so unreasonably high that it would seem unfair to make such a request. The frequency of such findings reinforces again and again the unusual burden of responsibility placed upon men in the coaching profession to represent the model of finest character formation within the educational system. This is not a fair demand, but it is a part of their professional reality.

Profile 2—problem university athlete and coach. This young athlete was tested as a junior college transfer who had received All Coast honors in football. His profile was plotted against that of his coach, who had one of the outstanding success records in the nation. The data provided sensitive insight into the athlete and prepared his coach to respond to certain aberrant behavior during spring training through the use of coaching techniques that helped the athlete to stabilize and grow emotionally. In a number of high stress situations, he was given the type of masculine emotional support that was essential if he was to continue to demonstrate his considerable motor giftedness. The psychologic insights into the extreme sensitivity to criticism and failure proved most valuable. The athlete's understanding that in spite of his unusual athletic ability, he still lacked self-confidence, had a difficult problem handling his emotions when under stress, and felt let down by his former coach contributed to the positive program that the coach utilized. The young man finished his two years of eligibility and was subsequently a high draft choice in professional football. The coach, who could also be negatively affected by failure or criticism, was able to use this sensitivity as a basis of remarkable understanding of this fine young athlete.

Profile 3—problem university team and coach. This comparison is offered as a psychologic model for developing a more effective coaching approach in terms of team performance. The coach was faced with the problem of relating to a team where the athletic program had been on the downgrade

**Personality traits of competitors
and coaches**

Bruce C. Ogilvie

for four years. The team was composed of a majority of athletes who had been recruited before his tenure and a minority he had brought into the program. There was a morale problem, along with an obvious lack of dedication and team cohesiveness. The psychologic profile was an objective confirmation of these facts; application of these clinical insights presented difficulties. In talking with the coach, it was necessary to tell him that this was the most narcissistic, self-centered, non-team-oriented group of athletes we had ever tested. The clinical impression was that, as a group, integration, united effort, and self-sacrifice would not be predictable qualities. In exploring various approaches, the coach asked how a clinical psychologist would handle such a situation. In the absence of any previous experience, I stated that my inclination would be to explain exactly what the team profile implied. His reaction was immediate; he said he was going from the phone to the team meeting and relate what the "team shrink" said.

Space does not permit a detailed description of what developed. According to the head coach and his assistants, the near verbatim report of my evaluation brought a period of silence, followed by a player sitting in the back shouting "right on, baby," followed in turn by other comments from within the group attesting the validity of the clinical impression. This developed into a painful open discussion where team members ventilated their feelings freely regarding specific instances of selfishness and other types of negative playing behavior. The meeting terminated with a consensus that the preseason training period would emphasize the many forms of behavior that could lead to team integration. The players made a commitment to each other that each would work to eradicate the negative influence of selfishness from the team. The coach was then able to move toward developing such positive team traits as drive and aggressiveness, with the result that, by the second year, the team became a contender within the conference.

The traits in which this coach himself scored low deserve attention, since his profile suggested he was a person with traits similar to those of his team. He had compensating strengths, but it was important in terms of our learning about the AMI to determine what significance these traits might have played in his own outstanding career as a university and professional athlete. A second question was that of his personality in relation to his selection of recruits. When his profile was reviewed, he admitted the most rebellious forms of athletic behavior, which eventually led to his being thrown off his team in mid season. He was forced to beg his coach to be allowed to return

51

the following season; he then went on to gain a national reputation. Our professional relationship has extended over a decade, which may account for his openness and willingness to use counsel. The profile suggests, however, that he remains rebellious and resistant to anyone who represents authority.

Profile 4—professional team and new coach. This professional team was tested in the early part of a season at the request of their new coach. While his

PROFILE 1. OLYMPIC GOLD MEDALIST

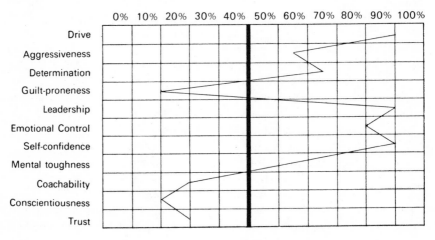

PROFILE 2. PROBLEM UNIVERSITY ATHLETE AND COACH   Coach _ _ _ Athlete _____

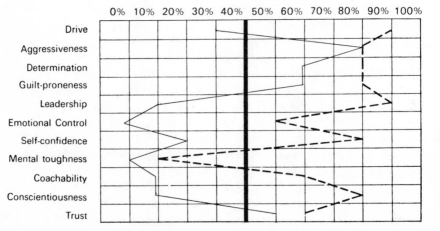

**Personality traits of competitors
and coaches**
Bruce C. Ogilvie

primary interest was a greater understanding of the individual athletes, the team profile offered a model for extending our thinking about the team. The apparent difference between team and coach suggested that they would be operating on quite separate frames of reference with respect to sport.

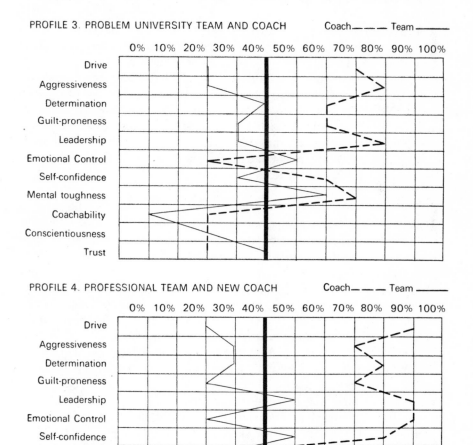

PROFILE 3. PROBLEM UNIVERSITY TEAM AND COACH   Coach _ _ _ Team _____

PROFILE 4. PROFESSIONAL TEAM AND NEW COACH   Coach _ _ _ Team _____

The team was in last place and had ended in this position the previous season. Their depressed psychologic profile was a function of defensiveness where they began to withdraw their ego identification from sport when their intelligences suggested that there was low probability for athletic success. Rather than have their athletic pride continually bombarded by the devastating effect of constant failure, they began to invest their egos in other areas of life where the probability of success was greater. This failure syndrome was contagious, because even the newly acquired professionals were subtly influenced by it.

The coach considered this a challenging situation that he felt sufficiently qualified to modify. His profile suggested it would have been difficult to find anyone better equipped psychologically to meet such a challenge. He integrated methods into his training program that would have a positive effect upon team drive, aggressiveness and determination. He recognized the fact that he was going to have to work full time to reestablish a positive attitude toward the role of coach. He designed team strategy to utilize those members whose attitudes and skills were high as a stabilizing influence during highly critical playing situations. These select individuals acted as a reintegrating force when team play seemed to get out of hand.

FUTURE APPLICATIONS OF AMI

The future application of this variety of approach to the measurement of athletic traits depends on a number of important assumptions. First, that coaches will accept the challenge of developing skills in an area where they have received the most cursory educational background. Second, that they accept the fact that 11 traits form only a limited basis for evaluating a team or the personality of an athlete, and that this knowledge must be considered as a base for further exploration of each individual's and each team's motivational system. It has been our experience with hundreds of coaches who have experimented with the AMI that they are personally changed by this new focus in their teaching. Only a few told us that these insights add to their already too great coaching burden, so they chose not to be so informed and not to change their coaching philosophy.

We have learned that psychologic information cannot compensate for professional deficiencies or for lack of technical knowledge about a sport. We hope the inventory will be used to refine coaching communication skills that can provide a sounder basis for the goal sought by each athlete. Most important, we feel this approach will greatly increase the possibility that new levels of personal fulfillment will obtain when coaches' and athletes' goals merge.

**Personality traits of competitors
and coaches**

Bruce C. Ogilvie

REFERENCES

Albaugh, G. R. A. "Comparative Study of the Ability of Basketball Coaches to Assess the Personality Traits and Profiles of Their Players." Ph.D. dissertation, University of Utah, 1970.

Coffer, C. N., and Johnson, W. R. *Personality Dynamics in Relation to Exercise and Sport. Science and Medicine of Exercise and Sport.* New York: Harper and Row, 1960.

Hendry, L. B. "Assessment of Personality in the Coach-Swimmer Relationship, and a Preliminary Examination of the Father Stereotype." *Res. Quart.* 39(1968):543-555.

Heusner, L. "Personality Traits of Champions and Former Champion Athletes." Research Study, University of Illinois, 1952.

Kane, J. E., and Warburton, F. W. "Personality Related to Sport and Physical Ability." In *Readings in Physical Education,* edited by Frank Warburton. London: The Physical Educator Assn., 1966.

Ogilvie, B. C. "Psychological Consistencies in High Level Competitors." JAMA 205(1968): 780-786.

Ogilvie, B. C., and Tutko, T. A. *Problem Athletes and How to Handle Them.* 2nd ed. London: Delham Books, 1967.

Ogilvie, B. C., and Tutko, T. A. "What is an Athlete?" Proceedings of the American Association of Physical Education, Health, and Recreation, Las Vegas, 1967.

Biofeedback and related training: potential for physical education

Kathileen A. Gallagher
University of San Francisco

This paper is intended to draw to the attention of physical educators the value of biofeedback in dealing with symptoms of stress. The author believes that physical educators may make a vast contribution to health by learning to use biofeedback and related training programs to acquaint students with the value of knowing their bodies and maintaining a more desirable level of bodily function.

Researchers in biofeedback have found that when the subject becomes aware of the particular state of his bodily functions, he can begin to modify them. In biofeedback training, the individual is given information about specific changes within his body through the use of electronic instruments that detect moment-by-moment changes in

Biofeedback and related training:
potential for physical education
Kathileen A. Gallagher

the heart, circulatory system, muscle group, or brain waves, and so on. These biological changes are usually indicated to the subject by means of a light or sound which serves as a cue to his physiological state. In this way, the individual can compare his subjective experience with objective cues, and be continuously informed as to his progress toward a desired internal state.

Biofeedback training presents promising procedures for combating debilitating states of many psychogeneric syndromes. It is being investigated with respect to the prevention of stress-related disorders, such as ulcers; in training insomniacs to achieve sleep; and as a substitute for drug addiction. Budzynski and Stoyva (1970) found sufferers of severe tension headaches had all or most of their pain alleviated by learning to relax their forehead muscle with the aid of an electromyograph (EMG). Eventually, they were able to counteract their tension without the use of the EMG. Other patients with serious cardiac disease are learning to control their symptoms. Engel (1967) achieved marked improvement in patients with arterial fibrillation by providing them with external feedback of their cardiac activity and reinforcing slower heart rate.

Hypertension, a form of high blood pressure that may lead to strokes or heart attacks also seems to be amenable to biofeedback training. Shapiro and Turnsky (1969), in developing a method for the treatment of patients with essential hypertension, found that systolic blood pressure can be modified by the use of external feedback and reinforcement.

Some investigators have suggested that brain wave biofeedback might be effective in combating anxiety. Brain wave patterns recorded by an electroencephalograph (EEG) during waking and sleeping are divided into alpha, beta, theta, and delta categories which correspond to the number of cycles per second recorded from the surface of the scalp. The alpha wave (8-12 cps) has been recorded while subjects were experiencing a "pleasurable state of relaxation." Kamiya (1969) found that through biofeedback, many subjects have been trained to control their brain waves, so that they achieve and sustain alpha waves for prolonged periods. Subjects describe this experience as producing marked tranquility and calm.

However, voluntary control of physiological functions was known long before the current biofeedback experiments. For hundreds of years Zen Buddhists and yogis have claimed to be able to slow their heartbeat, to increase their body temperature, to survive with little oxygen, and to influence other bodily functions which were thought to be involuntary and not sub-

57

ject to modification. Yoga and Zen are thus the focus of increasing scientific interest.

One of these Eastern techniques that has been the subject of recent experiments is Transcendental Meditation (TM), which was developed by Maharishi Mahesh Yogi. The Students' International Meditation Society estimated that 90,000 persons in the United States have started practicing TM in the last six years (Wallace and Benson, 1972). The technique requires no change in life style and can be learned in a relatively short training period. Practice involves sitting a few minutes in the morning and evening with the eyes closed, concentrating on a particular sound or thought. During this time the mind is said to experience subtler states, as physiological changes occur which correspond to this refined mental activity. Meditation is described as a unique state that is restful, yet alert, which is refreshing both physically and mentally, (Wallace, 1970). Kamiya (1969), in his work with the biofeedback of alpha waves found that his results so closely resembled descriptions of Zen and yoga meditation that he invited several Zen meditators to participate in his experiments. These experienced meditators learned to control their alpha waves far more rapidly than did the average person.

A number of studies have described certain biological differences between meditators and non-meditators. During meditation, oxygen consumption and metabolic rate decrease markedly and resemble the rates observed during a deep state of rest (Wallace, 1972); the breath rate decreases, indicating relaxation (Allison, 1970); skin resistance increases significantly, indicating deep relaxation and reduction of anxiety (Wallace and Benson, 1972); cardiac output decreases markedly, indicating a reduction in the work load of the heart (Benson, 1970); and the concentration of blood lactate decreases (Wallace and Benson 1972)—high concentration of lactate in the blood has been associated with anxiety neurosis, anxiety attacks and high blood pressure.

The foregoing research shows that many body functions may be controlled voluntarily. Through such control, perhaps man will be able to adapt to the stress of his environment. Until recently, an ever increasing dependency upon the use of drugs has been the answer to psychogeneric disorders resulting from stress. One of the reasons for the wide use of psychopharmacological agents is that use of the chemical requires no knowledge or skill other than the swallowing of a pill. As we have seen, alternative systems that may produce similar effects require training to produce a desired state. One might assume most people would prefer to take a pill rather than to take the time to be trained, but the universal acceptance of such solutions may be a thing of the past. At this point, there appears to be a readiness in our

Biofeedback and related training:
potential for physical education
Kathileen A. Gallagher

society to reject the ostensible efficacy of drugs and to pursue a more natural way to deal with the problems of contemporary existence. This change may be witnessed in the recent interest in personal health. For example, an interest in natural foods is no longer thought of as solely a concern of the food faddist. Homemakers the world over are demanding better food products and questioning the additives, preservatives, and hormones in many commodities. Aerosol products with ingredients damaging to the respiratory system are either being used more cautiously or are being taken off the shelves. In addition, the public is more cognizant of drug addiction, so that far more attention is being given to possible deleterious side effects of medicine. This growing distaste for and suspicion of chemicals indicates a readiness to seek a more natural alternative to the alleviation of stress. Biofeedback training is one such alternative since unlike drugs, it offers the individual greater autonomy and responsibility for his own health.

Since physical education typically involves training programs that lead to improved performance of motor skills, physical educators may be able to make a major contribution to personal health by offering training in the control of and sensitivity to those organic functions governed by the autonomic nervous system. It may be that combining information about biofeedback with a program for controlling bodily processes may serve to offset the current high incidence of psychogeneric pathology. In other words, trained control of bodily states could well be added to the physical education curriculum, and so help create a healthier public.

To implement such a program into the curricula would require that physical educators become familiar with the literature pertaining to biofeedback training and that they work with those in science and medicine to set up programs for conducting research in the relation of biofeedback training to physical education. Through study, we may find that physical education can explore yet another way of training the individual for a full and healthy life.

BIBLIOGRAPHY

Allison, J., "Respiratory Changes During Transcendental Meditation." *The Lancet*, April 1970. p. 833.

Biofeedback and Self-Control. Chicago: Aldine-Atherton, 1971.

Budzynski, T., and Stoyva, J. "An Instrument for Producing Deep Muscle Relaxation by Means of Analog Information Feedback." *Journal of Applied Behavior Analysis* 2 (1969): 231-237.

Budzynski, T.; Stoyva, J.; and Adler, C. "Feedback-induced Muscle Relaxation: Application to Tension Headaches." *Journal of Behavior Therapy and Experimental Psychiatry*, 1970, 205-211.

Engel, B. Paper read at Pavlovian Society, Princeton, N. J., November 1967.

Engel, B., and Chism, R., "Operant Conditioning of Heart Rate Speeding." *Psychophysiology* 3 (1967): 418-426.

Engel, B., and Hansen "Operant Conditioning of Heart Rate Slowing." *Psychophysiology* 3 (1967): 176-187.

Engel, B., and Melmon, K. "Operant Conditioning of Heart Rate in Patients with Cardiac Arrhythmias." *Conditional Reflex* 3 (1968): 130.

Kamiya, J. "Operant Control of the EEG Alpha Rhythm and Some of its Reported Effects on Consciousness." In *Altered States of Consciousness*, edited by C. Tart, pp. 489-50. New York: John Wiley, 1969.

Mayr, O. The Origins of Feedback Control." *Scientific American* 223 (1970): 111.

Miller, N. "Learning of Visceral and Glandular Responses." *Science* 163: 434-445.

Shapiro, D. Turnsky, B.; Gershon, E.; and Stern, M. "Effects of Feedback and Reinforcement on the Control of Human Systolic Blood Pressure." *Science* 163 (1969): 588-590.

Timmons, B.; Salamy, J.; Kamiya, J.; and Girton, D. "Abdominal-thoracic Respiratory Movements and Levels of Arousal." *Psychonomic Science* 27 (1972): 173-175.

Wallace, R. "The Physiological Effects of Transcendental Meditation." *Science* 167 (1970): 1751-1754.

Wallace, R., and Benson, H. "The Physiology of Meditation." *Scientific American* 226 (1972): 84-90.

Weiss, T., and Engel, B. "Operant Conditioning of Heart Rate in Patients with Premature Ventricular Contractions." *Psychosomatic Medicine* 33 (1971): 301-321.

Issues in physical education and sports

2 PHYSIOLOGICAL

Fitness and
cardiovascular health

Fred W. Kasch
California State University, San Diego

Degenerative heart diseases are killing and debilitating millions of Americans annually. Each year 1.2 million die of coronary heart disease (CHD), of which about one-half are premature. Many victims of heart attacks live in fear of another attack. The World Health Organization has called heart disease man's worst epidemic.

The decline in cardiovascular fitness in Americans is inversely proportional to the rise of CHD. Is there a cause and effect relationship? We are not sure. We do know from evidence in England, Israel, Africa, Asia, and the United States that occupations leading to physical fitness appear to deter the severity and incidence of CHD. Mann (1972; Mann and Others, 1972) believes that physical fitness deters CHD in the Masai people of Africa, although some atherosclerosis exists. He also states that cardiovascular fitness is the most promising thera-peutic medium available for combatting the CHD epidemic.

How can this high incidence of disease exist in the face of our advanced medical technology? The answer is that these diseases are non-infectious and therefore cannot be controlled by drugs. In 1970 a Copenhagen Sym-posium on CHD and Physical Fitness (Larsen and Malmborg, 1971) concluded that environmental factors appear to be responsible for the high incidence of CHD. These factors include lack of adequate physical activity, diet, cig-arette smoking, anxiety, and obesity. Additional contributing factors include high blood pressure (hypertension), diabetes, excessive use of alcohol, ECG abnormalities, and heredity. Thus, it is the private citizen and not medicine that can do the most to counteract the incidence of CHD, since he alone can control his environment.

THE NEW ROLE OF EXERCISE IN CHD

At a recent Seattle symposium entitled "The World of the Heart and Lung," it was recognized that physical exercise is of prime importance as a thera-peutic medium in both prevention and rehabilitation of CHD and pulmonary disease. No longer is it prudent in medicine to advise only rest and drugs for the heart victim. He must be rehabilitated and returned to full employ-ment and a normal life. This cannot be done in every case, but CHD pro-grams are successfully rehabilitating many patients in San Diego under Kasch and Boyer. Other successful therapists include Hellerstein in Cleve-land, Balke in Madison, Pyfer and Bruce in Seattle, Brock in Denver, and Zohman in New York. Rehabilitation is succeeding primarily through exer-cise, although diet, elimination of smoking, and the control of body weight, anxiety, diabetes, hypertension, alcohol, and ECG abnormalities also seem to be of value. It must be pointed out that physical exercise modifies every CHD risk factor. It lowers body weight, lipids, blood pressure and glucose, eases the effect of anxiety by the utilization of adrenalin, and lessens arryth-mias of the heart. In addition, the desire for cigarette smoking and alcohol are often overshadowed by the motivation to improve one's health. Neither drugs nor cardiac surgery can make these claims.

WHAT ABOUT PREVENTION?

As valuable as these successful rehabilitation programs may be, they do not get to the "heart" of the matter—prevention. Here is where the greatest gains can be made. The public must be made aware of the problem and then be convinced to do something about it. CHD starts in infancy. It is a pediatric problem which progresses into adult life and is then recognized as a disease.

Karlsberg (1971), a Swedish pediatrician, has stated that the human uses one-fourth to one-third of his life in growth and development in preparation for the remainder. This means that a sound heart and other body organs can only be developed by vigorous physical activity in about the first twenty years of life. Present-day ten- and eleven-year old boys and girls have developed only 65 percent of their cardiovascular capacity, as reported by Cumming and Danzinger (1963). It is quite possible that this insufficient development of capacity for work may be a contributing factor to heart disease in later life. In addition, this low level of cardiovascular development, the result of inactivity, may lead to poor micro- and macro-coronary circulation, low cardiac reserve, myocardial neuro-hormonal imbalance, faulty lipid-glucose metabolism, obesity, and hypertension.

CARDIOVASCULAR HEALTH AND THE SCHOOL

In the school we develop the child mentally, socially, and occupationally, only to let him die prematurely as an adult because we neglect his organic development. The school must become the primary agent in the prevention of CHD, because in controlling the child's environment for many hours each school day it has the means of teaching the child about exercise, smoking, diet, obesity, anxiety, hypertension, diabetes, alcohol, ECG problems, and heredity-family tendencies. But even more important, the school can help supply the many hours of vigorous exercise required for the child's full physiological development. Aside from heredity, this vigorous physical activity is the primary source of organic health. One cannot gain it by sleep, food, or anything else, but only through adequate daily exercise. Because it is the only part of the school curriculum that uses exercise, physical education is thus ideally equipped to train young people in the principles and practices leading to organic vigor and to help develop life-long recreational habits for maintaining that vigor.

For more than fifty years physical education has emphasized fitness through sports. But today we have scientific proof that most American school sports are too low in their cardiovascular demand to develop the heart and circulatory system. In addition, through fifty years of observation we can see that America is becoming more unfit, although sports have flourished.

The answer is clear—with a few exceptions, American sports do *not* lead to fitness. We must change our approach and start using fitness techniques to become fit. We must run, swim, cycle, skate, row, hike, and then put these activities into the physical education curriculum.

WHAT IS CV HEALTH?

The criterion of a machine is its ability to work. The human machine's work is dependent upon oxygen (O_2). It can work for short periods of time without O_2 (anaerobic work), but in sustained (aerobic) work, O_2 is essential. O_2 is transported from the lungs to the tissues by the heart and circulatory system. Thus, if we measure the O_2 consumed over a period of time, we now have a measurement of human work. In practical terms, cardiovascular fitness is the ability to work continuously for 15 minutes at about 70 percent of maximum heart rate (HR) capacity and the ability to repeat this task daily or even more often. If we have disease or a breakdown and we cannot work at high intensities, this means that the cardiovascular system's capacity is diminished (Simonson and Enzer, 1942). If we determine the increase in absorption of O_2 (VO_2), we now have a valid, repeatable measurement which can be compared with other people. We also have a measurement of the function of the cardiovascular system. These measurements can be made in the laboratory using tests for stress, including the bicycle ergometer, treadmill, or step test. The greater the VO_2 max, generally speaking, the better the cardiovascular machine, or cardiovascular (CV) endurance, although natural endowment and state of training are also factors which must be considered.

HOW TO OBTAIN CV ENDURANCE

Cardiovascular fitness or endurance results from a sustained circulation of about 15 minutes or more at about 70 percent of max capacity. For example, with each heartbeat, arterial blood flows from the heart to the cells of the working muscles and is then returned through the venous system by muscle action to the lungs for removal of CO_2 and replenishment of O_2. Finally, it flows back to the heart for the next cycle. Rhythmic activities like running, cycling, swimming, rowing, skating, and walking or hiking, all of which use gross muscle action, are the best sources of sustained work at 70 percent of capacity. Such activities require a large amount of O_2 and consequently a great amount of circulation. By measuring the O_2 uptake we can indirectly measure the approximate amount of circulation and the

**Fitness and
cardiovascular health**
Fred W. Kasch

increase in work over the resting state. The VO_2 at rest is 3.5 ml/min/kg of body weight and is termed one MET. Endurance activities increase the number of METs, or the metabolic cost of work. Generally speaking, the MET level should be increased 8-9 times in order to develop CV endurance. Table 1 displays the METs (Balke, 1960) for several rhythmic activities and compares their relative merit in producing CV endurance.

Thus, to improve CV endurance one must select rhythmic activities of adequate MET level. Isometric or non-rhythmic exercises are inadequate and may be dangerous or even fatal, particularly to those with heart disease. Many sports involve only anaerobic spurts of activity—they are only intermittently strenuous and at other times are too low in intensity. Rhythmic activities are aerobic and are constant in intensity. They can therefore be prescribed more precisely and usually more safely.

TABLE 1
METs LEVELS FOR SEVERAL SPORTS

Sport	MPH	Mets	
Running	7.0	12	
Swimming	1.6	9	
Cycling	14.0	9	Adequate CV endurance
Rowing	11.0	13	
Skating	13.0	10	
Golf		4	Inadequate CV endurance
Tennis		6	

STANDARDS OF CV FITNESS

Table 2 shows that the VO_2 max in Swedish boys from 7 to 17 years is equal, while about a 15 percent decline occurs in teenage girls, as compared to their younger counterparts. This is primarily due to the increase in adipose tissue in adolescent girls.

The data in this table is the ideal. American youngsters at age 10 and 11 have a VO_2 of 37 ml/min/kg for boys and 34 ml/min/kg for girls (Cumming & Danzinger, 1963). They have the same potential as Swedish children and should be their equal.

TABLE 2
VO₂, AGE, AND MAX HEART RATE IN SWEDISH CHILDREN*

Age	MALE		FEMALE	
	ml/min/kg	Max HR	ml/min/kg	Max HR
7	58.7	203	56.0	209
9	56.8	206	56.4	215
11	56.9	207	52.9	210
13	56.5	213	48.7	208
15	59.7	202	44.7	202
17	58.2	201	47.9	201

*Adapted from P. O. Astrand (1952).

Figure 1 illustrates the adult decline in VO_2 with age. That this decline in men can be minimized is seen in the data in Table 3. These men trained two to three times a week to make these VO_2 gains. Thus, proper application of cardiovascular exercise can forestall the usual decline in cardiovascular function.

Females decline in VO_2 from 2.08 L/min at age 30, to 1.98 L/min at 40, and 1.78 L/min (–15 percent) at age 50. Males decline 22 percent during the same time period. The effect of long-term training on patients with CHD and men without CHD is presented in Table 4.

Although the actual VO_2 values for CHD patients are much lower than for normal men, the percent of increase with training is equivalent, that is,

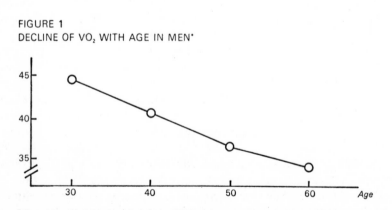

FIGURE 1
DECLINE OF VO_2 WITH AGE IN MEN*

*Adapted from W. Hollman and H. Knipping (1961), I. Astrand (1960), and Robinson (1938).

**Fitness and
cardiovascular health**

Fred W. Kasch

TABLE 3
REVERSAL THROUGH EXERCISE OF VO$_2$
DECLINE IN MEN WITH AGE

Age	n	ml/min/kg	L/min
30–39	14	37.6	3.09
40–49	50	38.4	3.14
50–59	48	35.9	2.87
60–69	9	36.1	2.62

TABLE 4
EFFECTS OF LONG-TERM TRAINING
ON MEN

	Normals	CHD
Mos.	VO$_2$ ml/min/kg	VO$_2$ ml/min/kg
0	31	24
3	—	29
6	38	31
12	40	31
24	40	31

29 percent. It is this increase in circulatory function that may be of greatest significance in rehabilitating CHD victims and in preventing CHD in normal subjects.

Oxygen uptake, the criterion of O$_2$ transport and cardiovascular function, has been reviewed in relation to age, sex, and disease. Another approach, much simpler, but less accurate, is the use of recovery HR from standard exercise. The reader is referred to Astrand & Rhyming (1954), Sharkey (1971), and Gallagher (1967) for step tests. The three minute step (Kasch, (1961; 1968; 1970) has been chosen for our purpose here, because it can be used for all ages and both sexes. It is mild enough for even diseased subjects, yet it gives a wide range of response, as may be seen in Table 5. This step test uses a 12-inch bench, 24 steps per minute rate, for 3 minutes.

Although six- to twelve-year-old girls have higher HR than the same age boys, their percent of increase over resting are identical. Young men, proba-

69

TABLE 5
SUGGESTED STANDARDS OF RECOVERY HR IN A
0–1 MINUTE POST-EXERCISE PERIOD

Classification	6–12 yrs		18–26 years		33–57 yrs
	Boys	Girls	Men	Women**	Men*
Superior	64–72	69–80	62–68	67–75	50–62
Excellent	73–82	81–92	69–75	76–84	63–76
Good	83–92	93–104	76–83	85–94	77–90
Average	93–103	105–118	84–92	95–105	91–106
Fair	104–113	119–130	93–99	106–116	107–120
Poor	114–123	131–142	100–106	117–127	121–134
Very Poor	124–133	143–154	107–113	128–138	135–148
Mean	98	111	88	100	98
Range	74–126	83–142	72–104	—	60–150
SD	12.0	14.8	9.8	—	18.7

*No data available for women, use figures for men 33–57 yrs and add 10.
**Arbitrary data.

bly because of their superior strength, have lower HR than children. Adult men often have sub-clinical and actual clinical disease and thus an even wider range of HR occurs. Broad differences in cardiovascular responses in children and adults can be distinguished by this test, but sensitive differences are not possible. The tables should be interpreted in this broad sense, using the results as a guide in exercise prescription, but *not* as a critical evaluation of the cardiovascular system. Additional and more definitive studies are needed for that purpose.

NEED FOR TRAINED PERSONNEL

A new philosophy of health must be developed in our society. The school should be paramount in this change. Emphasis on prevention of disease, particularly CHD and degenerative diseases, is the new order for health and physical educators, physicians, nurses, and para-medical personnel. In-service training of physical and health educators, administrators, and teachers must start now. We cannot wait for change to occur by means of new teachers from the teacher training institutions—that may take twenty to forty years while the epidemic is killing us now.

**Fitness and
cardiovascular health**

Fred W. Kasch

Teacher training curricula must be revised immediately, along with curricula in elementary and secondary physical and health education. Emphasis must be placed on environmental health and cardiovascular endurance activities. The old games of low cardiovascular return should be eliminated. At least half the time and emphasis should be on endurance and physical fitness.

Additional college curricula should be instituted for the training of paramedical personnel in rehabilitation and prevention of CHD of adults. These personnel might include CV exercise leaders, exercise technologists, exercise program supervisors and directors. One- to five-year programs would graduate the personnel needed to initiate nation-wide programs.

SUMMARY

CHD and other degenerative diseases are annually killing and debilitating millions of Americans unnecessarily. Since physical exercise is the most essential element in the prevention and rehabilitation of coronary, pulmonary, and degenerative disease, physical education curricula, including teacher training, should be revised to include programs promoting the principles and practice of cardiovascular health, especially with respect to smoking, obesity, hypertension, diet, alcohol, and anxiety.

Exercise aids the circulatory system by improving micro- and macro-coronary circulation, expanding myocardial reserve, decreasing peripheral resistance and blood pressure, controlling catecholomines and balancing the myocardial oxygen supply and demand, balancing lipid-glucose metabolism, and improving of cardiac arrythmias.

Cardiovascular function or fitness is the ability to sustain a high level of oxygen transport by means of the circulating blood over a period of at least 15 minutes. This type of endurance is obtained only through participation in 15 minutes of rhythmic exercise such as running, swimming, skating, rowing, or cycling, with prior gradation to develop this extended tolerance.

Standards of cardiovascular endurance are related to the criterion measurement of the oxygen transport system, VO_2 max. These standards are reported above for all ages, both sexes, and in relation to CHD.

A less desirable, but simpler measurement of circulatory endurance is the heart rate. This is reported above for all ages and both sexes, using a simple and inexpensive step test. Its limitations are discussed.

71

CONCLUSION

In view of the present epidemic of coronary and degenerative disease in America, it is past time to develop cardiovascular health through CV exercise and other controllable risk-environmental factors. The responsibility lies with the individual, but he must be made aware of the problem. To accomplish this goal, a nation-wide educational program must be initiated for school children as well as adults.

REFERENCES

Astrand, I. "Aerobic Work Capacity in Men and Women." *Acta Physio. Scand.* Supp. 169 49(1960):1-92.

Astrand, P. O. *Experimental Studies of Physical Working Capacity in Relation to Sex and Age.* Copenhagen: Munksgaard, 1952.

Astrand, P. O., and Rhyming, I. "A Nomogram for Calculation of Aerobic Capacity from PR during Submaximal Work." *J. App. Phys.* 7(1954):218-21.

Balke, B. "The Effect of Physical Exercise on the Metabolic Potential, a Crucial Measure of Physical Fitness." In *Exercise & Fitness*, pp. 73-81. Chicago: Athletic Institute, 1960.

Cumming, G. R., and Danzinger, R. "Bicycle Ergometry Studies in Children." *Pediatrics* 32(1963):202-207.

Gallagher, J. R. et al. "Is Your Patient Fit?" *JAMA* 201(1967):117-118.

Hollman, W., and Knipping, H. "The Ascertainment of Physical Capacity from Clinical Point of View." In *Health and Fitness in the Modern World*, pp. 17-30. Chicago: Athletic Institute, 1961.

Karlberg, P. "Pediatric Work Physiology Forward." *Acta Pediatrics Scandinavica* Supp. 217, 1971.

Kasch, F. W. "Exercise Physiology Laboratory Manual." San Diego, Ca.: San Diego State College, 1970.

Kasch, F. W. "A Comparison of the Exercise Tolerance of Post-Rheumatic and Normal Boys," *J. Assoc. Phys. & Mental Rehab.* 15(1961):35-40.

Kasch, F. W., and Boyer, J. L. *Adult Fitness.* Palo Alto, Ca.: National Press Books, 1968.

Larsen, O. A., and Malmborg, R. O. *Coronary Heart Disease and Physical Fitness.* Baltimore: Univ. Park Press, 1971.

Mann, G. "The Saturated vs. Unsaturated Fat Controversy." *Proceedings of the Meat Industry Research Conference.* Chicago: American Meat Institute Foundation, 1972.

Mann, G. V.; Spoerry, A.; Gray, M.; and Jarashow, D. "Atherosclerosis in the Masai." *Amer. J. Epidemiology* 95(1972):26-37.

Robinson, Sid "Experimental Studies of Physical Fitness in Relation to Age." *Arbeitsphysiologie* 10(1938):251-323.

Sharkey, B. *Physiological Fitness and Weight Control.* Missoula, Mont.: Montana Bureau for Research on Physical Activity and Sport, Univ. Montana, 1971.

Simonson, E., and Enzer, N. "Physiology of Muscular Exercise and Fatigue in Disease." *Medicine* 21(1942):345-419

Fitness testing

Benjamin Ricci
University of Massachusetts

Rare indeed is the physical educator who misses an opportunity to define and discuss physical fitness. Yet he often simply accepts and promulgates, unquestioningly, the previously pronounced definitions and concepts of the "leaders" of physical education. Nurtured on method offered by solid conservatives, the physical educator is channelled into a course of action and mode of behavior which leaves little room for skepticism. Indeed, the physical educator has been endowed with a veritable pharmacopoeia of *physical fitness* tests.

By comparison, *fitness* testing sounds learned and respectable. By avoiding the prefix "physical," users of the term may possibly be demonstrating a desire to avoid controversy. Yet, controversy cannot be avoided.

73

What factors compel one to dissipate energy as well as finances on fitness testing? Because the exhortation to evaluate, given all prospective teachers, enjoys an extremely slow extinction rate—roughly comparable to the half-life of radium, which is 1600 years. Besides, the gathering and statistical manipulation of data creates an aura of respectibility. After all, members of the scientific community constantly test hypotheses, so why shouldn't physical educators? Furthermore, data tables containing means, standard deviations, standard errors of means, F ratios, and levels of significance, with possibly a smoothed ogive graph or two, may impress school administrators and board members and perhaps some college administrators. Then too, results of fitness tests might even be used to justify modification of course offerings. Above all, the human subject who produced the data may enjoy a spin-off—the elimination of flawed responses to test batteries. Abundant health! Progress!

At this juncture, the reader may surmise a ripple of satire and may be moved to challenge the testing program, which uses up energy and consumes time. Why, the reader might ask, should I administer fitness tests? Is my test battery valid? Should I bother to define physical fitness, or just plain fitness, or total fitness, which includes such profundities as mental, spiritual, and emotional fitness?

In recognition of and respect for the complex biomechanical composite which is a human being, and in keeping with the Law of Parsimony, we suggest obtaining estimates of the responses of particular systems to the taxing effects of a variety of physical tasks through the use of stress testing. Stress is exhibited along a continuum as is response to stress. Irrespective of the avowed purpose of testing, the cardiopulmonary, metabolic, heat regulatory, and neuromuscular systems of the human organism respond to any challenge that threatens homeostasis. Physical stress may be imposed by exercise, or work, or by a variety of human performances reflecting displacement, force, acceleration, speed, velocity and so forth. Although marvelous, human systems cannot differentiate between terms. This is left for the mind to ponder. The quantification of stress with respect to particular sub-systems, rather than to total body response, becomes the challenge.

Should one be impressed with norms? Yes, provided the norms—the average accomplishments—are carefully obtained from randomly selected sub-populations. Random selection implies that the laws of chance relative to selection are allowed to operate—that all possible subjects are equally likely to be selected as representatives. Yet norms which reflect diligence as well as adherence to rigorous statistical procedure can reflect a complete disregard for biomechanical interplay. Pull-up, or chinning, norms, which are typically presented as a function of sex and chronological age are an example of disregard for biomechanical interplay. Table 1 presents a set of published norms on pull-ups.

The above pull-up accomplishments reveal that biomechanical interplay has been disregarded. One can readily observe that all twelve-year-old males are not carbon copies of each other relative to somatotype, muscle girth, hormonal level, muscle infra-structure, limb length, or motivation level. Especially during the onset of puberty, the range of heterogeneity is remarkable. Pull-up accomplishment, by sex and chronological age, for each of at least three somatotype categories would greatly enhance the robustness of the procedure.

Without an expression of mass displacement and subsequent work accomplishment, or of accomplishment expressed as a function of body mass, the pull-up task is devoid of meaning, as Table 2 illustrates.

Note that subject B must perform double the number of pull-ups to achieve the same pu/kg body-weight index as A achieves. Yet, when ex-

TABLE 1
PULL-UP NORMS, BOYS UNDERHAND GRIP*

Age	12	13	14	15	16	17	18	Percentile
No. Pull-ups	9	14	16	20	20	20	21	99th
	1	2	4	6	7	7	8	40th
	0	1	2	4	5	5	6	25th

*From E. A. Fleishman (1964).

TABLE 2
EVALUATING PULL-UP ACCOMPLISHMENT*

Subject	Weight (kg)	Pull-ups (pu)	pu/kg	Displacement (m)	Work (kgm)
A	50	3	.06	1.5	(50 × 1.5) = 75
B	100	6	.06	3.0	(100 × 3.0) = 300
B	100	1.5	.015	0.75	(100 × 0.75) = 75
B	100	3	.03	1.5	(100 × 1.5) = 150

*From B. Ricci (1970).

pressed as kgm work, B's accomplishment is four times greater than that of A. To attain the same work output, B (third entry) need perform only half the number of pull-ups as A, which amounts to one-fourth the pu/kg index.

As shown in the last entry, the accomplishment of equal numbers of pull-ups (3) by persons of very different mass (50 kg versus 100 kg) could lead to three conclusions: (1) the individuals are equal in terms of pull-up accomplishment; (2) A is to be ranked above B because of achieving a greater pu/kg index; or (3) B is to be ranked above A because he performed twice as much work. This point need not be belabored. Suffice it to say that sweeping reforms are long overdue, in fact urgently required, to translate items on so-called tests of physical fitness into expressions which consider—rather than totally disregard—biomechanical factors.

Pull-up achievement is also a function of grasp, hence the measurement of grasp must be standardized. Greater pull-up accomplishment resulting from the reverse grasp (palms facing the performer) is rooted in a biochemical explanation (Ricci, 1971). In the execution of pull-ups, irrespective of grasp, the greatest force in the upper limbs is produced by the extensors of the humerii. The forces produced by the flexors of the forearm are also pronounced and are distinguished by type of grasp. With the forward grasp, forces about the elbow joint are of a sustained nature in comparison with a variable, rhythmical force application around the elbow joint resulting from the reverse grasp. Data from the author's on-going research, in which blood lactate levels are estimated, substantiate the hypothesis of variable versus sustained forces. Using the reverse grasp, lactate levels were *less* following the execution of a *greater* number of pull-ups than when the forward grasp, was used.

Quantifying adaptation to stress by estimating gross metabolism provides an opportunity to exhibit a respectable level of research competence along with the opportunity to demonstrate ignorance of active tissue mass involvement. For example: individuals A (♂) and B (♀) of comparable age (individuals of the same sex and comparable age but of different somatotype could be substituted), show an oxygen consumption during the 4th to 6th minute of running performance on a motor driven treadmill of 4181 cc/min. for A (♂) and 2500 cc/min. for B (♀). What conclusion might the unwary or uninformed researcher be tempted to draw? That the male is capable of greater oxygen consumption? That the female is more efficient because her oxygen consumption was 60 percent less than the male's? Actually, both conclusions are indefensible.

Oxygen consumption reflects the involvement of active tissue mass, notably muscle mass which may comprise 40 percent of the total body mass.

Since muscle mass thus elevates the oxygen consumption values, it must be considered in the conclusions. Options are available. One would be to express oxygen consumption as a function of muscle mass or lean body weight. Obviously this would entail an added estimation. More simply, the oxygen consumption could be expressed as a function of body weight, as is shown in Table 3.

Now the data become more meaningful. The female performer, heretofore seemingly inferior in terms of her metabolic adaptation to stress emerges as the one who is the equal of the male. Once again, the opportunity for error is present. What accomplishments are to be recorded? Subject A performed approximately 58 percent more work than Subject B: 7769 kilogram-meters versus 4489 kilogram-meters. The male also consumed approximately 60 percent more oxygen than the female and performed 58 percent more work. Yet adaptations to stress in terms of oxygen consumption as a function of muscle mass are approximately equal.

At the time the research was being conducted, the subjects cited in the above example were superbly conditioned runners. As stated earlier, subjects of the same sex and age but of different somatotype would offer an opportunity for faulty conclusions, unless the estimation of metabolic adaptation to stress reflected the mass involved.

Sound research design must be utilized before sound conclusions can be drawn. A justifiable estimation of the response to metabolic stress imposed by such physical tasks as bench stepping, treadmill running, or stair climbing can easily be accomplished by subjecting individuals to a uniform work

TABLE 3
EXPRESSION OF OXYGEN CONSUMPTION*

	Ht/cm	Wt/kg	O_2 Consumption cc/min (during 4–6th min)	O_2 Consumption expressed as a function of body weight VO_2 cc/kg/min
A ♂	189	92.6	4181	45.1
B ♀	164	53.5	2500	46.7

*Adapted from B. Ricci (1970).

load, then expressing oxygen consumption estimations as a function of mass being displaced.

Estimation of cardiac response to stress imposed by a variety of physical tasks represents another estimation which can result in erroneous interpretation. This parameter is further subjected to unscientific labeling which equates heart rate (cardiac frequency) with pulse rate. Admittedly, the units of measurement are both frequency per minute or adjusted to minutes. However, the similarity ends there. The frequency of heart muscle contraction, which imparts force to blood, yields heart rate, that is, the rate of cardiac muscle contraction. By comparison, the *result* of the muscle force imparted by the left ventricle, further affected by the elasticity of the arteries, yields pulse rate. Obviously the resiliency of the blood vessels will determine to a great extend the rate of transformation of energy from potential to kinetic.

Cardiac frequency (heart rate) only partly reflects the response of cardiac tissue to stress. Actually, the heart propels blood, and the rate of blood delivery per unit time is the product of rate of ventricular contraction times the amount of blood ejected during each contraction. Of particular interest is the rate of contraction of the left ventricle as well as the volume of blood ejected into systemic circulation during each contraction, that is, the stroke volume. Admittedly, estimation of stroke volume in humans presents technical difficulties which are surmounted by relatively few well trained physiologists and medical doctors.

The ease with which the heart rate is obtained adds to its appeal and use. Moreover, the use of this variable is considerably strengthened and made respectable when it is expressed as a percentage of maximum. For a variety of reasons, all persons do not possess the same maximum heart rate. Estimations of cardiac adjustment to stress (as revealed by cardiac frequency alone) by persons A and B are justifiable when expressed as a percentage of maximum for A and for B. Obtaining maximum heart rates demands the use of safety precautions as well as dedication on the part of the subject.

With respect to neuromuscular parameters the term "force," which expresses magnitude as well as direction, is advocated as a replacement for strength, which is usually incorrectly used. Strength obscures such essential considerations as muscle cross-sectional area or the presence of torque. After having been subjected to a hand dynamometer, A's accomplishment is 50 percent greater than B's. What can one rightfully conclude? Here again, the greater compression of the dynamometer by A over B (who might even possess equal upper arm and forearm lengths) lacks meaningful interpretation, for the hand flexor cross-sectional area might be twice as large for

A as for B. The force expressed as a function of muscle cross-sectional area would probably be equal for A as well as for B.

In some of the preceding examples, sex was conveniently introduced. While recognizing hormonal and configurational differences, male and female accomplishments can often be compared if expressed as a function of another parameter. Sometimes, however, sex differences may be taken into account in such a way as to further obscure rather than clarify the measurements sought. For example, in the Harvard step-test, bench heights for females were arbitrarily lowered—the advocates of the lowered bench heights were women. No consideration was given to the disadvantaged short-legged male versus the advantaged long-legged female. Sex mattered most and males were doomed to the 50.8 cm bench height, while females were privileged (primarily because of sex) to adapt to the stress imposed by stepping onto a 43.18 cm or a 45.72 cm bench at a prescribed cadence. (Ricci et al. [1966] describes the somewhat surprising results.) Sex differences aside, the unsuccessful completion of the Harvard step-test may merely reflect motivation levels and discomfort tolerance levels rather than cardiopulmonary response to stress imposed by bench stepping.

Irrespective of sex, how well or poorly a person adjusts to stress imposed by physical work or exercise can be measured in part from estimations reflecting adaptations of particular systems. When interpreted with care—when expressed *as a function of* mass, for example, or displacement or cross sectional area, or torque, or limb length—data can become meaningful, defensible, and worthy of detailed statistical manipulation.

But we have a professional and public mentality to deal with and to update. For a host of reasons, notably the methods orientation of physical educators, our schools are not equipped with the apparatus essential for performance estimates. (Money could not possibly be an issue, because essential apparatus for respectable estimates can be purchased for a fraction of the amount expended for athletics). Furthermore, the physical educator has been content to adopt, without questioning, so-called physical fitness tests which can be administered to large numbers of persons within a relatively short time, generally without apparatus, without regard for psychological and biomechanical considerations, and with total reliance on norms, some of which seem to have been handed down with the Ten Commandments.

Are physical educators prepared to enter the scientific world? Hardly, for until their curriculum begins to reflect replacement of method with content, they are at the mercy of the "leaders in the field"—some of whom are with us only in spirit. Until quality research becomes an established, honored practice, the physical educator is destined to remain a consumer rather than a producer of knowledge. And, in the words of UCLA economics professor William R. Allen, "Research is to teaching, what sin is to confession: without the one, you have nothing to say in the other" (National Association of State Universities and Land Grant Colleges Circular Letter, May 31, 1972).

REFERENCES

Fleishman, E. A. 1964. *Examiner's Manual for the Basic Fitness Tests.* Englewood Cliffs, N. J.: Prentice-Hall.

National Association of State Universities and Land Grant Colleges Circular Letter. Number 10, May 31, 1972.

Ricci, B. 1971. Kinetics of pull-ups: overgrasp vs. undergrasp. *Medicine and Sport* 6:236-39.

Ricci, B. 1970. *Experiments in the Physiology of Human Performance.* Philadelphia: Lea & Febiger.

Ricci, B. 1970. *Physiological Basis of Human Performance.* Philadelphia: Lea & Febiger.

Ricci, B., and others. 1966. Energy cost and efficiency of Harvard step-test performance. *Arbeitsphysiologie* 22:125-30.

Changing requirements for the ph.d. in physical education with a specialization in exercise physiology

George A. Brooks
University of California, Berkeley

The body of knowledge which constitutes the core of "physical education" is material from many other disciplines, including psychology, sociology, philosophy, history, the performing arts, physics, mechanics, biological chemistry, nutrition, medicine, and physiology. However, the focus that distinguishes physical education from other disciplines is its interpretation of the human as a kinesthetic being and its high regard for the benefits of exercise and sports.

In many respects the study of exercise physiology, one of the bases of physical education, is enormously exciting and gratifying. It affords the individual a rare opportunity to probe the mechanisms underlying performance in the sports activities so intimately a part of our culture. In effect, those who can qualify as exercise physiologists acquire a means for continued involvement with the motor activities that one invariably learns to appreciate at an early age. The field of exercise physiology, along with other specializations in physical education, continues to attract many of the most inquisitive students with experience in physical education and athletics. However, the job of the exercise physiologist is changing, and with it, the qualifications necessary to meet the present and future demands upon an exercise physiologist are changing also.

We should consider, first, whether physical education should encourage research in an area which could be considered a branch of applied physiology. Should not physical educators rely on pure scientists and medical personnel to develop and elaborate the foundations on which to base our profession? While strong arguments could be found for both sides of this question, in a practical sense, such discussions are superfluous. In the past, the contribution of medical people and pure physiologists to the realm of exercise physiology has been substantial. However, the number of investigators studying exercise in medical schools and departments of physiology is on the decline today, compared to several decades ago, during the genesis of studies on metabolism, when many physiologists were interested in direct and indirect calorimetry. Physiological and biochemical research has become involved in increasingly detailed studies of very confined areas. As a result, many of the questions raised by physical educators have gone unattended and unanswered. An example of this is the phenomenon of post-exercise oxygen consumption, formerly called the "O_2 debt." Quantifying the amount of excess O_2 consumed in recovery from exercise has in the past been considered a method of assessing an individual's anaerobic work capacity. The O_2 debt measure was based on the assumption formulated by physiologists and biochemists that the excess O_2 consumption after exercise represented, in whole or in part, the reconversion to glycogen of the lactic acid formed in exercise. Recently, it has come to light that the lactic acid formed in exercise is not reconverted to glycogen during recovery from exercise, and although the metabolic basis underlying post-exercise O_2 consumption has been only partially elucidated, it is now obvious the O_2 debt is not a valid measure of the anaerobic metabolism which occurs during exercise. The problem of post-exercise O_2 consumption is but one example of the overlapping boundaries between physiology and physical education. How much longer would the attempts at quantifying post-exercise O_2 consumption have continued, had not a physical educator taken the time to learn some elementary physiology and biochemistry, to read the literature, and to perform the necessary experiments?

82   Another example of how basic research has failed the physical educator

Changing requirements for the ph.d. in physical education
with a specialization in exercise physiology

George A. Brooks

is to be found in the sport of weight training. There are almost as many schemes for achieving maximum strength gain as there are coaches. This should not be taken as criticism of those involved physical educators working in weight training—on the contrary, it is a criticism of the failure of basic research to serve physical education. I am sure that weight training coaches would find some common approach if only the biological mechanisms of strength gain and muscle growth were understood. It has not really been established if an increase in muscle bulk is requisite to gain in muscle strength, or if the increase in muscle size (hypertrophy) associated with weight training is accomplished by the hypertrophy of existing muscle cells or by an increase in the number of muscle cells (hyperplasia). Solution to the above problems of muscle growth may well have to await a physical educator who can master the necessary experimental techniques and afford to spend several years in the laboratory.

Obviously, the solutions to the practical problems of physical education will have to come from within the profession. What kind of preparation, then, is appropriate of those Ph.D. candidates in physical education who will be our researchers? For the prospective exercise physioligist the course of preparation is harrowing. In order to perform physiological research, either pure or applied, within or outside the confines of physical education, a thorough training in basic physiological and biochemical concepts and research techniques is required.

That a thorough scientific preparation of physical education researchers is necessary is easily understood if we compare knowledge to an apple tree: Most of the fruit low on the tree has already been picked. Reaching the higher fruit requires a firm, far-reaching grasp, and considerable effort and the construction of a solid supporting structure from which to operate. Again the illustration of recent advances in the field of post-exercise O_2 consumption (O_2 debt) is helpful. Our level of comprehension was hopelessly mired because of the inability to reach beyond simple O_2 consumption and blood lactate measurements. In actuality only a little more technical sophistication was required to completely change our outlook.

Preparation of the exercise physiologist is also complicated by the tendency for scientists to specialize. This has been the case for a decade or more in several physical education schools and departments around the country. It is no longer unusual in fact, to find physical educators who have had intensive scientific training. Finally, the prospective candidate should be

83

aware that the exercise physiology job market has become saturated. At present and in the foreseeable future, even those with the best of preparations, including the intensive research experience of post-doctoral training, will find it difficult to find a job as an exercise physiologist. It is therefore important for students of human motor performance to be constantly alert to new areas in which they can fill a need. In the future, health services may be an area in which exercise physiologists may make great contributions. Working with physicians and other medical personnel, exercise physiologists may devise and direct exercise programs for cardiac rehabilitation, obese, and geriatric patients. In private industry, exercise physiologists could be employed as part of a preventive medicine program to set fitness standards and to direct exercise programs for workers. In view of the current aerobics and jogging craze, the possibility even exists for exercise physiologists to try their hand at the health studio business. This last suggestion is admittedly a far cry from the goal set in training a student for a Ph.D. But in view of the present overproduction of physical educators specialized in exercise physiology, it is not unlikely that some of those with primarily academic interests will be forced to mark time in a related field of endeavor until colleges and universities again begin to demand personnel.

Below is to be found a suggested course outline for the Ph.D. degree with a specialization in exercise physiology. The courses suggested below are, of course, *in addition* to minimal requirements expected of all Ph.D. candidates in physical education. It is understood also that the outline will vary from university to university because of differences in course offerings. The intent has been to leave the program as flexible as possible so that course sequences can be tailored to the needs and interests of students.

Curriculum for the Exercise Physiology Ph.D. in Physical Education

I. *Prerequisites*

 *Undergraduate Exercise Physiology—one or two semesters
 *General Chemistry, including laboratory—two or three semesters
 *Organic Chemistry, including laboratory—two semesters
 Physical Chemistry—one semester
 *Mathematics—two semesters of calculus
 *Physics—one semester

II. *Physical Education*

 *Exercise Physiology Seminars
 *Other Physical Education Seminars
 *Research Method Seminars

**Changing requirements for the ph.d. in physical education
with a specialization in exercise physiology**

George A. Brooks

Journal Club Seminar

Individual Research

III. *Education*

*Other Physical Education degree requirements; School of Education
requirements, if any

IV. *Physiology*

*Graduate Survey Mammalian or Human Physiology with laboratory

*Cardio-vascular Physiology

*Cell Physiology

Renal Physiology

Endocrine Physiology

Environmental Physiology

Comparative Physiology

Animal Care

Animal Surgery

Others

V. *Biochemistry*

*Graduate Survey Biochemistry with laboratory

*Advanced Laboratory Techniques:

Chromatography

Uses and Handling of Isotope

Techniques in Manometry

*Whole Animal Energetics

Mitochondrial Energetics

Muscle Energetics

Others

VI. *Statistics*

*Three graduate level courses on Parametric and Non-parametric
Statistics

VII. *Zoology*

Selected courses to substitute for or augment other outlined courses

VIII. *Nutrition*

Selected courses to augment other department offerings

---

*Required courses

Note that the above outline places an enormous reliance on the talents and facilities of departments outside those of physical education. Aside from the absurdity of departments of physical education attempting to duplicate the facilities of other departments, it only makes sense to tap existing resources. Moreover, students benefit greatly from contacts outside the department. Such contacts are often intellectually stimulating and many provide the opportunity for establishing relationships which may lead to collaborative research.

It must be emphasized again that the maximum flexibility concomitant with the needs of the students should be allowed. Scrutiny of the university catalogue of course offerings may reveal that the courses suggested above appear in departments other than the most obvious one. For example, excellent courses in physiology and biochemistry often are given in departments of zoology. Frequently, excellent courses in biostatistics are offered in schools of public health. It is equally likely that departments of education or psychology also offer work in statistics. Departments of nutrition should not be overlooked, as they offer excellent opportunities to increase the student's understanding of human physiology and nutritional requirements. Schools of agriculture often contain the best courses on nutrition, chemistry, statistics and physiology. No stone should be left unturned; major universities contain many sources of untapped potential for physical educators.

As challenging as the above outline appears, it makes no mention of the undergraduate prerequisites of chemistry, physics and mathematics, which may be nearly as challenging as the graduate program itself. Promising undergraduates interested in exercise physiology should be encouraged to fulfill the Ph.D. prerequisites, so that graduate work is shorter, more rewarding, and perhaps less traumatic. Although it is sometimes possible for graduate students to petition to have certain prerequisites dropped, this is not usually a good idea, since the background of physical education students must be comparable with that of students in medicine, dentistry, other scientific fields with whom they will be competing in their advanced classes.

A frequent criticism of the type of program suggested here is that it is absurd to expect physical education students to compete against students specializing in physiology, biochemistry and other biological sciences. There might be some support for this argument if graduate students in physical education are not prepared to take advanced course work in the basic biological sciences or are academically inferior to students in other fields. The prerequisites outlined in the preceding paragraph are therefore designed to afford advanced students in exercise physiology the same background as

Changing requirements for the ph.d. in physical education with a specialization in exercise physiology
George A. Brooks

most students in the other biological sciences. Hence arguments based on their lack of preparation need not apply. With respect to academic competence, the only real way to maintain the quality of our profession is to insist that its members be as competent in the area of their specialization as members of other professions are in theirs. For exercise physiologists this means that they compete successfully with members of other professions on the ground common to both. Too often statements are made to the effect that although some research in exercise physiology is not really good physiological research, it is good research for physical education. However, either a piece of research is competent, or it is not. Research in physical education is good if it possesses intrinsic value and if it is germane to physical education. The fact that someone donned a white laboratory coat, amassed some numbers, and performed a series of statistical manipulations is irrelevant. Perhaps no better screening procedure exists for the selection of Ph.D. candidates in physical education with a specialization in exercise physiology than the gauntlet of a thorough schooling in both the basic sciences and physical education.

Under Roman numeral II in the suggested curriculum outline, the section "Seminars in Physical Education" needs to be elaborated, since it is the link by which students in the proposed curriculum remain physical educators. Seminars on the physiology of exercise must be taken to familiarize the student with the field of exercise physiology, but students should supplement this seminar with other graduate seminars in physical education, including the seminar in research methods usually required of all physical education students. Particular emphasis in this seminar should be paid to the art of grantsmanship, since the research budgets in most physical education departments are meager, reflecting the fact that most departments in most institutions of higher learning depend heavily on outside support. The record shows, however, that physical educators who have competed for grants have done remarkably well. Thus the term paper for the research methods seminar might consist of the construction of a research grant proposal. The Journal Club Seminar (1 unit) should be taken every term. While this seminar properly should be very informal, for instance, over lunch Friday noon, its intent is to nurture the interests and habits necessary to achieve and maintain the status of respected researchers. In this seminar students should be introduced to the practice of scrutinizing the *Index Medicus* monthly and *Current Contents Life Sciences* weekly. Additionally, students

87

should be regularly assigned to report on their own research or recent papers of interest to the group. Particular attention should be applied to the scrutiny of reviews of the literature, methodology, and statistical analyses.

In reading this outline of a course of study for a Ph.D. in exercise physiology, some people will probably feel that I have not gone far enough, others will think that my ideas are completely out of line with their concept of physical education. In my defense I would say that I am not alone in my conclusions, and frankly much of what I have said has been borrowed from others and already existing programs. Physical education and exercise physiology appears to be undergoing a period of rapid change, as reflected in the emergence of several young researchers at the helm of AAHPER research and in the recent growth of the American College of Sports Medicine. This curriculum in exercise physiology is therefore designed to enable students of exercise physiology to meet immediate and foreseeable demands. No doubt, of course, the curriculum will continue to change as it evolves with the field.

The movement medium

Blanche Jessen Drury
California State University, San Francisco

Movement is psychologically and biologically necessary to man. Psychologically, it offers him a means of expressing himself, through overt gesture, of the hands, facial expression, or through the muscles that help him to speak. Pantomime and dance are the art forms of movement. Throughout history, man has used them to express his innermost thoughts, his relationship with the divine, and his relationship with the forces of nature. Movement is also, of course, a biological need. Traditionally, this need has been met through work, but in a society in which work no longer means physical movement, man must seek some other form of activity to meet this biological requirement. As life becomes more sedentary, hypokinetic diseases, particularly those of the heart and circulation, take their toll. Why has man turned away from movement as a means of continuous development? Part of the answer lies in the fact that a positive attitude toward movement has not been established at an early age.

In the early stages of infancy, the baby is absorbed in exploring and moving his body. Each new movement represents new learning. In the first year of life during the uncurling from the foetal position, normal growth and development takes place through body movement. Concepts of laterality, directionality, and purposeful movement develop, until the child is self-sufficient in his movement. The gross movements give way to refined movement as neuromuscular development occurs. In a rich environment neuromuscular control develops normally, but removed from a rich environment, exploration and movement become limited and learning suffers.

Around nine or ten years of age, or about the third or fourth grades, physical activity becomes highly important for the child. Movement—running, jumping, kicking, turning, tumbling—becomes almost a compulsive urge of the organism. It is at this time that attitudes toward movement are established. Yet it is also at this crucial time that programs in physical education are the most limited. Beautiful buildings, large fields, swimming pools, and physical education apparatus are absent from the elementary school; they are all reserved for the senior high school. We know that unless a person learns to swim by age 14 he is not likely to become much of a swimmer. But those who have taught nine- and ten-year olds or younger children to swim know that the naturalness of learning is frequently lost. How many other skills are never mastered because we fail to recognize the moment of readiness to learn? Much has been done in the study of reading readiness, but little in movement readiness. Moreover, studies performed through the Joseph P. Kennedy Foundation for the Mentally Retarded show the need for movement in the development of learning. If this is so true for the retarded, how much more important is it for normal children?

Some researchers, such as Dr. Otis Cobb, have suggested that we add another scale to our judgment of child development, that of the Coordination Coefficient. This scale would evaluate the child's ability to move all parts of the body in a concerted purposeful manner. Ratings on the Coordination Coefficient would lead to information about the readiness to learn. Motor learning may be specific, but the basic neuromuscular ability to learn can and should be evaluated.

Researchers and teachers in early childhood education have long realized the importance of perceptual motor learning and movement exploration. These concepts are slowly being accepted by the physical education profession. However, as long as teacher training programs, particularly for men, train "coaches" rather than instructors, high schools will continue to per-

The movement medium
Blanche Jessen Drury

petuate a program of sports for the glory of the few. I suggest the focus of physical education change completely and that the profession focus all its attention on physical education programs for the young child. The movement-oriented Headstart program has shown how learning potential can be improved. The current proposal in California to establish early childhood education before the kindergarten is a a step in the right direction. But how much training in understanding movement skills would teachers in such a program receive? Early childhood education should be based primarily on movement. Readiness to learn comes through exploration, and exploration means movement in an enriched environment. Many years ago Rousseau saw the need for movement in the education of the child; the Montessori method and the philosophy of Dewey are based on activity. But what has the profession of physical education done to assist in the training of teachers in early childhood education? We plan a curriculum based on the physical fitness facts received from the 18 year olds who are rejected from military service! Perhaps these young people would not have been rejected if a truly good program of early physical activity had existed. True, physical activity cannot, of course, insure freedom from disease, but it can teach a healthy attitude toward physical activity.

Although many areas in physical education need research, no one has proposed a long-term study, such as Terman's study of gifted children. Some issues would not need to take years to resolve, if the profession were willing to cancel all the mediocre studies of master's or doctoral candidates and concentrate on a national study of the physical activity needs of children and adults. Then perhaps we might have some answers as to the amount and kind, of exercise appropriate for people of all ages in our society. Presently most state and national physical fitness tests stop at age 18, or at least statistics beyond that age have not been forthcoming. In addition, the growing number of elderly people certainly deserve some attention to their needs and abilities for physical activity.

Kinesiology is broadly defined as the study of movement. Most institutions require a basic course in kinesiology in the preparation of physical education teachers. For over twenty-five years, the writer has taught kinesiology in a teacher training program. In retrospect it seems futile to expect students to get an adequate grasp of the whole field through one course. To divorce the study of movement from all activity makes a single course very limiting. Actually, elements of kinesiology should be included in every physical education lesson, starting in grade school. Learning to kick a ball

91

is an excellent time to experience the laws regarding the application of force to an external object. Exploration of where to place the foot, how much force it takes, what happens to body balance, and how the arc of movement is increased are all questions which are best presented as the movement is learned. Since third graders seem to have few problems learning algebra, they could undoubtedly learn the basic principles of the physics of movement at this early age. The chasing and fleeing games of the first graders would be excellent opportunities for showing the control of the body in space, of the need for a broad base, and of how to lower the center of gravity. These lessons can be explained in the classroom with objects, and transferred to the body movement on the playground. Since young children are interested in the exploration of outer space and have some understanding of gravity and weightlessness, why not capitalize on this knowledge in teaching them how to tumble—what it feels like to bounce in the air on a trampoline and why it is easier to propel oneself through air than water.

As part of a course in kinesiology, the writer has frequently assigned students to activity classes so that they might observe many people performing similar movements. Some students have actually been surprised to hear a karate teacher, for example, explain some of the laws of physics in the execution of a particular movement. It would seem, then, that the study of kinesiology has become an isolated part of the physical education program, instead of the underlying girder. How much better it might be if the physical educators, who so quickly defend the principle of "education through the physical," were to spend more time explaining the how and why of physical activity in the daily instructional program.

The writer does not wish to imply that all physical education can be reduced to a study of the neuromuscular system, recognizing the part sociology and psychology play in the performance of movement. Moreover, the selection of activities is generally based on a cultural concept of needs. Different ethnic groups place different values on particular types of movement. To divorce dance from black culture would be impossible, for it is an integral part of the culture. In addition, the emotional impact of movement must be thoroughly understood. Why is an aspiring Olympic performer willing to set such a grueling training program for himself? His body becomes the instrument through which he acquires satisfaction, and movement becomes the road to glory. Although the range of ability is great between the Olympic performer and the student in the gymnasium, each should understand how his body functions and why it moves as it does.

Psychology has always been interested in learning, and yet many of the studies have been limited to muscle fatigue of the trigger finger, or eye blinking, with few studies that consider the complete organism in a given situation. Through telemetering and other instruments, a study of body functioning under stress can be done while the performer is on the field in the thick of the contest. What might we learn if psychology, physiology, sociology, and physical education were to collaborate in a study of movement and learning? In fact, it is only through interdisciplinary cooperation that a real study of human movement and learning can be accomplished.

Physical education should muster all its forces to study all manifestations of movement, from early childhood to geriatrics, and in an ever changing environment. Instead of each master or doctoral degree candidate searching for a suitable subject of study, the profession could set up a series of subjects to be studied for the year, in research involving hundreds or thousands of subjects, so that valid scientific conclusions could be made. With concerted effort we might come up with some real answers about the impact of movement upon learning, so that physical education may finally assume its rightful place in the educational picture.

BIBLIOGRAPHY

Bell, V. L. *Sensorimotor Learning*. Pacific Palisades, Ca.: Goodyear, 1970.

Brown, R. C., and Cratty, B. J. *New Perspectives of Man in Action*. Englewood Cliffs, N.J.: Prentice-Hall, 1969.

Brown, R. C., and Kenyon, G. S. *Classical Studies on Physical Activity*. Englewood Cliffs, N.J.: Prentice-Hall, 1968.

College Entrance Board. *The Challenge of Curricular Change*. Princeton, N.J.: College Entrance Board Publications, 1966.

Cratty, B. J. *Movement Behavior and Motor Learning*. Philadelphia: Lea & Febiger, 1964.

Davis, M. *Understanding Body Movement*. N.Y.: Arno Press, 1972.

Foshay, A. W. *Curriculum for the '70s: An Agenda for Invention*. Washington, D.C.: N.E.A. Center for the Study of Instruction, 1970.

Godfrey, B. B., and Kephart, N. C. *Movement Patterns and Motor Education*. N.Y.: Appleton-Century-Crofts, 1969.

Kroll, Walter P. *Perspectives in Physical Education*. N.Y.: Academic Press, 1971.

Mackenzie, M. M. *Toward a New Curriculum in Physical Education*. N.Y.: McGraw-Hill, 1969.

Neill, A. S. *Summerhill, a Radical Approach to Child Rearing*. N.Y.: Hart, 1960.

Sharer, R. E. *There Are No Islands*. North Quincy, Mass.: Christopher Publishing Co., 1969.

Slusher, H. S., and Lockhart, A. S. *Anthology of Contemporary Readings: An Introduction to Physical Education*. Dubuque, Iowa: Wm. C. Brown, 1966.

Vendien, C. L., and Nixon, J. *The World Today in Health, Physical Education, Recreation*. Englewood Cliffs, N.J.: Prentice-Hall, 1968.

Issues in physical education and sports

3 CURRICULAR

Mission, omission and submission in physical education

Muska Mosston
Director, Center on Teaching,
Trenton, N.J.

Rudolf Mueller
East Stroudsburg State College, Pennsylvania

This paper is a declaration of indictments, past and present, of physical education instruction.

Even those among us who have been dedicated to the development of physical education cannot escape some blame for the behavior of thousands of teachers, teachers who are *our* products. They have all been in our classes. The time has come at last for us to look at ourselves with boldness and frankness.

Historically, physical education has lacked an independent internal framework which would give it recognizable shape and structural strength. The lack of internal consistency is compounded with other problems, including the discrepancy between what the academics and physical educators regard as important, the distance between what physical educators recommend and what really occurs in the gymnasiums of America, and the continued attacks on physical education by others. The accompanying uncertainty has produced a number of pressures, anxieties, fears, frustrations, and threats to the profession (individually and collectively). It has caused a professional neurosis and has resulted in an elaborate system of personal and professional defense mechanisms, including the kinds of compensating behavior, which we might call justification by association, justification by absorption, and justification by uniqueness.

Justification by association is an identity-seeking technique which supposedly allows the profession to shine a little brighter by reflecting the light of an established, accepted discipline.

Physical educators are not physicians, psychiatrists, psychologists, sociologists, biologists, physiologists, or para-medical people—not by training, knowledge or function, even though we should and do utilize their knowledge. Physical educators are also not religious leaders, military trainers, fashion designers, policemen, or judges—and the profession's preoccupation with rigid standards of personal appearance, ideas, interests, aspirations and abilities does not help legitimize its image. Teachers must realize that clothes, haircuts, facial hair, beliefs, personal likes and dislikes are not the criteria by which one judges people and their worth to society. Further, physical educators are not athletic coaches, athletic trainers, recreational leaders, or athletic officials. Athletic competition and recreation are separate fields from physical education, with their own objectives and principles. Although physical education may use similar tools, there should be a significant difference in how they are used so that athletics and recreation do not come to dominate physical education.

Justification by absorption is another way that the profession has attempted to legitimize itself. This technique involves expanding one's own territory until one becomes a formidable foe—any potential critic must be willing to challenge the whole field. Today, it is almost impossible to criticize physical education without being accused of challenging God, the flag, motherhood, purity, goodness and maybe even apple pie.

In the name of physical education, we profess expertise in military fitness training and presidential fitness training; we profess expertise in dating, marriage, sex, drugs, safety, first aid, athletic training, weight control, nutrition, biology, physiology, driver education, rhythm-dance, movement education, body building, perceptual training, motoric development, etc. Is this what physical education is all about?

Mission, omission and submission
in physical education
Muska Mosston and Rudolf Mueller

This absorption-proliferation process in itself weakens the profession, but we compound it by insisting on the importance of subject matter over people; adhering to outdated organizational patterns; imposing conformity through requirements for uniforms, showers, pace, etc.; building the class around an omniscient authority figure; promoting the concepts of esprit de corps and the correct form; excusing from class members of athletic teams; and developing competitive climates in which child is pitted against child. Thus the profession is on record as placing group needs above individual needs, group conformity above individual expression, group control above self control, authority above self discipline and dependence above independence.

Further, the entire profession continues to skate on thin ice when it tries to justify itself by citing its uniqueness. What is it that is unique? Is it the subject matter? the child? the tools? the product? the medium? Or is it really just the set of assumptions that makes us different? Couldn't other social agencies do exactly what we do? Isn't our presence within the school system the only really unique aspect of this profession? Couldn't our work be carried out by some other agency, as is the case with such similar fields as athletics, recreation, and physical skill training?

Certainly, at this juncture in the profession's development, one might legitimately ask, "What is physical education, in its present form, doing in the American public school?" Colleges and universities are presently reviewing their required physical education programs with just this question in mind. When current practice is compared to current educational theory, the incongruities become clear and any claims to uniqueness become relatively unimportant. Soon elementary and secondary schools will be asking the same question about their physical education programs.* The future of physical education might depend not only on how we answer, but on who asks the questions that initiate the process of change.

Let us examine the future of this profession by identifying some of the paradoxes that are deliberately being perpetrated in the field. (If we do not

---

*Some high schools have already questioned their physical education programs and have reduced or even abolished them in their traditional formats. This paper was written in 1970, and the reader will recognize that some other predictions which follow have also come true.

assume deliberateness, if the current state of the field developed haphazardly, then, indeed, it needs intensive scrutiny.)

The first paradox pertains to philosophy and curriculum. To repeat here the philosophy of physical education or even to cite the usual collection of objectives, aims, and principles would be boring to the reader and insulting to those of my colleagues who have reiterated that assemblage of noble and nebulous statements fed to our undergraduates as purposes and principles. Had our curricula remotely approximated the philosophy, it would have been enough. But our curricula move in the direction opposite to our stated philosophy. Physical education has generally allied itself with the main objective of American education, that is, "education for all." But when one examines the programs in schools, it becomes quite obvious that the movement experiences commonly offered are *not* designed for all. In fact, they are a priori designed for exclusion! Exclusion, not inclusion, is the principle guiding the practices in American gymnasiums (Mosston, 1969). For example, let us look at the high jump as an educational experience. We are not concerned here with the use of the high jump in athletic competition, where the exclusion principle is congruent with philosophy and practice. We are examining the *design* of the high jump experience in light of the stated educational objective. After several "innings" the rope or bar excludes most participants. If the raising of the bar continues, it soon excludes all! The design of the activity is obviously hardly congruent with the philosophy of physical education.

The emphasis here is on the word "design". We have designed it! We have been teaching this design to generations of teachers, causing millions of children to be excluded from participation in this activity. Let us examine an alternative design. Place the bar at a slant, so that it represents variable height, with its intrinsic quality of *inclusion*. Experimenting with this alternative with children all over the country we have found that all children participate, including those with various physical handicaps; all children participate willingly and are motivated to begin; all children experience frequent success, for they *always* begin where they know *they* can be successful; and all children become engaged in competition. In fact, they discover that they can compete with themselves or with others, and they learn to choose for themselves the kind of competition they want. Since this arrangement never excludes the top performers and since the availability of choice provides plenty of motivation to continue, all children are always included.

Multiply this example by a thousand and figure out the kind of programs we could have, had it not been for a deliberate omission. Exclusion and pressure on children are important issues (Theory into Practice, 1968;

Mission, omission and submission
in physical education
Muska Mosston and Rudolf Mueller

Flemming and Doll, 1966; Gordon, 1966); Mosston (1969) suggests that "every decision made by a teacher in every act of teaching has the consequence of inclusion or exclusion. These decisions serve as a powerful and sometimes irreversible antecedent to what actually occurs *to* the learner, *for* or *against* the learner."

Mosston (1969) further accuses physical education of mass exclusion when he states:

> Our field of human movement intrinsically possesses and produces the quality of high visibility. The difference between those who can and those who cannot is quite apparent. The most indicting aspect of the visibility factor is its range of exclusion which potentially includes so many: the extreme somatotypes, the handicapped, the unwilling, the racially different, and combinations of all these.
>
> Indeed, the physical educator, particularly the one who has been brought up with the professional myth of Greek standards of beauty, harmony and perfection, must learn to grapple with the reality of a pluralistic society and re-examine his notions of standards and norms.

There is a second sense in which the curricula in physical education have not been developed according to the stated philosophy of the field; that is, that the intellectual purpose of education in a free society is to seek the truth, not to present scattered and carefully selected instances as the whole truth. Thus, intellectual honesty demands an exploration of all the possibilities of a discipline. Decisions concerning the feasible and desirable must be carefully weighed and often postponed until this inquiry has been completed. Any assembly of feasible activities (such as basketball, wrestling, or gymnastics) invariably represents merely a small part of curriculum and movement possibilities; a still smaller selection of possible activities occurs when measures of desirability are applied to the selective process. In physical education these measures of desirability have too frequently been results of decisions based on personal taste or power position, on the standards set by a committee, on the politics of a professional organization, or on the traditions of teacher education programs at various colleges.

All these sources of decisions concerning feasibility and desirability are inconsistent with intellectual integrity, which requires full exploration of all possibilities (Mosston, 1969). Let us look at one aspect of gymnastics, the mount onto the parallel bars. As a rule, mounts are presented as a strictly defined collection of exercises that represent the only ways a person should   101 get on the parallel bars. Such a set of mounts is acceptable as a model for competitive gymnastics, in which all individuals are measured against a single performance model and those who cannot reach the model are excluded. But such a model must never be used for educational purposes, because it prevents the investigation of the possible by excluding much of the potential.

The question of the participant ought not to be "How do I perform the few selected mounts?" The question should be, "How do I interact with this part of my environment?" The number of mounts which result from all possible combinations of posture, direction, speed and the variable conditions of the environment itself is great. This, then, constitutes the subject matter. This is the intellectually honest base upon which a course of studies could be developed. Multiply this example by the number of environments with which man can interact via movement and a different picture of the possible curricula emerges.

A second major paradox in physical education curricula is the emphasis on the group at the expense of individual development. Class organization is geared primarily to the group; in fact, individuals are usually manipulated to satisfy the group arrangement.

Uniforms are imposed so that the group will look good. Equipment is distributed to fit the group organization, quite often at the expense of individual learning. Often in a gymnasium only 10 percent of the equipment and floor space is used in order not to spoil the group arrangement and control. (One can see this waste of space, equipment, time and the consequent non-learning in basketball, tumbling, and so on, where only a portion of the available equipment is used. The rest is either arranged neatly on a dolly in the corner of the gymnasium or hidden in cabinets in the director's office.)

Control and discipline are attempted through the group. Systems of rewards and reprimand have been devised whereby group pressure is either overt or implicit. The concept of the group has been elevated in physical education to an unprecedented level; it has become an undisputed value. However, when one examines what such procedures and beliefs do to people, one discovers that they intrude upon and often violate the very essence of individuality. The imposition of group arrangements, group standards, group morality, group aesthetic values always intrudes upon the right and the very ability of the individual to make choices. The individual must conform, or his conduct is identified as deviant behavior. Tumin

(1957) says:

Mission, omission and submission
in physical education
Muska Mosston and Rudolf Mueller

Real creativity is viewed with suspicion and distrust because it means, above all, difference, intolerance, and insistence on achieving an individual identity. Real feeling is viewed with equal distrust and hostility because it almost always means bad manners, spontaneity, unpredictability, lack of realism, failure to observe routines. Well-rounded, adjusted, happy—these are the things we are told it is important for us to be. No points, no sharp cutting edges, no despairs and elations. Just nice, smooth billiard balls, rolling quietly on soft green cloth to our appointed, webbed pockets, and dropping slowly into the slots under the table to be used in the same meaningless way in the next game. Chalk one up for mediocrity. For it is the only winner in this game.

Schwab (1969) discusses group dynamism as a doctrine of education and says:

Once a group is fully formed, [the individual] . . . has little or no status . . . in his own right but only as a member of the group. It is the group that determines what will be done and, in effect, does it. And it is the group character, furthermore, that determines what is acceptable and unacceptable, good or bad, true or false.

He further states:

The very nature of inquiry, whether scientific or practical, is thus altered. It ceases to be a procedure whose ultimate measure is the completeness and verity of the knowledge acquired. It ceases to be a process whose fruits are measured by carefully nurtured *diversities* of criteria.

It becomes, instead, a procedure whose ultimate measure is the continuing and increasing solidarity of the group.

Physical education abounds with procedures and programs that exemplify this statement. In fact, we have even developed words, phrases and slogans that create public shame for anyone who does not adhere to the group doctrine.

And we have even gone farther. We often violate the privacy of our students. Consider, for example, the arrangement of classes by height. Height is a personal thing, it is of one's own, it is private. How does a person who happens to be quite short feel when he is always made to stand first in line, day after day, year after year, always under the visual scrutiny of the teacher? Or, conversely, what about the very tall person who is always at   103 the end, never close enough to enjoy the warmth of the teacher? Let us consider the privacy of appearance. There are only three or four professions in our civilization that still require a uniform. By what right does a teacher demand that all her girls wear black leotards? What about the girl who knows she looks best in blue? Or the boy who prefers to wear long pants because his own self-image does not permit him to appear in shorts?

And by what right do we violate the privacy of personal movement, movement for self-development, movement for self-expression, or for any other purpose? Everything we do in the gymnasium is open and visible to the eyes of friend and foe alike. In fact, the very architecture of our gymnasiums is a violation of privacy. Libraries, laboratories, even classrooms, contain booths or corners for privacy and individual learning. But no such privacy is allowed in physical education. One can conceive of different designs for gymnasiums: buildings divided into small areas by low partitions, containing different levels, varied lighting, different colors—areas conducive to personal engagement in learning about oneself, areas available for the student's choice and need. Such areas would not invite public pressure and stigmatization, but rather would invite fuller participation and self development.

Morris (1969) addresses himself to this issue by saying:

> Consider the matter of privacy and quiet reflection. How much opportunity is there in a typical school in America for a youngster to sit still and quiet and go over the personal choices he must take that day? . . . We have elevated gregariousness to the status of a moral commitment for today's youth. It is now suspicious behavior to declare that one wants to be alone.

A third paradox has to do with the separation of men and women in physical education. Clearly the separatist movements in this field belong to a past social, economic, and certainly philosophical era. Cless (1969) decries the situation and says:

> Higher education in the United States was designed exclusively for the white, upper-class or middle-class male. Its procedures, its rigid uninterrupted time table, and its cost all but prohibit its use by women despite well meaning, sometimes desperate, twentieth century attempts to provide appropriate schooling for every qualified American citizen.

Paradoxically, men and women in physical education confront this dilemma by perpetuating the myths of their own separate domains. In the second half of the twentieth century—an era of new examination of sexuality, new

**Mission, omission and submission
in physical education**
Muska Mosston and Rudolf Mueller

insights into self-concepts and emotional conditions, and new freedoms of association—we still hold fast to the antiquated arrangements represented by that magic, omnipotent partition separating the boys' gym from the girls' gym.

The fourth and final paradox refers to the gap between current knowledge in the behavioral sciences and observed teaching behavior in gymnasiums. Despite the prevalence of data, research, and new teaching models, physical educators, in the main, still adhere to, perpetuate, and defend the S-R learning model, translating it into a Command style of teaching. Physical educators seem to refuse to consider the data which so powerfully demonstrates the ill effects of using a single teaching behavior, particularly the command style of teaching, which by its very nature excludes alternative responses and fails to accommodate variability in learning and performance. Some of the noble attempts by individuals in the field who have demonstrated the feasibility and desirability of alternative teaching styles in addition to the command style have been largely ignored—*the behavior of teachers has changed little.* Mosston's "spectrum of teaching styles" (1966) is perhaps the only unified teaching theory within physical education, and yet, despite indications of curiosity on the part of colleagues and scattered attempts to put it into practice, no significant change can be observed in the behavior of teachers across the United States.

How can we expect to be considered a part of education when we so thoroughly ignore the primary aim of education—the development of independent thought, ideas, questions, and experimentation on the part of our students? Such student responses can come about only by means of alternative teaching styles. In physical education, the development of free, responding, thinking, and critical students remains verbal—the omission is clear and frightening, and the submission is dangerous.

These four paradoxes, then, are the legacy we bestow upon our undergraduates in our teacher education programs, a legacy laden with irrelevancies, hampered by serious omissions and sadly leading to submission. The '60s saw an attack on and the vanishing of service programs. The '70s will bring similar attempts on our professional programs. The '80s may well witness the death of a potentially glorious field. Let us not participate in that swan song; let us face *now*, openly and boldly, the painful task of self-surgery, of self-renewal. Let us embark now on our very necessary tasks of reconstruction.

105

REFERENCES

A.S.C.D. *Humanizing Education*, Washington, D.C.: N.E.A., 1967.

A.S.C.D. *A Climate for Individuality*, Washington, D.C.: N.E.A., 1965.

A.S.C.D. *Perceiving, Behaving, Becoming*, Washington, D.C.: N.E.A., 1962.

Cless, E. L. A Modest Proposal for the Education of Women. *American Scholar*, Autumn 1969, pp. 618–627.

Dinkmeyer, D. C. *Child Development*, Englewood Cliffs, N.J.: Prentice Hall, 1965.

Flemming and Doll, *Children Under Pressure*, Columbus, Ohio: Charles E. Merrill, 1966.

Goffman, E. *Stigma*, Englewood Cliffs, N.J.: Prentice Hall, 1963.

Gordon, S. (Ed), *Pressures That Disorganize in Secondary Schools*, N.J. Secondary School Teachers Association, 1966.

Mosston, M. Inclusion & Exclusion in Education—II. Paper read at the Symposium on Innovation in Curricular Design, University of Pittsburgh, Feb. 1969.

Mosston, M. *Developmental Movement—Evolving Structure for Human Movement.* Paper read at the Oregon HPER Convention, October 1969.

Mosston, M. *Teaching Physical Education: From Command to Discovery.* Charles E. Merrill, Columbus, Ohio: 1966.

Mueller, R. A Learning Climate for Children Who Can Not, Paper read at the East Central District Conference of N.J.A.H.P.E.R., Princeton, N.J.

Schwab, J. J. On the Corruption of Education by Psychology in *Theory of Knowledge and Problems of Education*, Ed. D. Vandenberg, Urbana: University of Illinois Press, 1969.

Schwebel, M. *Who Can Be Educated*. New York: Grove Press, 1968.

Theory into Practice, February 1968, Publ. by College of Education, Ohio State.

Tumin, M. Popular Culture and the Open Society. In *Man Culture*, ed. B. Rosenberg and White Glencoe, Ill.: Free Press, 1957.

Van Cleve, M. Personal Choice. In *Teaching and Learning*, ed. D. Vandenberg, Urbana: University of Illinois Press, 1969.

Concept curricula, experiential learning and teacher education

Christopher L. Stevenson
University of California, Berkeley

Concept curricula, experiential learning and teacher education may appear to be strange bedfellows indeed, but I am convinced that bedfellows they will have to be if physical education is to play a viable part in the education.

As one part of the total educational process, physical education has the same general objective as that process, namely the socialization of the young. As the family circle has abrogated some of its responsibilities in this area, it has fallen to education to ensure that each succeeding generation is willing and able to function satisfactorily in society. Educationally-based socialization is not merely the transmission of discipline-oriented information which enables the recipient to acquire a niche in the occupational sphere; it also includes the diffuse socialization of those values, behavior patterns,

107

attitudes, expectations, and goal orientations without which a person is unable to operate satisfactorily in society. Physical education curricula unquestionably contribute greatly to the physical development of the child, but I have doubts as to how much they contribute to diffuse socialization.

The reason for this ineffectiveness, I suggest, is that the physical education curriculum generally is either completely based upon team sports, or such sports constitute a substantial part of the program. There has been a consistent controversy over the socialization that sports provide. On one side of the argument are those who believe that sports are effective socializers of such desirable personal and social traits as leadership, self-discipline, cooperative behavior, sportsmanship, and respect for rules (A.A.H.P.E.R., 1962; Larson, 1964; Oxendine, 1966; Cooker, 1970). On the other hand, critics of sports have refuted these claims and have condemned team sports in particular as a menace to education (Crosby, 1963; Brown, 1968; Taylor, 1971).

In considering this issue, it is important to remember that the *de facto* content of socialization is not simply that which is deliberately presented to the student; rather, it consists largely of material and experiences to which he is incidentally exposed. Sports do not inherently transmit desirable or undesirable socialization information; they simply reflect the values of their social environment. Consequently, the socialization content of contemporary American sports is to an extent the result of the complex of big business, entertainment, and the instant media-produced superstardom that surrounds and pervades them. Because of this societal background, sports abound with instances of emotional self-indulgence, anti-social behavior and contempt for authority, on the part of athletes, physical educators and coaches (Keating, 1965; Brown, 1968).

It is my contention that the inclusion of and the emphasis on sports in contemporary physical education is unfortunate, leading as it does to the transmission of socially undesirable values and personality characteristics. Admittedly, sports in the Physical Education class are often protected from the influence of the surrounding complex. Nevertheless, the mere use of sports enables the child to imitate the stereotypic behaviors and attitudes of his major league sports heroes, figures which are more often than not imbued with the undesirable influence of the sports-big business-entertainment complex. We are all aware, I am sure, of the difficulties in breaking bad athletic habits that have been acquired through the imitation of sports heroes. Our teaching jobs would be much easier if such exposure to bad influences never occurred. Infinitely more difficult is the rehabilitation of

values and personality traits.

Concept curricula, experiential
learning and teacher education
Christopher L. Stevenson

What can be done about this situation? I suggest two alternatives: either replace sports in the curriculum, or continue to use sports but in a manner and an environment that controls undesirable socialization and makes the desirable information explicit and effective. Both of these strategems, it would seem, are gaining ground in contemporary curricula. The college level curriculum for physical educators is becoming increasingly diversified. It is beginning to include exercise physiology, treatment of sports injuries, the history of physical education, movement education, and so on. Hopefully this trend will continue and will result in the development and the inclusion of activities expressly designed to transmit desirable socialization information. In recent years innumerable simulation games have been created, and are being used in educational programs. Although the majority of these games involve no more activity than is required to act out a role or move a counter on a board, it should not be too difficult to develop activities which involve physical activity along with the transmission of information.

The second strategem leads directly to concept curricula. A concept curriculum is one which is developed around concepts, rather than around activities, as is predominantly the case at present. The concepts that compose the curricula include not only those related to facts, for example, in anatomy, physiology and health, but also concepts of movement (types of body movements, prepositional movements, bodily shapes) and concepts of normative social behavior, such as fair play, sportsmanship, and cooperative behavior. Because the major concern of the curricula is the transmission of these concepts, the activities which make up the curricula are selected specifically for this purpose, on the basis of their applicability and their potential effectiveness. Ideally then, a concept curriculum goes some of the way towards providing a controlled environment in which sports activities may be used explicitly for desirable socialization. It is also a curriculum that is amenable to the inclusion of specifically designed socialization activities.

The next question is how to teach a concept curriculum effectively. It cannot be taught in the fashion of the traditional skill-oriented physical education curriculum. It is not sufficient merely to expose the student to an activity and expect that he will automatically derive certain concepts from that experience. To clarify the direction which the teaching of physical education and its concept curricula will have to take, let me describe my experience at Stanford in the team teaching of an experimental course in the sociology of education. This course is essentially experiential, that is, it communicates sociological concepts largely by involving the students in experiences relating directly to those concepts. These experiences are predominantly simulation exercises and field activities. The simulation exercises are often exercises used in cross-cultural sensitivity training programs, such as those run by Vista and the Peace Corps. The field activities take the student out into the field to gain real experience of sociological phenomena. We have discovered time again with experiential learning that we cannot rely simply on the experience to convey a concept. It is of the utmost necessity to follow the experience with a period of reflection, discussion, evaluation, and conceptualization. Then and only then can we feel confident that the concept has been communicated.

The traditional learning model (Figure 1) is used in the vast majority of disciplines, from kindergarten through graduate school. Certainly, physical education uses this model exclusively in its teaching methodology. The experiential learning model (Figure 2) is increasingly used in disciplines concerned with developing creative students, particularly the sciences, which have developed the Nuffield programs in math, biology, chemistry,

FIGURE 1
TRADITIONAL LEARNING MODEL (MODIFIED FROM WIGHT AND HAMMONS, 1970)

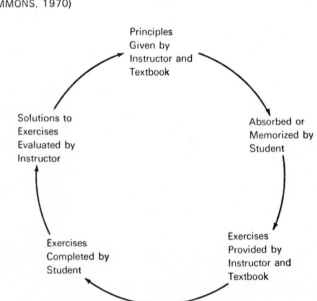

**Concept curricula, experiential
learning and teacher education**
Christopher L. Stevenson

and physics (Halls, 1968). Physical education is above all else an experiential discipline, since its very being is the experience of physical movement (Ulrich and Nixon, 1972). Physical education, therefore, should be using the experiential learning model, and it should be using it most especially with its concept curricula.

In the experiential model, the starting point is the experience, which, depending upon its structure and its circumstances, may involve action, affectivity, the solving of problems, the collection of data, or all of these. Reflection is the next stage. It is during this vital phase that the experience is analyzed, evaluated, and internalized, and that insights and concepts are culled from it. After the conceptualization stage, the concepts derived from a specific experience are generalized to a broader context. The very act of generalization generates questions and problems which may be resolved by further exploration experience, completing the cycle.

FIGURE 2
AN EXPERIENCE-BASED LEARNING MODEL (MODIFIED FROM WIGHT AND HAMMONS, 1970)

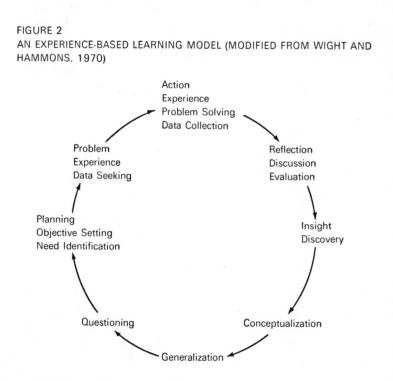

111

I think it needs to be stressed that this is a student-oriented model. The *student* "experiences," conceptualizes, generalizes, poses questions and generates new experiences. The student, therefore, is involved in his own learning process. This contrasts sharply with the teacher-oriented traditional model.

The parts of the model that I wish to emphasize for physical education are the reflection and the conceptualization stages. These stages are critical for the effective teaching of concept curricula. It is vital that time be taken to include these stages, to reflect, to evaluate, and to discuss the experiences that have just been presented, so that the concepts may be made explicit and hopefully understood and internalized. The implication is that the current approach to teaching physical education, and the teaching methods employed need considerable modification if they are to teach concept curricula effectively. The old notions geared to an activity class will have to be discarded. We must be prepared to be less active physically, and to spend more time in discussion, reflection, and education.

The problem is to reconcile the need for a new approach to the teaching of physical education with the style of teaching that predominates in the profession. Unfortunately, physical education is presently preoccupied with coaching. This is a problem which, in my opinion, cannot be overemphasized. In high school the physical educator is popularly recognized and respected as a coach. Certainly, he is not known for his achievements as a teacher. Although school budgeting, hiring practices and priorities, and public sentiment have all contributed to this problem, it still remains the responsibility of the physical education profession to attempt to correct the situation.

It might be argued that professional preparation physical education works against the preoccupation with Coaching, rather than reinforcing it, since its mandate is the education of teachers. Indeed this is so, as far as the administrative mandate is concerned, but the situation is, nevertheless, that the coaching style of teaching, and the eulogization of it, is very much in evidence in the professional program. Implicitly if not explicitly, the coach is upheld as the professional model, deferred to and often courted by faculty members, or at least by those faculty members who do not themselves have coaching responsibilities. The administrative, financial, and material dominance of the athletic department is a fact of life for many professional physical education programs. In the eyes of the student physical educators, the direct association of success with such obvious departmental and individual dominance tends to devalue the goals and attitudes recommended in his professional preparation. Even the teaching practicum experience reinforces

Concept curricula, experiential
learning and teacher education
Christopher L. Stevenson

coaching as the model teaching style. Student teachers are not only guided by incumbent high school physical educators, primarily coaches, they are encouraged to add extracurricular coaching duties to their practicum work loads. While this may be a realistic response to the existing employment situation, it does nothing to militate against the debilitating coaching ethic in which physical education has become entrapped.

It is clear that coaching, characterized as it is by aggression, dominance, intolerance, and authoritarian-submissive interpersonal relationships (Ogilvie and Tutko, 1967; Ogilvie, 1970), is incompatible with the teaching of concept curricula and the use of the experiential model. It is also clear that teaching styles cannot be changed over-night. Some evidence indicates that the adoption of a teaching style follows a cyclic process (Lortie, 1969). The basic model of a physical educator is provided for the student by his high school physical education teacher. This model is reinforced in the college physical education program, and becomes the basis of the future performances of the neophyte physical educator. Thus the coaching style reproduces itself.

If an alteration in teaching style is to occur, this cycle must be interrupted. It is my belief that the most effective place to interrupt it is in the professional physical education program. Wholesale changes in the philosophical outlook of the program and in the practical implementations of that philosophy will be necessary. There must be an ideological and a material divorce of the professional physical education program from the athletic department. Central to the new philosophy must be a realistic conception of the role that physical education plays in the total educational process, and a conception of the objectives of that educational process. It will be necessary to encourage the use of concept curricula and the experiential learning model for the teaching of physical education and the realization of its objectives.

Although the details of implementing this ideological change are beyond the scope of this article, two aspects of that change should be mentioned. First, the professional physical education program itself must use the experiential-learning model and the concept curricula mode in educating its students. This, of course, presumes that the faculty have already changed their teaching style. Second, the teaching practicum will have to be modified drastically. It will no longer be sufficient simply to release the students to the tender care of the local teachers. The practicum will need a more rigid system of controls, so that the student is supervised solely by the professional education faculty, thereby enabling him to practice-teach using concept curricula and the experiential model.

The change I am advocating is an enormous task. I recognize the immense inertia of any established system, and the extent of investment in the status quo. I simply present my observations in the hope that perhaps physical education can be rehabilitated, even in spite of itself.

BIBLIOGRAPHY

American Association of Health, Physical Education and Recreation. 1962. Athletics in education. *Journal of Health, Physical Education and Recreation* 33(1962):24–27.

Brown, S. R. "Competitive Athletics and Character." *Journal of Secondary Education* 43(1968): 60–62.

Cooker, N. G. "Value of Team Sports." *Times Educational Supplement,* 27 November 1970.

Crosby, J. "Athletics are a Menace to Education." *School Activities* 35(1963):11–14.

Halls, W. D. "England: Sources and Strategies of Change." In *Strategies for Curriculum Change,* edited by R. M. Thomas, L. B. Sands, D. L. Brubaker. Scranton Pa.: International Textbook, 1968.

Keating, J. W. "Character or Catharsis." *Catholic Educational Review* 63(1965):300–306.

Larson, L. A. *"Why Sports Participation?"* *Journal of Health, Physical Education and Recreation* 34(1964):36–37.

Lortie, D. C. "The Balance of Control and Autonomy in Elementary School Teaching." In *The Semi-professions and Their Organization,* edited by A. Etzioni. New York: Free Press, 1969.

Ogilvie, B. C. "The Challenge That Awaits the Physical Educator of the '70s." Address at the Annual Conference of the National College Physical Education Association for Men, Portland, Ore., 1970.

Ogilvie, B. C., and Tutko, T. A. *Problem Athletes and How to Handle Them.* London: Pelham Books, 1967.

Oxendine, J. "Social Development: The Forgotten Objective." *Journal of Health, Physical Education and Recreation* 37(1966):23–24.

Taylor, M. A. "Day of the School Team is Done." *Times Educational Supplement,* 5 March 1971.

Ulrich, C., and Nixon, J. E. *Tones of Theory.* American Association of Health, Physical Education and Recreation, 1972.

Wight, A. R., and Hammons, M. A. *Guidelines for Peace Corps Cross-cultural Training.* Washington D. C.: Office of Training Support, Peace Corps, 1970.

The principle of specificity and the physical educator

Richard S. Rivenes
California State University, Hayward

Effective physical education programs should be based upon facts about human physical activity. These facts and the theories and principles derived from them form a body of knowledge called kinesiology, which studies physical activity from physiological, psychological, biomechanical, sociological, historical and philosophical perspectives.* Kinesiologists and allied scientists have discovered a great deal about the nature of physical activity, sport, and dance, but unfortunately, most of this knowledge has not been utilized by those who plan curricula, teach physical education classes, or coach athletic teams.

---

*See discussion on separation of the *discipline* of Kinesiology and the *profession* of Physical Education in Jerry N. Barham, "Toward a Science and Discipline of Human Movement." JOHPER, October 1966.

A prime example of this gap between knowledge and practice concerns the principle of specificity of neuromuscular performance. There is probably more fundamental information regarding human skill in this area than in any other, yet the profession of physical education has largely ignored it. In this chapter primary attention is given to the principle of specificity and its implications for the physical educator who is concerned with becoming a more effective teacher, rather than to questions of kinesiological evidence and theory. For a comprehensive examination of the data which support the principle, readers are referred to excellent reviews by Morford (1964) and Alderman and Howell (1969).

THE PRINCIPLE OF SPECIFICITY

Nearly fifty years ago experimental psychologists focused on a question of considerable importance for physical educators. Simply stated, they asked whether motor abilities were general or specific in nature? The following is a sample of the conclusions of these early researchers:

> It seems quite patent that motor ability is not general, but that it is some-what definitely specialized (Perrin, 1921, p. 49).
>
> Motor skills are so specific that the foremost students in the field of motor measurements refuse altogether to think in terms of a general motor capacity. Knowledge of an individual's performance on any particular motor test tells us little or nothing about his probable performance on any other motor test (Long, 1932, p. 2).
>
> The independence of the skills measured in these tests argues against any theory of general motor ability and in favor of specific skills (Seashore, 1930, p. 62).

FIGURE 1
COMMON AND SPECIFIC VARIANCE IN THE PERFORMANCE OF TASKS A AND B

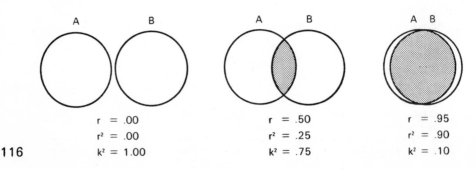

The principle of specificity
and the physical educator
Richard S. Rivenes

Although the validity of these pioneer studies may be challenged retro-spectively on the basis of their relatively primitive design and statistical treatments, it is significant that psychologists found ample evidence at the outset of their research to effectively support the specificity position and a large amount of subsequent data have reinforced these early conclusions. Such evidence from a variety of disciplines concerned with human behavior indicates that there should no longer be any controversy on the matter. Viewed as a whole the vast amount of data lead to one general conclusion: the relation of any one neuromuscular performance to another is almost universally low. This conclusion is widely known among behavioral scientists and many physical educators. Not so commonly understood, however, is the interpretation of this information.

Understanding of interrelationship is based upon one's familiarity with the correlation coefficient.* A coefficient of correlation (r) is a number falling in the range -1.0 to 1.0, which indicates the degree to which two measures are related. In analyzing the degree of specificity, the r has limited value when viewed directly. However, by squaring the coefficient and converting it to percent (X 100), a meaningful and useful value may be calculated. This figure is the proportion of the variance of the two measures which is common or general. From a practical standpoint, r^2 may be considered representative of the common factors among two performances (see Fig. 1). Fleishman (1961), for example, examined the relationship between the number of sit-ups and the number of push-ups completed by a group of subjects. He found the r in this case to be .30; therefore, r^2, or common factors, amount to 9 percent of the total. Very little of the ability to do sit-ups is related to (or affected by) the ability to do push-ups.

Whereas the coefficient of correlation indicates the strength of relationship, the coefficient of alienation (k) indicates the lack of relationship. Thus:

$$k^2 = 1 - r^2 \text{ and } k^2 + r^2 = 1.00$$

The quantity k^2 may also be converted to percent to establish the amount of independent variance which is specific to either or both measures. Thus,

---

*For a comprehensive discussion of the interpretation of the correlation coefficient, see Quinn, McNemar, *Psychological Statistics* (New York: John Wiley and Sons, 1962), pp. 116-135.

k^2 is reflective of the performance factors which are uncommon or specific in nature (see Fig. 1). In the above example in which the r between push-ups and sit-up performance was found to be .30, k^2 is 91 percent. The large majority of the abilities measured are specific to the individual tasks. It is important to note at this point that the reliability of each of the measures correlated must be high in order for this type of analysis to be valid.

Although the procedure is somewhat more complicated than described here, calculating the derivatives r^2 and k^2 from raw correlation coefficients enables one to estimate the degree of generality (r^2) and specificity (k^2) associated with any two performance measures. If $r^2 > k^2$, a generality position is supported. If, as has been repeatedly established, $r^2 < k^2$, specificity is a more valid descriptor. It is not necessarily a matter of either generality or specificity, but the relative magnitude of such factors must be considered in order to assess the nature of neuromuscular performance.

IMPLICATIONS

Most of the physical education books devoted to curricular topics are written with the assumption that general abilities exist. As Henry (1956) has pointed out, "By their actions, it is clear that our curriculum planners would spell coordination with a capital C—certain activities must be included in the school programs because they develop the coordination." This is a strong indictment, but one that is easily substantiated. For example, there is an almost universal practice of referring not only to *coordination*, but also to *agility, balance, reaction time* and other alleged abilities as if they represent

TABLE 1
INTERCORRELATIONS AMONG BALANCE PERFORMANCES

	2	3	4	5	6	7	8
1. 1 Ft. Length Bal. Eyes Op.	.16	.47	.23	.27	.06	.24	.14
2. 1 Ft. Length Bal. Eyes Cl.		.13	.46	.29	.44	.21	.13
3. 1 Ft. Cross Bal. Eyes Op.			.34	.47	.32	.23	.08
4. 1 Ft. Cross Bal. Eyes Cl.				.24	.28	.32	.17
5. 2 Ft. Cross Bal. Eyes Op.					.47	.18	.04
6. 2 Ft. Cross Bal. Eyes Cl.						.11	.06
7. 2 Ft. Length Bal. Eyes Op.							.30
8. 2 Ft. Length Bal. Eyes Cl.							

[1]From E. A. Fleishman, P. Thomas, and P. Munroe, *The Dimensions of Physical Fitness—A Factor Analysis of Speed, Flexibility, Balance, and Coordination Tests*. Office of Naval Research, Contract Nonr 609 (32), Technical Report 3, Yale University, September, 1961.

The principle of specificity
and the physical educator
Richard S. Rivenes

some unitary characteristic of the performer that may be called upon as the situation demands. If such abilities exist, then the r among the various tasks which purport to rely upon such abilities must yield r^2 proportions which are greater than k^2 (necessitating an r of .71 or larger). This has not been the case. Data on balance performance serve as an excellent illustration. Table I shows the intercorrelations among a number of very similar balance tasks. By calculating the r^2 and k^2 values for each coefficient, it may be determined that even among such similar tasks utilizing nearly identical musculatures, there are many more specific than common factors. Of the total performance variance in Table 1, 92 percent is task specific and only 8 percent common. The only valid conclusion is that there are probably as many balance abilities as there are balance tasks, very little general balance ability, and certainly not *a balance*. Similar findings are inescapable if one examines the evidence dealing with other abilities, including physiological parameters such as strength and endurance type performances. There are coordinations, not a coordination; agilities, not an agility; strengths, not a strength.

It is no longer tenable to assert that "handball is good for hand-eye coordination." Rather it must be recognized that handball contributes primarily to handball ability. Baseball does not develop some general attribute called timing as is often suggested; nor does skipping rope develop rhythm. By the same token one cannot accurately categorize performers as being fast, flexible or explosive. The performances in each of these cases is composed of highly specific factors relatively unique to that activity; the general abilities referred to simply do not exist. The principle of specificity may be difficult for physical educators to accept in a time when the profession is striving for more educational objectives for its programs. But the data are in, the principle is valid, and the implications in this respect are quite clear.

The principle of specificity is also incongruous with many of the testing and evaluation practices within the profession. Techniques of measurement, which involve the quantitative assessment of a performance, have become very refined in a number of areas and may use valid and reliable tools. When a measure is used as a predictor of some other behavior, it becomes a *test*, and this use of neuromuscular performance measurements involves serious theoretical problems. The principle of specificity has no quarrel with measurement *per se*, but it stands in opposition to most, if not all, forms of testing. If one performance is to be a predictor of another, the r^2 value must be high, i.e., there must be a large proportion of factors common to both performances in question. There are few, if any, tests used in physical education that can meet this criterion, because performance tends to be highly specific in nature. A football coach who screens athletes using a 40-yard dash as a test of speed can not be sure that those who run the fastest will be the better players, or for that matter, will be the fastest at shorter or longer distances. Not only is the ability to run fast highly specific to distance, but a given speed does not relate highly with actual sports skills in most areas. Physical fitness testing is another prime example of malpractice. How can one justify the use of a nationally recognized test which includes pull-ups, sit-ups, shuttle run, standing broad jump, 50-yard dash, softball throw for distance, and 600 yard run-walk as a predictor of physical fitness when fifty years of research indicates that the vast majority of that which is measured by these items is the items themselves? Pull-ups measure pull-ups, and such performance reflects very little about any other performance capacities. Morford (1964) and Alderman and Howell (1968) have examined this issue in full and concur with these contentions. It is clear that the current practice of using a few specific performance measures to test for a highly questionable general status labelled physical fitness is not in accordance with the available evidence.

It is common in sport programs for coaches to schedule vigorous exercise and conditioning programs as preparation for a contest or season. Calisthenics, running, weight training, and other activities are very popular. Is there any relationship between such activities and sports performance? Specificity evidence indicates that there are relatively few factors common to various conditioning tasks and sport skills. In fact, one study found a correlation of .00 between number of sit-ups and years of football experience at the high school level (Fleishman, 1961). Yet how often does one see the sit-up ritual performed *en masse* during a typical football season? There are usually *some* common factors, that is, r^2 is not typically zero, and this may account for the limited but beneficial effects attributed to various training programs on speeds of movement, strengths, etc. But the question of time and efficiency must be considered. If 10 percent of an hour's training is effective and related to a given sport performance, 90 percent of that time is wasted. The principle of specificity indicates that training activities should be as similar as possible to the actual needs of the athlete. A wrestler should wrestle to get into condition for wrestling, not run miles. Many of the standard calisthenics and exercise routines that have been a part of most sports should be abandoned in view of the evidence.

There are, of course, other implications of the principle of specificity, but those described briefly here are among the most important. Certain

The principle of specificity
and the physical educator

Richard S. Rivenes

program changes are in order in physical education, but perhaps more importantly, the communication gap between those who research the various parameters of activity and sport and those who implement programs must be improved if the field is to remain viable.

REFERENCES

Alderman, Richard B., and Howell, Maxwell L. "The Generality and Specificity of Human Motor Performance in the Evaluation of Physical Fitness." *Journal of Sports Medicine and Physical Fitness* 9(1969):31–39.

Fleishman, E. A.; Thomas, P.; and Munroe, P. *The Dimensions of Physical Fitness—A Factor Analysis of Speed, Flexibility, Balance, and Coordination Tests.* Office of Naval Research, Contract Nonr 609 (32), Technical Report 3, Yale University, Sept. 1961.

Henry, Franklin M. "Future Basic Research in Motor Learning and Coordination." *Proceedings of the College Physical Education Association,* 1956.

Long, John A. *Motor Abilities of Deaf Children.* Teachers College, Columbia University Contributions to Education, No. 514, Columbia University Bureau of Publications, 1932.

Morford, W. R. "Motor Abilities—Physical Fitness and the Specificity of Human Motor Performance." *Bulletin, Health and Physical Education Council, Alberta Teachers Association,* 4(1964): 35–52.

Perrin, F. A. C. "An Experimental Study of Motor Ability." *Journal of Experimental Psychology,* 4(1921):25–57.

Seashore, R. H. "Individual Differences in Motor Skills." *Journal of General Psychology,* 3(1930): 39–66.

Dance and the problem of departmental affiliation

Gay Cheney
California State University, Hayward

The question as to the proper department in which to locate is a much-debated one. Its solution has been discussed by people in dance, creative art, performing art, fine arts, and aesthetics, and by state committees, college committees, community, and departmental committees. Strangely enough, the only people who are not discussing it are the physical education people with whom dance lives most of the time, and under whose aegis dance first entered the area of education! Meanwhile, it has become fashionable to solve the problem of location by moving dance to the creative or performing art departments, unless it sets forth on a bold independent venture to build a structure of its own. And few physical educators seem to be oppressing this move.

Dance and the problem
of departmental affiliation
Gay Cheney

In the stages of the affiliation between dance and physical education, the latter considered dance to be an asset, adding depth experience and the dimension of art and creativity to movement programs. Dance people, in turn, were grateful for an entry into education and were interested in the forms of movement common to both kinds of physical activity. Both sides, however, have become less tolerant of the other. To many physical educators, dance is a kind of freak, tolerated only because it happens to exist in their department. Because it is often not within the experience of physical education teachers, it is looked at askance or ignored altogether. The unspoken thought might run something like this: "We don't understand you, but you're here, and, as long as you don't make any waves, we'll give you room." No wonder dance teachers, faced with this reception, want to move toward the arts, a place where they feel their concern with the subjective will be better understood. Many times, however, the jaded glance is deserved. Some dance people seem to have gone about making noisy demands, claiming superiority over their colleagues in sports. They have made great fuss trying to get their "art" out of physical education. While dance is undeniably an art form, those who must move to the art department to prove it would seem to be uncertain of this—or of themselves. When the move is so motivated, little is resolved.

Thus, as always, there are two sides to the story. There are also two issues to be considered in resolving the problem; the philosophical question as to the most logical place for dance to reside and the practical question as to where dance can reside and develop to its fullest. As a creative performing art through a physical movement, dance has a foot in both art and physical education. In common with the other arts, dance has a concern for technique, improvisation, composition, and aesthetic principles, along with creativity, communication, and formation of symbol. Dance might claim to be a cousin to painting and sculpture with its shared interest in line, design, and shape; it could establish a conjugal tie with music in a common concern for rhythm, tempo, meter, phrasing, and form; it might consider drama a distant relative also involved in performance and communication through the body. Philosophically, dance could join this area as the art of motion. The arts seem to stand in adjacent positions, joining at mutually shared points. Dance shares elements with all, becoming the point of meeting of the temporary and the spatial arts, encompassing both spheres in movement. 123

Practically, dance could exist easily in the performing arts buildings, where there are studios and practice rooms equipped with barres and mirrors, leotards and tights, accompanists, records, drums, and also a fair share of rehearsal and performance time and space, equal publicity, attention, respect. But if the teacher is not careful he may find himself continually serving the needs of his cohabitants. He can spend full time choreographing "Damn Yankees" and "Blood Wedding," adding visual interest to a chorale and training actors in moving. He can learn to squeeze movement in and out of sets, around the dialogue and plot, and between the measure marks of the score, but was this his dream for dance? In his eagerness to affiliate with the arts, he has allowed the dance to take a back seat. It was for the perpetuation of dance in its own right that he made this alliance, but he must be realistically aware that performing arts departments, too, are looking for affiliations which are to their best advantage.

Movement, the essence of dance, is also, of course, shared by sport. Dance deals with time, space, and energy; it is organized rhythmically, spatially, and dynamically; it is concerned with economy, efficiency, control, and meaning. Balance, compensation, elevation, momentum, coordination, opposition, sequence, climax are all involved. It is a form of expression; it is communication; it is performance; it is occasionally an aesthetic experience. Which of these things could not be said of all other physical education activities?

Each form, of course, has its unique qualities: while performance aspects of both are similar, the creative effort of each has different emphasis and result; while sport is spontaneous and immediate—the real thing, dance is a repeatable *symbol* of the real thing; while sport arranges movement to achieve a particular pragmatic goal, dance arranges it to provide a meaningful experience for the audience; while competition is a built-in essence of sport, it has nothing to do with the basic nature of dance.

In addition, dance is an art, and although gymnastics and diving might be exceptions, sport is not usually so designated. Even so, an athlete may claim, for example, that there is nothing more beautiful than the moment of suspension at the top of a pole vault, that hanging on thin air just before the vaulter starts the descent. Another might feel that the style with which he handles the ball, turns, jumps, and reaches for the basket is highly self-expressive. And marathon observers tell of being moved to tears watching a runner return from miles across country, to cut first through the finish line. In all these cases, the movement of a human being has had a powerful effect. The movement is meaningful, it communicates, it "feels" to the performer, it evokes feeling in the spectators. Is this not the ultimate goal of dance?

**Dance and the problem
of departmental affiliation**

Gay Cheney

Philosophically, then, dance could quite naturally join sport in the physical education family as the communicative and aesthetic aspect of movement.

Practically, too, dance may be provided for quite well in terms of space, money, and time within physical education departments. Despite all the space and time, however, there may exist an atmosphere stifling to dance. Although dance and sport both derive from movement and share many aspects of it, the competitive aspect of sport can be so distorted as to make it basically imcompatible with dance. Ideally, sport competition should sustain a competitive situation which evokes one's finest and most beautiful performance. But all too often competition evokes one's will to win at almost any cost. The winning supersedes the importance of agonism, beauty, finesse, style, meaning. Rather than the phenomenon of movement experienced for its own sake, it is the end of that movement that is significant, whether it is measurements, seconds, inches, points, punts, pennants, cups, jackets, letters, scores, or scholarships. The individual experience of transcendence is lost in the race for records.

In such an atmosphere, dance cannot coexist. The language of winning is foreign to dance. It focuses on the direction a piece of choreography must take, on fully realizing the potential of a movement, on becoming absolutely *with* an audience. It can understand an athlete who feels the whole team interconnected as one, who feels an inseparable part of the energy of the wave, who feels his own effort relax and some greater force take over in a continued running. But it cannot exist where winning means to "beat the hell out of 'em!" In a situation, however, where the athlete gives the finest performance he is capable of within the framework of his competition— winning or losing, incidentally—dance can exist. In a department and with a staff dedicated to the study of movement and the movement experiences of all human beings, dance can thrive. In fact, such a physical education department is a natural home for dance. And hopefully more physical education people will protest the moving of dance to another location. Philosophically and realistically, dance can stay in physical education only when it becomes a healthy and sound place for the development and personal expression of movement.

Our other job—
teaching why

Paul A. Metzger
John F. Kennedy High School, Willingboro, N.J.

Physical education is based upon concepts that deal with both the physical and the mental aspects of life. The following concepts are examples and should not be taken as a complete inventory of the concepts underlying physical education.

1) *Exercise increases muscular strength.* Although experts differ about what actually takes place within the muscles to make them stronger, considerable experimental and empirical evidence indicates that exercise increases strength.

2) *Capillarization is an effect of exercise.* An exercising muscle must have a means of getting nourishment and eliminating waste products, functions which depend on the capillaries imbedded in the muscle tissues. Muscles which perform large amounts of work become more efficient by developing

more capillaries. This phenomenon occurs in the cardiac as well as the striated muscles (Morehouse and Miller, 1967, p. 255).

3) *Vigorous exercise aids in maintaining cardiovascular health.* There is much evidence that physically active individuals suffer fewer heart attacks (Fox and Haskell, 1968).

4) *Exercise aids in weight control.* If more calories are ingested than are used, the extra calories are deposited as fat in the body. Since the number of calories used by the body is dependent upon the length and intensity of muscular action, the effect of exercise upon weight is easily seen. In fact, "inactivity is more of a factor in overweight than is the amount of food consumed" (Heim and Ryan, 1960).

5) *The acquisition of motor skills aids the development of personality.* Children who lack physical skills are frequently excluded from peer groups. In addition, a child who displays a high level of gross motor skill is usually accorded a higher place in the status hierarchy than one who does not. Thus the acquisition of physical skills is a prerequisite to this social and personality development.

6) *Physical activity provides a healthy outlet for emotional tension,* thereby contributing to personal and social adjustment.

7) *Physical activities develop leadership and followership.* The ability to lead and the ability to follow are acquired through practice. Physical education offers innumerable opportunities for individuals to practice being both leaders and followers.

If physical education is to gain increased public respect it will be necessary to teach these and other concepts to the students presently enrolled in our elementary and junior high schools. To refrain from teaching the concepts of the field until high school is a waste of valuable time. In fact,

> our schools may be wasting precious years by postponing the teaching of many important subjects on the grounds that they are too difficult. . . . the foundations of any subject may be taught to anybody at any age in some form. (Bruner, 1960).

If we adhere to this idea, we must attempt to stimulate the cognitive as well as the psychomotor and affective aspects of our students. Even kindergarten and first grade students should be made aware of the physiological, emotional, and social concepts of physical education. Naturally, any teaching at these early levels needs to be extremely elementary, yet,

127

the first objective of any act of learning, over and beyond the pleasure it may give, is that it should not only take us somewhere, it should allow us later to go further more easily. (Bruner, 1960).

Physical education needs to develop a curriculum which emphasizes the basic concepts involved. So far the field has given great attention to skill development at the expense of this general understanding.

The primary responsibility of physical education to its students is to develop the desire to pursue an active life once they have terminated their formal schooling. To succeed, physical educators must help their students develop knowledge and attitudes as well as skills. Since people tend to use their recreational time doing the things that they do best, the development of a number of physical skills is important. Learning to understand these skills makes their continued use even more attractive. Further knowledge of the physical, emotional, and social benefits of activity enhances the development of a positive attitude toward physical activity.

The students, therefore, must understand the concepts of physical education. The best way to implement this understanding is to have a quality program which reaches all of the students. This program should be as diverse as possible, so that each student has an opportunity to achieve some degree of success in at least one activity. One success leads to an interest in the development of greater skill, which in turn leads to further successes.

Many of the physiological principles upon which physical education is based can be demonstrated by simple experiments. The hypertrophy and atrophy of muscle tissue can be shown in conjunction with a weight training unit. It is only necessary to have the students measure the girths of various parts of their bodies six weeks before the beginning of the weight training unit, again at the beginning of the unit, and also at the completion of the unit. If presented in this manner the "overload principle" will have increased meaning and will thus become a more lasting type of knowledge than it would be if it were merely discussed.

The atrophying effect of muscular disuse can be demonstrated by comparing the size of the non-affected and the broken limb of an injured pupil at the time that the cast is removed. Although this type of teaching cannot be planned for in advance, there are usually some students who suffer fractured limbs in each school each year.

The effect which vigorous exercise has upon cardiovascular endurance can also be exhibited. After the relationship between distance running and this type of endurance is explained, each student could be timed in a dash. He can then be timed in a distance run, the length of which is a multiple of the dash distance. The relationship of these two times then becomes an endurance ratio. After several weeks of training in distance running, the dash and the longer run times could again be compared. Any improvement in the endurance ratio could be observed. After this experiment the teacher could then point out the positive effects of vigorous exercise upon the heart. If the students realize that the heart is a muscle and if they compare their pulse rate before and after distance running, the value of exercise to the heart becomes apparent.

Many of the basic concepts cannot be experimentally demonstrated in a limited amount of time. Students may, however, gain an understanding of these topics through discussions. Since it is important that they become involved in any discussion, some background library work should be required, so that the discussion is not simply a teacher-centered lecture. Topics which can be handled in this manner include the effect of activity upon weight and upon aging, the relationship of physical skill to leadership qualities, and the role of physical activity in relieving emotional tensions.

Much can be gained from discussion which follows or even interrupts motion pictures. Social relationships which develop during the playing of games can also be pointed out in class discussion. The wealth of teaching aids for physical education concepts includes pamphlets, film strips, movies, and posters. Catalogs which contain sources of materials are generally available through departments of education.

If physical education is to achieve and maintain its rightful place in education, physical educators must teach more than activities. The concepts which emphasize the need for activity must be understood, for, as Dewey said, "the only possible adjustment which we can give to the child under existing conditions is that which arises through putting him in complete possession of all his powers" (Dewey, 1897).

REFERENCES

Bruner, Jerome. *The Process of Education*. New York: Vintage Books, 1960.
Dewey, John. *My Pedagogic Creed*. New York: E. L. Kellogg, 1897.
Fox, Samuel M. and Haskell, William. "Physical Activity and the Prevention of Coronary Heart Disease." *Bulletin of the New York Academy of Medicine*, August, 1968.
Heim, Fred, and Ryan, Allen. "The Contributions of Physical Activity to Physical Health." *Research Quarterly*, Part 2, May 1960.
Morehouse, Laurence E. and Miller, Augustus T. *Physiology of Exercise*. Saint Louis: C. V. Mosby, 1967.

Developing a boys' secondary physical education program*

Donald B. Davies
Los Altos High School, Los Altos, Calif.

This essay deals with the boys' physical education program at Berkeley High School in Berkeley, California. It attempts to show how several administrative problems common to most secondary school physical education programs were solved. The solution

---

*This article and the following one concern the organization and implementation of a new curriculum in the Berkeley, California, school system. They were written by the Director of Physical Education for the system and the Department Chairman of Boy's Physical Education at Berkeley High School. A comprehensive three-year school, it enrolls about 3200 students, equally divided between boys and girls. The school was founded in 1880 and has been in its present plant for 71 years.

Since Berkeley High is the only public high school in the city, it is a melting pot of racial backgrounds, political beliefs, and educational philosophies. Its problems are very similar to those of many urban or inner-city high schools throughout the United States today. We hope that the methods and solutions proposed by these authors may contribute to the developmental process in other systems.

**Developing a boys' secondary
physical education program**

Donald B. Davies

required changes in administration policies or techniques that were often complicated, involving many interrelated issues. But as these changes were made and as each problem was solved, a gradual improvement in the quality of the boys' physical education program took place. By no means is it implied that the program developed was or is ideal, by no means do we have all the answers. But the solutions worked for this school at this particular time, and perhaps they can be of some help to others facing the same problems.

THE WAY IT WAS

As was the case for many school districts fifteen years ago, the physical education program for the 11th and 12th grade students consisted of throwing the ball out in football, basketball, and softball. The 10th grade students had a minimal amount of instruction in the above sports plus swimming and volleyball, but here too, it was mostly play. No intramural program existed. The interscholastic athletic program consisted of eight varsity sports involving about 17 percent of the male students at the school. Athletic coaching assignments were carried out after school with no extra compensation and no released time.

The basic philosophy of the physical education staff was that they had been doing things this way for years, and they saw no reason to change now. Unfortunately, many secondary school physical education programs operate on this same stereotyped philosophy, because of poor leadership at the school or district level in physical education, and because most male physical education teachers are interested in coaching athletic teams far more than in teaching physical education classes.

PHILOSOPHY AND OBJECTIVES

The members of a physical education department must have a sound philosophy as to what they are trying to do for the students and a plan to follow in accomplishing their goal. Much of their basic philosophy will stem from the state code and then from the local community by way of elected representatives. The local board, however, usually relies on the physical education staff to develop the district's philosophy. In other words, the physical education staff is usually quite free to develop its own philosophy.

College and university physical education teachers continually stress the importance of physical education objectives and the development of a sound philosophy. But few professional physical educators at the secondary level can effectively communicate with the board of education, parents, administrators, teachers, and students as to what the objectives of physical education are and what basic philosophy will be stressed while attempting to meet these objectives. This lack of communication is one of the profession's greatest weaknesses. Basic reasons for this weakness include poor communication skills, lack of understanding as to what they are trying to do, and making everything so complicated that they fail to reach the various publics. Objectives, therefore, must be sound, understandable and so simply put that communication problems are eliminated.

The objectives we settled on were physical fitness, recreational competency, and social efficiency, or, put simply: fitness, skill, and citizenship. There is nothing new about these objectives, and most physical education teachers have similar ones. Having objectives and communicating with the various publics about them are two different stories. Objectives are the tools by which we can sell our program, by using them to answer questions about it. The ramification of the objectives must be so familiar to the staff that they can be discussed well with all publics. It is not necessary to discuss objectives in detail here, because there are hundreds of books and articles on the subject, but it is necessary to repeat how important objectives are in developing a sound program.

The understanding and communication of objectives is by far the most important base on which to build a successful program. Once we understood our objectives and were willing and able to communicate with our various publics, the solution to other problems became much easier.

WORK LOAD

The most important objective of a public school educational program is English. A student should have a reasonable level of skill in reading, writing, speaking, and listening. The next priority is math, to the point where the basic skills are mastered and the individual has a satisfactory knowledge of the basic mathematics used in the society of which he is a member.

Fortunately our public schools can go far beyond these basic objectives and can provide a broader experience for students, not only in academic subject matter but in physical education, recreation, occupational preparation, and citizenship. This allows us to create a curriculum concerned with the development of the total individual. In that case, each discipline, as part of the total curriculum, is important to the education of the students.

Developing a boys' secondary
physical education program

Donald B. Davies

The argument that physical education classes require less preparation than academic classes can last forever. The truth of the matter is that each discipline has its own idiosyncrasies relative to work load and each usually balances out with any other discipline. Try telling a typing teacher that his job is easier than an English teacher's, or a woodshop teacher that his work load is smaller than a foreign language teacher's, or a football coach that his work is easier than the math teacher's. Work loads should be considered only as a function of the time actually in contact with the students. Most school districts now treat the teachers, in the various disciplines, including physical education, as equals. They pay them on a single salary schedule and give them comparable work loads.

This philosophy suggests that the interscholastic athletic program is merely an extension of the physical education curriculum, since in most California high schools athletic team participation takes the place of the physical education class. The state has approved this, and the districts usually welcome it. In effect an athletic team becomes a physical education elective class with a physical education teacher. It therefore becomes a part of the total curriculum and should be treated as such with respect to coaching assignments, which should be considered as class assignments and either paid for at the district's certificated rate or in released time. Some combination of these two processes is also acceptable. There is no other way, for to do so merely admits that physical education is not as important as other subjects in the curriculum. Paying the golf coach $250 for the season is an insult to the profession. Unfortunately, physical education and teachers of other subjects who also coach have been willing to be insulted because of their love for coaching.

It took three years against determined opponents to solve the work load issue successfully for the physical education teachers. The policy change indicated that coaching an athletic team was considered the equivalent of two class assignments. A class assignment for a school district averages about $1000 per semester. This means that released time actually cost the district around $2000 per coaching assignment, depending on the length of the season. If the released time concept is not used, then each coaching assignment should be worth about $2000 in extra pay.

It would have been difficult and unfair to ask teachers for their time and energy in building a new program when their work load was so unequal. But once the objectives of the program had been stated and communicated and the work load of the interscholastic athletic coaches equalized with that 133 of the total faculty, emphasis could then be shifted to developing a program which would offer the best chance of getting the job done.

COORDINATING THE THREE PHASES OF PHYSICAL EDUCATION

We are trying to meet our physical education objectives by exposing students to many physical education activities. We then wanted to develop a competency level in a few activities which would enable the individual to maintain his fitness level and his leisure time throughout life. Along with this we were attempting to develop a positive attitude toward physical education. To accomplish this for all students with all levels of ability, it was necessary to coordinate all phases of physical education.

The coordination of the service, intramural, and interscholastic phases of the program is all important. The director must view each phase in relation to the educational effort of the school. It would seem logical to claim that the service program should take first priority, because it involves all the students, and the athletic program last, because it handles the fewest students. But this argument is not entirely sound, because each phase handles a specific element of the student body. All three phases are important, and they must be solidly coordinated under the direction of one individual who is held accountable for the entire program.

Unfortunately the athletic program becomes the dominant phase of the physical education programs of many secondary schools. Too often there is a separate department chairman and athletic director, both responsible to the principal, which usually leads to inconsistencies and overemphasis.

Once it was established that the three phases would be coordinated under one administrative position, the next step was to develop each phase. In developing the service curriculum we decided what we wanted the students to have accomplished by the end of the 12th grade. It therefore became necessary to review the program from kindergarten through 12th grade. It was also important to understand the needs of children at the various levels, the society in which the educational institution is located, and what finances and facilities were available—in other words, to follow standard textbook procedures for curriculum development.

Although complete coordination was never achieved, it was felt that the K-3 program should emphasize the basic movement skills of running, throwing, kicking, etc., through a program of movement exploration, rhythms, games of low organization, and drills in simple skills. The 4-6 program should emphasize the fundamentals of the team sports common to our culture. Grades 7 and 8 should emphasize competition in team sports and the

Developing a boys' secondary
physical education program
Donald B. Davies

fundamentals of such sports as wrestling, gymnastics, and swimming. It is important to remember that finances and facilities help determine the content of the program. The 9th and 10th grades should emphasize instruction and competition in team and individual sports, plus a highly concentrated unit on the lifetime, carry-over sports. The 11th and 12th grade program could then become truly elective, emphasizing competency in a few activities of the students' choice.

This was the thinking behind the development of the 7-12 service program. The intramural and athletic phases would be extensions of this philosophy. It looked good on paper. However, it led to our next problem, overcoming the fact that most men in the physical education profession, especially at the high school level, are primarily interested in coaching interscholastic athletic teams, not in teaching physical education classes.

COACHING AS TEACHING

Many teachers at our college training institutions continually stress the importance of being a physical education teacher first and a coach second, of physical education before athletics. Our national and state association groups tend to reinforce this same philosophy. It is sound, but it has not worked. It *has* caused a split in the physical education profession: secondary coaches have heavily supported the coaches' associations rather than national and state physical education associations.

In reality, an extremely high percentage of the secondary school physical education teachers go into the field because they want to coach. We do have some dedicated individuals who sacrifice athletics to physical education, but they are few. So instead of continually expressing dissappointment in the priorities set by such teachers, it is much more logical to take advantage of this intense interest in coaching. After all, the interscholastic athletic program is an important part of the total program. Coaching is teaching. We simply turned our physical education program into a competitive-team coaching situation. We not only got good teaching in our physical education classes, but we got an atmosphere which was healthy for the entire program. We developed a situation which enabled the service, intramural, and athletic phases to be truly coordinated, and we ended up with a natural avenue for participation on our athletic teams. Everyone seemed to profit from the approach.

Specifically, each teacher became a coach for his class in each activity, and the class became the team for the within-period intramural competition. The classes from the same period then became a combined team with co-coaches for the between-period intramural competition held after school or in the evening. Units were timed to precede the sports season as much as possible. Points were scored by all participants. Ability classifications were set up to insure that all students had an important contribution to make toward their class period. Points were cumulative over the entire semester, creating a positive competitive spirit among the students and, equally important, among the coaches. The teaching in this situation was excellent and avoided too much emphasis on varsity athletics. This competitive emphasis also worked for the lifetime, carry-over sports in the elective program. Participation at this level exceeded 70 percent of the male students in the intramural phase of the program.

Once the physical education program had been reorganized to provide exposure and then competence, once the intramural program had been enlarged to make room for everyone, and once the physical education teachers began doing as good a job in their classes as with their teams, there was no reason why the athletic program could not be expanded.

THE EXPANDED ATHLETIC PROGRAM

In our high schools we spend thousands of dollars on the interscholastic football program, often having a teaching ratio of 20-1 and catering to only about 6 percent of the male students. Football is a great sport, it helps greatly the few boys it involves, and it is good for school morale and school discipline. There is no reason it should be eliminated. But if the interscholastic football program is so worthwhile, then the other students, both boys and girls, should have a chance for similar benefits from other sports. Many more athletic teams should be added and classification teams should be restored. It amounts to a simple expansion of the elective physical education offerings.

Viewing the athletic program in this way we were able to expand our program from the eight most popular sports (football, basketball, track, baseball, swimming, golf, cross country and tennis) which involved about 17 percent of the male students, to a fifteen sport program, adding gymnastics, wrestling, soccer, water polo, crew, handball and power volleyball and involving over 32 percent of the male students. Similarly, the girls' athletic program has expanded from zero to seven sports. Certainly all students cannot and will not wish to participate, and money will not be available for everything. However, we can indeed gradually expand our programs to

ISSUES IN PHYSICAL EDUCATION / CURRICULAR
Developing a boys' secondary
physical education program
Donald B. Davies

expose more and more students to the excellent educational benefits of an athletic program.

The expansion of the athletic program along with the expansion of the intramural program and the increased service class electives led to the ever increasing problem of finance, the next problem we had to solve.

SOLVING THE FINANCIAL PROBLEMS

If the service, intramural, and athletic phases of the program were to be considered part of the total school curriculum, then the district had the obligation to support all three phases. This had always been true for the service phase. A large share of the expense of running the intramural program was paid for out of the community service tax monies, so there were very few problems in expanding this phase. The athletic program, the most costly phase, was originally supported to a large extent from gate receipts and the student government. This procedure automatically placed the individual coaches and the entire athletic department in a subordinate position with respect to an always-changing group of student government officers, a difficult situation at best.

As inflation took its toll, and as the student body became less interested in interscholastic sports (as is the case in many large urban districts) supporting the existing program became difficult, and expanding it seemed impossible. Fortunately the district agreed to pay for transportation, officials, equipment, cleaning, and uniform purchases, a logical step if the three-phase program is considered part of the total school curriculum.

The next step was to remove the athletic phase of the physical education program from student control. This was done simply by an administrative decision allotting gate receipts to the physical education department. The monies were used to purchase athletic awards, provide meals for athletes on trips, support the cheerleaders, pay entry fees, purchase miscellaneous uniform items and serve as a general backup for the athletic budget supplied by the district. The student body card became an athletic card.

The student government was then able to spend its time conducting student government activities and was relieved of the headaches of running an athletic program. The loss of revenue did not amount to much, since most of the money taken in by the student government was from athletics and by far the greatest expenditure was for athletics. The student government 137 no longer needed large sums of money. However, a 5 percent tax was proposed for all fund-raising activities by all student groups, revenues from which could then be used for activities the student leaders wished to support. Solving these financial problems greatly helped to expand the athletic program and to develop the life-time activity aspects of the service class program.

Finally, by agreeing to fund the position of locker room-equipment supervision, the district also eliminated the great amounts of time wasted when the teachers are required to handle equipment problems, locker problems, uniform problems, clerical problems and so on. As it now stands, one classified employee, under the direct supervision of the physical education department chairman, handles all these nonteaching duties for all personnel in the three phases of the program. Coaches were not concerned with equipment, lockers, insurance, physicals, eligibility or maintenance. Their job was to teach and coach. The loss in uniforms due to this system is minimal, the teaching time saved is enormous and the value to the district is tremendous.

UNSOLVED PROBLEMS

This article has described how certain administrative problems in physical education were solved, leading to the improvement of the total program. This, however, is by no means the end of the story. The development of the program occurred between 1960 and 1970. But our objectives in physical education must continually be evaluated, and changed if necessary, to keep up with our changing society. The needs of students remain very much the same over the years, but we must continually modify the way we meet those needs.

Current issues which have a profound effect on the physical education program involve race relations, a more permissive attitude on the part of educators, the growing popularity of different recreational activities, alternative modes of education, subschools, the hippy impact, accountability and year-round schooling. The impact of these issues is causing fast and profound change in physical education programs. Some changes are constructive and worthwhile, many are destructive and inconsistent—but that is another story.

Coach your physical education classes

Paul A. Daniels
Berkeley High School, Berkeley, Calif.

It has often been said that some of the best teaching in education occurs in the inter-scholastic athletic program, and conversely, some of the worst teaching in education takes place in the Physical Education program. Consequently, several years ago, the Boy's Physical Education department at Berkeley High School initiated the present "coaching approach" in the teaching of its tenth grade physical education classes. The tenth grade classes were selected for this type of teaching because the tenth grade marks the culmination of the team sports program which began in the seventh grade and because in the eleventh and twelfth grades, physical education is an elective class.

This decision has had many beneficial effects on our physical education classes. First of all, our staff began teaching, or "coaching," their classes with greater enthusiasm. Second, the students became more motivated because fundamental skills were now being taught with some immediate purposes in mind. Third, the decision gave greater impetus to our intramural program, for the competition between classes became an integral part of that program. Finally, we began to discover many youngsters with hidden talents.

Classes were organized so that taking attendance and conducting group exercise were carried out quickly and effectively.

We required all of our students to run one lap before and after class, or a total of one-half mile a day. As soon as a student came to the track, he began running his first lap, which he had to complete before the tardy bell. While the students were running, the "coach" was taking attendance. As each student completed his lap, he gave the coach his attendance roll number. Thus we were able to take roll before the class actually began, and in addition, we had given the student some pre-class warm-up.

As soon as the tardy bell rang, we began our group exercises, which were executed in a continuous sequence. For example, we would do thirty jumping jacks, twenty alternating toe touchers, twenty trunk twisters, twenty push ups, ten sit ups, ten finger tip push ups, ten leg raisers, and thirty seconds of running in place. All of these exercises were done quickly, and without pauses between them. As soon as the class was about to complete one set of exercises, a preparatory command was given for the next exercise. The complete set of exercises took about four to five minutes of class time.

The rest of the class period consisted of coaching the students in the fundamental skills of a selected sport. For teaching a large group of students the basics of a sport, we preferred the "whole" method over the "part" method. Thus we taught or "coached" the whole skill or game initially. We felt this approach would help each student to quickly recognize his particular deficiencies and would help the coach gain a clear idea of what particular skills to stress in terms of both the class and the individual. For example, in the beginning of our tenth grade gymnastics unit, we demonstrated the various routines on each of the six different pieces of apparatus. At first this was overwhelming for many of the students, and some were even reluctant to attempt the complete routine. However, within a week's time some students had mastered the beginning routines and were moving on to difficult ones, while the average and slow students were not far behind, since they now knew the routines could be accomplished.

The "whole" method followed by the "part" method also helped us overcome our two main problems of insufficient time and overcoaching. We tried to move from one skill level to the next, as quickly as possible. Initially, the majority of the students in a class need about half the class time for the

Coach your physical education classes

Paul A. Daniels

complete routine. As the student became more proficient, however, three-fourths of the class period was used for the whole activity. Students who exhibited proficiency in a skill were allowed to move on quickly to the next activity, thus increasing economy of time and equipment.

As a student demonstrated the activity, the coach would evaluate him individually. In handball, for example, the coach would begin with a brief presentation of the objectives, fundamentals, strategies, and essential rules of the game during the first part of the period. During the second half of the period the students would play while the coach helped individuals identify their skill deficiencies. In addition, the coach would be making a mental or written analysis of what skills needed to be emphasized for both the group and the individual. This analysis might take the form of a mental note like the following: "They all need to work on their weak hands, especially Troy, Brent and Harold. About twelve of them need a great deal of work on returning shots off the back wall, and about five of them should be working on kill shots." During the first half of the class on the following day, the coach would begin with basic fundamentals for the entire class, followed by small-group work in terms of the previous day's analysis. Again, the second half of the class would be devoted to activity and continued skill analysis.

FALL PROGRAM

Cross-country and track & field   The tenth grade program begins with a three-week unit in cross-country running, followed by a three-week unit in track and field. Both these units serve as an ideal way of initially conditioning our students, while at the same time introducing them to activities with which most of them were not familiar. The third week of each unit consists of a week-long inter-class competition. In the competition, each coach enters as many students as he had in his class, dividing the students into two different divisions according to skill level. (In the cross-country meet the better students run a slightly longer course than the average student.) Each class receives a point for each student who performed. In addition, a class earns points based on individual performance during the meet.

Wrestling   Scheduling our physical education units either before or during the season of any particular sport yielded many beneficial results. In the case of wrestling, we use members of the wrestling team as coaching aides and referees during both the instructional phase and the competitive portion of the wrestling unit. During this unit the students are divided by both their weight classification and their wrestling skill. For the wrestling tournament in the ninth week of the semester, students are placed in two divisions, depending on their wrestling ability. Class points are awarded on the basis of student participation, and on the basis of each student's advancement during the wrestling tournament.

Swimming   The students are taught the basics of competitive swimming, including the various strokes, turns, and conditioning. Those few students who are unable to swim a minimum of fifty yards are taught basic swimming skills. In the competitive phase of the program students are again divided into two skill levels in each of the following events: 100-yard individual medley relay, 50-yard freestyle, 50-yard backcrawl, 50-yard butterfly, 100-yard freestyle, 100-yard individual medley, 200-yard relay, and diving. In addition, the beginning swimmers must swim a 25-yard freestyle, 25-yard backcrawl, and 100-yard freestyle relay. Classes earn points for student participation and student placement in each swimming and diving event.

Gymnastics   During the instructional phase of the gymnastic unit, the students learn routines for floor exercise, side horse, still rings, horizontal bar, parallel bars, and trampoline. In addition, all of the students participate in a compulsory floor exercise routine as a regular part of their daily calisthenics during this unit. The inter-class competition is composed of students competing in two divisions based on their individual gymnastic skill level. All of the students participate in the preliminaries, with the top ten students on each piece of apparatus competing against each other in the finals. As in the other inter-class events, each student is given a point for his participation. Points are also accumulated during the competition.

Fitness   We generally allow two to three weeks in the fall and spring for the students to complete six physical fitness tests, including pull-ups, sit-ups for 90 seconds, bar dips, obstacle course, endurance course, and a 600-yard run. At times we have included the fitness scores of individual classes in the inter-class competitions.

Overall class champion and awards   The class which accumulates the most points in the inter-class competitions throughout the fall semester is considered the over-all tenth grade class champion. In addition, we award first-through fifth-place ribbons to individual students in each event and give red and gold trunks to students who averaged 90 and 95 points on our physical fitness tests.

Coach your physical education classes
Paul A. Daniels

SPRING PROGRAM

Volleyball   The spring semester begins with a three-week unit in volley-ball. Each class enters two teams into a round-robin volleyball tournament, which takes place during the final week of the unit. Class points are awarded on the basis of student participation and team placement in the tournament.

Tennis   After the basic three-week instructional unit in tennis, we hold a 32-man singles tennis tournament on one day and 32-team doubles tourna-ment the next day. If time permitted, both these tournaments would be double elimination. We also use the Van Allen scoring system as a means of speeding up match play. Class points are awarded as previously indicated.

Handball   The handball competition is designed so that each coach enters four players in the singles handball tournament and eight players in the doubles portion of the tournament. This arrangement places 32 students in the singles tournament and 64 students in the doubles tournament. Again, class points are awarded on the basis of student participation and advance-ment.

Table tennis   The only significant difference in the organization of this event is that it is double elimination, beginning with two 32-man divisions. We award class points on the basis of student participation and their indi-vidual advancement during the tournament.

Badminton   We conclude our spring semester with a 32-man singles bad-minton tournament and a 32-team doubles badminton tournament, both of which are double elimination. The class which scores the most points through individual participation and advancement in the badminton tournament is declared the champion. The over-all spring semester champion is the class which accumulates the most points in all of the spring events.

CONCLUSION

We have been extremely pleased with our decision to incorporate this "coaching approach" into our tenth grade physical education classes. In fact, the fruits of our labors have proven so beneficial that we have begun to work out a similar program in our eleventh and twelfth grade elective classes.   143

For example, we have recently concluded a highly successful basketball tournament composed of students from our eleventh and twelfth grade recreational sports classes. We hope to initiate the same kind of program in flag football, softball, water polo, tennis, handball, paddle ball, badminton, and weight lifting.

In conclusion, let me add a word of caution: this approach to teaching physical education classes involves a great deal of work. However, if that prospect does not scare you, and if you want your students to be motivated and enthusiastic, then by all means you should coach your physical education classes.

Issues in physical education and sports

4 CULTURAL

Cultural considerations
for physical education

Jan Felshin

East Stroudsburg State College, Pennsylvania

Education is simply a social conception. Whether a particular society is "schooled" or "de-schooled," the beliefs about the past, present, and future that determine what is learned and what is taught express socialization and culture. Curriculum is always an institutionalized expression of these views and, as such, reflects somewhat pervasive attitudes toward persons, knowledge, and the process of education. This "contexture" of sources provides the bases for selection for the schools. Programs in schools do not duplicate the whole of sociocultural experience; rather, they exemplify and represent those dimensions that are considered appropriate and/or not provided for adequately in other institutionalized ways. Education is idealized, and programs are rooted in the affirmation of desirable values and knowledge.

147

PHYSICAL EDUCATION IN THE CURRICULUM

The role of physical education in the curriculum has been a tenuous one. Analysis of the contexture of education does not yield clear implications for the inclusion of physical education as an important and valuable aspect of knowledge or experience. In fact, educational positions that give priority to such concerns as rationality, literacy, and essential knowledge tend to diminish physical activity severly. The attempts of this profession to establish claims and contributions in contexts of rationality have been strenuous but largely absurd. Whether or not one has to "think" when one moves or plays is irrelevant; the focus of physical activities obviously is not cognition. Fortunately for the development of physical education, education in the United States has been conceived more broadly than education for literacy, but criticism of this subject area continually arises from a rationalistic base.

Another pervasive criticism of physical education in the curriculum relates to the idea that its concerns are "trivial" and unimportant in either the domain of knowledge or the serious endeavors of man. This has led to the limited acceptance of these activities as "extra-curricular" or as adjuncts to the "real" school program. Although physical educators have managed to retain instructional programs as well as after-school activities, they are often questioned, attacked, and even ridiculed. The educational coin of the realm is time, space, and money; and the exchange rate is in scheduling, credits, and grades. Physical education is incessantly devalued in contemporary bartering for curriculum status.

Even if the importance of physical education activities is granted, their necessity in the curriculum can be questioned. Schools, after all, are a specialized kind of institution. In this view, it is suggested that physical education is irrelevant because it duplicates available cultural learnings and does not require the unique capabilities of the school. Instructional time is precious and limited, and should not be squandered on those experiences readily available to children and youth in their everyday lives. Furthermore, both the unique functions of education and the extreme selectivity that is the basis of curriculum imply that time in school should be devoted to those things that require continual instruction. Physical education seems to utilize a great deal of "rehearsal time" in which students are supervised but actually only in practicing skills they already possess. This point of view, compounded by that of play as irrelevant to the school, leaves little room for sports and games in the curriculum.

Physical education, however, has endured in school programs and even flourished occasionally. This profession sought alliance with science and medicine and gained entry into the schools of the United States on the basis

**Cultural considerations
for physical education
Jan Felshin**

of its contributions to remediation and the needs of children and youth. Though no viable curriculum theory ever espoused "needs" as an exclusive source, it is obviously consonant with such principles as "educating the whole child" and "the optimum development of the individual." Furthermore, when the notion of "education for complete living" became popular as an outgrowth of the Seven Cardinal Principles in 1918, physical education developed an encompassing view of broad contributions to man through its activities. In doing so, physical education became an important methodology in the life of the school. Until the professional shift to delineating a body of knowledge for the field occurred in recent decades, physical education was characterized by its claims of contribution to a range of educational purposes and commitments.

After accepting a limited role in schools, physical education as a profession struggled to "catch up" with other fields in analyzing the contexture of education and defining its potential. In addition, there has been a conceptual revolution in this field, and the notion of a body of knowledge focused on man as he pursues movement and its forms either for their own sake or his own enhancement is generally accepted. The development of a discipline of knowledge is proceeding, and the corollary understanding that curriculum derives primarily from a focus on knowledge in relation to other aspects of the contexture of education is imminent. It is ironic that presently, when physical education is at the threshold of maturing as a field of study that is understood and capable of a significant role in education, it is threatened from another direction.

THE CONTEMPORARY CHALLENGE

Somehow, physical education has survived its own inability to develop a cohesive approach to curriculum and even its failure to reconcile theoretical points of view with reference to such aspects of its program as instruction, athletics, physical fitness, and sport, dance and exercise. The conceptual revolution that established the necessity of a defined body of knowledge was a bloodless one, and there is reason to believe that the argument over whether that discipline should focus on sport or on human movement will be reconciled. The contemporary challenge to physical education is an outgrowth of changing sociocultural values and attitudes wherein the virtues espoused by this field are in danger of becoming dysfunctional symbols for society and humanity. It is a staggering suggestion—that the one subject in

149

the curriculum most often criticized for being too social and playful in its orientation can be indicted on social grounds.

It is possible that the opportunities for social indictment have been enhanced by the shift of professional focus from the individual benefits of physical activity to conceptual concerns related to man in motion. Basically, however, physical education has developed behavioral models consonant with both the nature of some of its activities and their source in values attendant to competition, self-improvement, and hard work. Despite dramatic changes in psychological knowledge and attitudes, this field retained some pervasive commitments to a perfectability-through-effort model.

Physical education has become a symbol for obscene socialization. Authority, mindless compliance, sacrifice of self, performance conditions for self-worth, aggression, competition and the like values that attend many of the activities of this field are the socialization modes of an ordered and unpopular establishment. In accepting the competitive model, physical education has inappropriately generalized a conceptual error. That is to say, this profession has applied the principles of competition as though they were the cornerstones of organization, and *organized* physical activity does usually express the social attitudes and values most often found in public and highly organized competitive events. It is no wonder, then, that as both school and society are recognizing the limitations of an external and structured socialization model, physical education is designated as an offensive stronghold of support for that model.

Competition itself, of course, is not inherently evil or damaging either to human personality or to social contexts. In fact, competition does always imply cooperation and is a pervasive explanation for a great deal of human endeavor and interaction. Carried to extreme conclusions, however, the principles of competition are not consonant with contemporary understanding of humane concerns. Insofar as these conclusions imply conditional acceptance of self and others, the importance of external standards and goals for behavior, diminution of self-importance, compliance, sacrifice, aggression (both actual and symbolic) toward others, and acceptance of the constant need to improve and strive toward impossible perfection, they deny the integrity of the self and its social expression.

THE HUMANE FOCUS FOR PHYSICAL EDUCATION

In a world where neither culture nor counterculture is stable, where social organization and expectation are characterized by change and conflict, and where "establishment" has a pejorative connotation, socialization agree-

**Cultural considerations
for physical education**

Jan Felshin

ments do not obtain. The breakdown in these agreements dispels the notion of supervised and orderly progress toward adulthood and imposes upon the school the need for defining responsible social roles. Responsibility to rationality is no longer a sufficient identity for the school, if it ever was. The curriculum must be rooted in humane sources, and the skills and abilities that characterize the domains of knowledge must express these sources.

"Humane" suggests the enhancement and development of human potentialities and sensibilities. It is a concept that rests on the individual and his capacities for actualization, but it is based on recognition that these are developed in relation to other people. As a focus for education, it transcends humanistic psychologies in its basic tenet that what is good for the individual will benefit humanity, and what is best for humanity will benefit society. In this sense, the humane focus reconciles older dichotomies of the primacy of either the individual or the group. The centrality of the affective domain in human development, behavior, and interaction is an important theme.

Within the humane focus, curricular imperatives derive from concepts of *meaning and relevance* as these are actualized in *capacity and ability*. Education is *de*-humanized when it has no relation to the person and is disintegrative to his experience, especially of self. Meaning is requisite to self-integration and development. Only when people are engrossed and involved can they truly expend their finest efforts and experience the sources of their own meaning. Processes can be just as exciting as products, but growth as the exercise of abilities is fostered only when the person is captured in some way that enables energy, perseverence, curiosity, and inquiry. It seems apparent that

> The self is defined by what it can experience and has experienced. Each of us is known to ourselves as we are able to think, and feel, and act; and the discovery of capacity is crucial to the development of ability. The substance and processes of education are committed to the awareness and refinement of abilities and skills. The dimension of meaning and relevance must obtain for this to occur, and the human focus provides an inalienable framework for selecting and understanding how capacity and ability are related and when and why they are important.*

---

*Jan Felshin, *More Than Movement: An Introduction to Physical Education*. Philadelphia: Lea & Febiger, 1972, pp. 137–138.

Physical education is essentially a humanistic aspect of the curriculum. Its activities have been enduringly relevant and meaningful to man, and have survived and flourished in societies. Man pursues his own growth as an active organism expressing his abilities in behavior, and movement is basic to all his processes. Movement behavior is at once an expressive mode for the human and the source of data for behavior. Somehow, the humane focus for physical education must be clarified and its importance recognized for the best development of the field and of all who are involved in it.

IMPLICATIONS

Attention to the field of study underlying physical education has yielded a wealth of information and sufficient ordering of concepts to make it possible to deal with this field in a rational way. The study of sport, particularly, has revealed that it, like dance, is a significant phenomenon continuously fascinating and engrossing, and a social institution of some magnitude as well. The analysis of exercise has transcended a narrow focus on biophysiological effect and enabled understanding of its ritualistic sources as well as its relevance to body therapies and other psychological and spiritual systems. Play and games have been clarified as modalities of growth and expression. In sum, the conceptual revolution in physical education allows a confident and hopeful view of the field.

The role of physical education in the curriculum derives primarily from the insights of the field of study. The field encompasses an understanding of human movement and the movement forms of sport, dance, and exercise in both biomechanical and sociocultural contexts. Fields of study and school programs, however, are not identical. It is the whole contexture of education that gives rise to curricular imperatives, and physical education today must give greater cognizance to cultural considerations in determining its value modalities in curriculum.

It seems apparent that physical education must shift from programs based on the competitive models for human striving and behavior to bases in a humane focus in which meaning and relevance and capacity and ability are the primary values. This shift does not deny the traditional emphases and content of physical education programs; rather it suggests more clear and cogent expression of the importance of the field and its concerns.

If physical education is to be a viable force in the curriculum, the concerns of its field of study must be understood in their potential contribution to the life of man. Programs that express the importance of these contributions can

be developed, and the ensuing curricular change is likely to be more perma-

**Cultural considerations
for physical education**

Jan Felshin

nent and logically defensible than the "swing of the pendulum" and the temporary innovations that have characterized this field.

Physical education has always been concerned with *fitness*. In contemporary focus, however, this means an individualized program in which people can analyze themselves, set considered goals, and utilize the knowledge available in planning programs for their pursuit. Mass programs in which groups are "exercised" by others are anathema to this concept, for it is clear that the human pursues those things that are personal and meaningful to him.

Since movement is the primary mode for human development, *skill and mastery* is a basic concept for physical education. The self is defined by its capacities and abilities, and confidence and competence are inextricably related to the development of skill and mastery. It is true that "skill" suggests a predetermined model of excellence, and physical education has always been concerned with developing skills, but the humane focus lends greater importance to the affective domain, and to the satisfactions basic to the pursuit of skill and the attainment of mastery. Programs must allow for individuals to pursue their own development; exposure to a wide variety of activities for minimal lengths of time does not provide for this. The whole notion of "carry over" probably depends more on feelings about one's competence and ability than on some superficial acquaintance with an activity. It is important, too, in the contexture for curriculum that skill and mastery be understood to include the perceptions of the individual. The notion of "skill" applied indiscriminately to all people has led to the kinds of exclusion and public failure that are some of the dysfunctional effects of physical education.

Cultural participation in movement forms is perhaps the best understood focus for physical education. Programs based on the so-called "lifetime sports" are examples of this understanding. Unfortunately, those programs seem based on a conception of education as "preparation for life" rather than as an important experiential domain in the life of youth. Sport and dance are exceedingly important in society, and programs should provide for individuals to participate in culture. The most crucial culture for youth could, however, be the school; and it is on this basis that intramural and athletic programs function in the curriculum. It is important that physical education programs fulfill this focus in dynamic ways. Contemporary culture is characterized by new forms of sport and dance, and these should be en- 153 thusiastically welcomed into the curriculum. It is true that the recognition of lifetime sports helped shift programs from four major sports a year, but a broader concept is needed to insure that surfing, spelunking, karate, and a host of other attractive forms of movement find their way into programs.

The humane focus suggests, finally, that the *meaning and significance of movement activities* must be recognized. The symbolic forms of sport and dance provide unparallelled opportunities for the exploration and actualization of self and ability. It is not only that these forms seem to be relevant and meaningful to youth; rather, this focus suggests that there is meaning and significance uniquely inherent in movement activities. It is the concept of significance that explains why man creates symbolic and expressive forms; and as they endure, it becomes obvious that they contain this satisfying potential. As this focus is recognized, programs will reflect it. It negates the movitations of the competitive model in which one values winning rather than playing and recognition rather than experience. Striving and excellence are human values, and contesting is a logical setting, but the essence of sport and dance must be sought in the experiencing of self rather than in external outcomes or "teams" or trophies.

Physical education needs no apology. As expressive and significant forms of human behavior gain cultural primacy, attempts to justify their existence in rationalized ways are unnecessary. The concerns and activities of physical education are important considerations in the life and culture of man. It would be a tragedy for this field not to seek its sources in itself and fulfill them in programs, and this tragedy can be averted. The socialization model for physical education lies in the hopeful, humane dimensions of culture and its own ecstasies.

Sport and the radical ethic

Jack Scott
Oberlin College

I'm not sure if radical or revolutionary are really the most appropriate adjectives to describe the sport ethic I discuss in this chapter. This is particularly true in view of the connotation these words have as a result of manipulation and distortion by the mass media. A distortion which it must be admitted is partly the fault of many well meaning and perhaps some not so well meaning young revolutionaries. To me, what I have to say is simply old-fashioned common sense. Yet, since what I propose is fundamentally different from the contemporary American ethic of sport, it probably is appropriate to call it radical or revolutionary. For those who see some similarity between the radical ethic and the Christian ethic I need only remind you that Christ was a revolutionary. His ideas were revolutionary when he lived, and they would be even more revolutionary in twentieth-century America. If Christ chased the money changers from the temple, one can only enjoyably fantasize what he would do with Pete Rozelle and Walter Byers, never mind Richard Nixon and the corporate executives of IT&T. I start by describing what I see as the dominant ethic in American sport today. I then discuss the counterculture's criticism of that ethic and describe the position of the counterculture. Finally, I discuss how I see the radical ethic as a synthesis of these two positions. A way to conceptualize what I will attempt to do is to view the American ethic as the thesis, the counterculture ethic as the antithesis, and the radical ethic as the synthesis.

In my opinion, the dominant American sport ethic is best captured in Vince Lombardi's famous and often repeated remark that "winning isn't everything, it's the only thing." If this ethic only ruled the relatively small realm of professional athletics, it might be of no serious concern, but as we all know, it is the Lombardis, Tom Landrys, and Darrell Royals who are the high priests of the American athletic world. The Lombardian ethic is the rule of the day from the professional ranks, through the colleges, high schools, and junior high schools, down to the Little Leagues. Though educators may not have documented this phenomenon yet, many of our country's finest sport journalists have. Even some conservative figures in the American athletic establishment such as Fran Tarkenton and Harry "the Hat" Walker have begun to speak out in alarm about the influence of the Lombardian ethic on Little League and Pop Warner sports.

However, rather than simply ridicule the work of the Knute Rocknes, Vince Lombardis, and Paul "Bear" Bryants, I would like to speak briefly of their many accomplishments. However one may feel about these people, it must be admitted that the Lombardian ethic has guided those who live by it to some of the highest levels of athletic excellence known to man. This ethic is a product-oriented one to be sure, but it must be acknowledged that the product it turns out is an excellent one in most cases. In any sport that Americans have taken seriously, we have invariably developed some of the finest teams and individual athletes seen anywhere in the world. Though we sometimes get carried away with our own chauvinism, such as when we declare the Super Bowl a world championship, our myriad accomplishments in the international athletic arena including the Olympic Games speak for themselves.

For the most part, the men—I say men, because women have been pretty much excluded from serious competitive sport—the men who have followed the Lombardian ethic have been dedicated, hard-working individuals. The average big-time college football coach works at least as hard if not harder than the most dedicated professor. Only a fool would fault Woody Hayes for not being dedicated enough to the goals he has set for himself. We also often see what could be called an heroic struggle in sporting contests guided by the Lombardian ethic. At a time when one of the most crucial factors in determining who will be the President of the United States is which politician can afford the best make-up man, there is something very real and authentic about a hard-fought athletic contest, whether it be a sandlot baseball game or the World Series.*

It is also no wonder why so many American athletes put up with the present sports system, given options available to them. As Dave Meggyesy, Chip Oliver, and George Sauer have discovered, the problems and excesses that made them decide to leave football often exist to an even greater degree in society at large, while the jobs available in society at large seldom have any of the intrinsic satisfaction that they experienced in athletics. I am not attempting to apologize for the existing sports system. What I am attempting to do is point out the degree of alienated labor in American society.

Though we often hear many pious and hypocritical utterances to the contrary, Lombardi's comment that "you have to have that fire in you to play this game, and there is nothing that stokes the fire like hate" reflects how followers of the Lombardian ethic view their opponents. In American sport, the opponent is the enemy—an obstacle in the way of victory. In an interview that I did with George Sauer announcing his retirement from professional football, George commented that this aspect of American sport was one of the primary reasons he chose to leave the game despite his tremendous love for football. Sauer had this to say: "We shouldn't be out there trying to destroy each other, but some people try to make the game that way. They have the idea that in order to be really aggressive and obtain the height of football excellence, you have to almost despise your opponent,

---

*My reference to politicians and their make-up men is in regard to the famous television debates between John F. Kennedy and Richard Nixon in which it was claimed Nixon lost because he looked haggard and drawn—a result of improperly applied make-up. Commentators at the time pointed out that Nixon came off as second best not because of the substance of the debate, but as a result of his appearance. This whole phenomenon of image making is described in Joe McGinniss' excellent book, *The Selling Of the President*, a description of Nixon's 1968 Presidential campaign.

or even hate him. I think when you get around to teaching ideas of hatred just to win a ballgame, then you're really alienating people from each other and from themselves and are making them strive for false values."

Let me summarize the Lombardian or American ethic as I see it. It is a product-oriented system that has turned out an excellent product as a result of the sacrifices and hard work of many dedicated men. One of the ways this excellence has been developed has been by believing winning isn't everything, it's the only thing. Not too surprisingly, the opponent is viewed at best as an obstacle, at worst an enemy that must be overcome in order to achieve victory. Of course, this entire struggle takes place in a rigidly authoritarian structure. This position should be viewed, as I pointed out earlier, as the thesis.

Now let me go on to the antithesis—the counterculture ethic. Though it was around a long time before the birth of the counterculture, a saying that sums up this ethic is one I'm sure most people are familiar with: "It's not whether you win or lose, but how you play the game that counts." The counterculture ethic looks at the myopic product-orientation of the Lombardian ethic and demands that we stop being so product-oriented and focus on the process instead. The counterculture says we should enjoy sport for sport's sake, not for any extrinsic reward it might bring, including winning. Not too surprisingly, some counterculture proponents have even suggested that we abolish scoring. They see the value of the activity in the process, not the product; while to keep score is to focus attention on the outcome— the product. A counterculture runner wants to be concerned with how his run felt, not with how fast he covered the distance.

The counterculture has looked at the extreme competitiveness of the Lombardian ethic and has quite correctly been upset with its many abuses. Many counterculture proponents have suggested we replace competition with cooperation, since they see being competitive as trying to increase one's own stature by putting others down. Thus they frown on aggressiveness and competitiveness and offer gentleness and cooperation in their place.

According to the counterculture, since the rigid authoritarian structure of the Lombardian ethic stifles self-expression and spontaneity, this structure must be eliminated in order to allow these qualities to emerge. Consequently, hierarchical and role-specific relationships must be abolished. Likewise, since teamwork under the Lombardian ethic is often developed at the expense of individuality, so the counterculture usually prefers individual sports over team sports whenever possible.

The Lombardian ethic views sport as a masculinity rite from which

women are excluded. (Lombardi often motivated his players by indicating none too subtly that to lose a game was to lose one's manhood. One of his greatest players, Willie Davis, after a Green Bay Super Bowl victory commented, "We went out and won the game and preserved our manhood.") Upset by this super-masculine, square-jawed, steely-eyed approach to sport, the counterculture advocates coeducational sporting activities. Frisbee, where there is no violent body contact, is seen as a replacement for football.

In fact, the counterculture ethic reverses every value of the Lombardian ethic. Cooperation replaces competition, an emphasis on the process replaces an emphasis on the product, sport as a coeducational activity replaces sport as a stag party, a concern for enjoyment replaces a concern for excellence, and an opportunity for spontaneity and self-expression replaces authoritarianism. It should be clear by now why I call the counterculture ethic the antithesis of the Lombardian ethic.

The counterculture ethic, however, profoundly misunderstands the true nature of sport. They are like the "parlor athletes and some splendid though misguided sportsmen [who] talk about sport for sport's sake and condemn winning. They neither understand nor contribute to the problem. Sport for the sake of sport might be the worst dilettantism possible. As a slogan expressing abhorrence of corrupt practices, it is admirable; as argument that victory should not be striven for, it is mere nonsense" (J. Williams and W. Hughes, *Athletics in Education*, 1937). This quote, although referring to certain sport critics of nearly forty years ago, is still pertinent today. To tell a competitive athlete, man or woman, who is training three and four hours a day, day in and day out, year after year, not to be concerned with victory is liberal snobbery; or at best it is the remark of someone who simply does not understand the agonistic struggle which is an integral part of the competitive sport experience. *It is just as wrong to say winning isn't anything as it is to say winning is the only thing.*

Let me offer an often-told story to help explain what I see as the underlying reason for the development of the counterculture ethic. Remember the ugly old witch who, when she looked in the mirror and didn't like what she saw, smashed the mirror in frustration and anger? We see that the witch's action was futile, for the mirror was only reflecting her own ugliness and was not the cause of her appearance. Similarly, sport serves basically as a mirror reflecting the underlying values of a society. Consequently, all the strengths as well as all the abuses and excesses of American society are going to be reflected in American sport. But out of frustration and anger with the 159 cultural manifestation of sport in American society, the counterculture strikes out at sport itself. The counterculture has performed an invaluable service by highlighting the abuses of the American system, but its alternative has been rejected by the overwhelming majority of American people; it has been rejected quite correctly, I think, for it does not offer a sound, rational, humane and viable alternative. In short, it's the other side of the coin, but still the same old coin.

Sport cannot exist separately from the reality of American society. Sport, like all other institutional activities, reflects and in turn helps reinforce dominant American values. If the dominant values of a society are alienating and destructive, then any major institutional activity in that society will reflect these values. Not understanding this relationship, the counterculture looked at the institutional manifestation of sport in American society, saw its dehumanizing nature, and concluded that something was wrong with sport itself. The mistake was in not distinguishing between sport and the institutional manifestation of sport.

The radical ethic of sport says there is nothing fundamentally wrong with competitive sport. It says that the agonistic struggle in sport of team with team, man with man, man with himself, or man with nature is a healthy, intrinsically valuable human activity. It does not view sport as either solely a competitive or solely a cooperative venture. As many fine physical educators have tried to point out in the past, there is a vital interplay between competition and cooperation in healthy sport activity. *Competitive sport is in trouble when this balance is lost either in the direction of competition or in the direction of cooperation.*

Rather than replace the Lombardian emphasis on the product with the counterculture's emphasis on the process, the radical ethic refuses to view human experience in such a fragmented manner. The radical ethic recognizes the excellence of the outcome as important, but sees how that excellence is achieved as equally important. It does not go along with Lombardi, whose philosophy that "winning isn't everything, it's the only thing" could easily be translated into "the ends justify the means." It is not victory at any price. The radical ethic does not support authoritarian coaching techniques or the plying of athletes with anabolic steriods and amphetamines in the quest for victory—practices which are the rule of the day in high level competitive sport under the American ethic.

On the other hand, the radical ethic believes there is nothing wrong or dehumanizing about a person who wants to take pride in his work, whether it is in athletics or any other human endeavor. The radical ethic has no quarrel with the Lombardian quest for excellence. It only says that the means by

160

Sport and the radical ethic
Jack Scott

which that excellence is achieved is as important as the excellence itself. In fact, since it has a deep underlying faith in man, the radical ethic believes the sport experience will be even richer than it is under the Lombardian ethic when a humanistic approach that encourages man to develop his full potential replaces the present dehumanizing system.

The radical ethic also assumes women will have equal access to competitive sports. There are no sound psychological or physiological reasons why this experience should be denied to women. Though not opposed to coeducational sports on a recreational basis, the radical ethic does not see allowing women to compete against men as an adequate solution to the problem of providing women with equal opportunity. Because of size and strength limitations, only an extraordinary woman athlete will be able to compete against an average male athlete in most sports. Consequently, rather than sound the drum for coeducational activities, the radical ethic says that women who want to engage in competitive sports should be provided with the same economic and institutional support that men receive.

The radical ethic views the athlete as an artist who is struggling to express himself, but like the followers of the Lombardian ethic, radical proponents understand the need for dedication and hard work. No matter how esthetic a setting may be, a counterculture long distance runner will not have a peak experience during a long distance run if his physiological conditioning is such that he has a gut ache and cramps after the first mile. As anyone who has attempted to do any distance running knows, a lot of hard work is needed before one reaches a level of fitness that enables him to enjoy the process.

The radical ethic sees nothing wrong with team sports as long as the team spirit stems from a genuine development of community rather than from authoritarian intimidation. Sharing and cooperating with others in a healthy team setting makes a person more human rather than less. Under the radical ethic, team spirit would flow from a genuine concern for one's teammates rather than from a superficial and imposed conformity of blue blazers and crew-cuts.

But perhaps the most fundamental aspect of the radical ethic of sport is reflected in how one sees his opponent. The opponent is not simply an obstacle in the way of victory. Neither is he simply an instrument to be used for one's own glory. In a very real sense, the opponent is a brother who is presenting the athlete with a challenge. He cannot experience the 161 agonistic struggle of sport without the cooperation of his brother—his opponent. The radical athlete has an intense desire to achieve excellence and victory, but he just as intensely wants to seek out and experience the struggle. The champion radical athlete rather than attempting to maximize his chances for maintaining the victor's throne, will share his knowledge and skill with lesser athletes in the hope that they will rise to his level. Since victory is not the only concern of the radical athlete, he takes little pride or satisfaction in a victory easily won over a less skilled or weaker opponent. His pride in victory comes when he struggles courageously in the face of a real challenge.

Since the degree of alienation between participants would be minimized under a system of radical athletics, the sporting contest could be guided by a general ethic of sportsmanship, with specific rules and regulations kept to a minimum. Today, when athletes enter the arena viewing each other as enemies, an ever-increasing number of rules are required to regulate their behavior, for they will take advantage of each other in any way possible in their single-minded quest for victory.

Rather than denigrate the many accomplishments of those who have been guided by the Lombardian ethic or the counterculture ethic, the radical ethic attempts to build a system based on the achievements of these two systems, while avoiding their abuses and excesses. The radical ethic understands its indebtedness to men like Knute Rockne and Vince Lombardi for their accomplishments, but it does not see them as representing the apotheosis of the sport experience. *The radical ethic in sport has a commitment to excellence integrated with a desire to achieve that excellence by a process that will humanize rather than dehumanize man.*

For those who think that the ideas I have offered are not radical or revolutionary, I must admit that in some ways I would tend to agree. However, anyone who would attempt to implement the radical ethic on any significant scale in the American athletic world today will quickly discover just how radical and revolutionary these ideas are! *The fact, though, that a rational, humane ethic must be classified as radical or revolutionary should tell us something about the nature of contemporary American society.*

Men and women in sport: the "manhood" myth

Jack Scott
Oberlin College

As any American male who has participated in athletics can attest, athletic competition is our culture's masculinity rite. It is on
the playing fields of America where boys are
made into men. It was brought home to me
how this phenomenon even pervades the
counterculture when, on a visit to the Fill-
more East, I saw the long-haired, macho-
tripping male ushers decked out in football
jerseys! Apparently considering themselves
too hip for regular cop uniforms, they opted
for the next best thing.

Unlike in most primitive masculinity rites,
where after certain specific acts a boy is
declared a man for ever after, athletic competition requires males to prove their masculinity continually. Not surprisingly, most
coaches quickly learn that their chief motivational tool is the dispensation of manhood.

163

And if the coach is going to grant others their masculinity, he of course must personify all that a man is supposed to be. (In six years of commenting on the American athletic scene, nothing I have ever said or written has so infuriated the coaches' fraternity as a remark I once made that coaches' phobic reaction to long-haired male athletes might be indicative of latent homosexuality.)

The most complimentary remark a coach can make about a male athlete is to call him a "real stud" or "animal," and the most derogatory thing he can say is to intimate that the athlete may be effeminate. As Dave Meggyesy so aptly pointed out in *Out of Their League,* even an All-Pro professional football player can usually be totally intimidated by a coach who uses his doomsday weapon and calls the player a "pussy."

In American athletics, the successful coach is usually one who can keep his athletes insecure enough so that they are continually trying to prove their manhood. No coach was a better master at this form of manipulation than the late Vince Lombardi. Lombardi, who himself fit the ideal male stereotype, had the players on the Green Bay Packers convinced that to lose a football game was to lose their manhood. Willie Davis, a perennial All-Pro defensive end during his playing days and captain of Lombardi's world championship Green Bay teams, is an example of just how effective Lombardi was at this tactic. The average football fan who witnessed the hulking Davis terrorize NFL quarterbacks on many an autumn Sunday afternoon may find it difficult to believe that Davis' feelings about his own masculinity were in constant jeopardy, but during his playing days, Davis' sense of masculinity was only as secure as his most recent victory. In an interview with his former teammate Jerry Kramer, for Kramer's book, *Lombardi: Winning Is the Only Thing,* Davis talked about the motivation that led him and his teammates to one NFL championship: "We went out and we whipped them good and preserved our manhood." It is ironic but not surprising that it is football players—those athletes engaged in the most macho of all popular American sports—that seem to be the most sensitive about their masculinity.

The efforts of American males to assert or prove their masculinity through athletic participation can often take on sad as well as absurd dimensions. One such occasion occurred recently when a paunchy, middle-aged Norman Mailer decided to box Jose Torres, the former world light-heavyweight champion of the world, on the Dick Cavett show. As a former boxer myself, I'm not so uptight as to believe Mailer's desire to box automatically qualifies him as being into a macho trip. It was just his time and location choice as well as his selection of sparring partner that made the whole event seem quite pathetic. (On the other hand, the argument could be made that Mailer

Men and women in sport:
the "manhood" myth
Jack Scott

is so secure in his masculinity that he simply doesn't give a damn what others say or think about him. Mailer's track record, however, would seem to indicate this is not the case.)

Apart from the obvious dangers of making manhood or maturity synonymous with violent, physically aggressive behavior, using athletics as a masculinity rite also works to attenuate, if not totally negate, the intrinsic value of athletic participation. As Timothy Leary so brilliantly pointed out during a philosophical discussion of handball in *Jail Notes*, "It's the play off not the pay off" that's the real value of athletics. When males are participating in sports as a masculinity rite, they are usually so tense and anxious that they are unable to experience or enjoy the intrinsic value of athletics. The actual athletic participation eventually comes to be seen primarily, if not solely, for its utilitarian value rather than its inherent value. One need only look at the physical condition of the typical high school, college, or professional football player within a year or two after he is through competing to see how little he enjoys physical activity for its own sake. And even those relatively few former ballplayers who do keep physically active are usually doing so for some utilitarian purpose such as jogging to avoid a heart attack, rather than running for the simple joy of an exhilerating but exhausting run.

Given the reality of athletic participation as a masculinity proving ground, it is not surprising that women who participate in competitive sports are faced with a degree of discrimination and oppression that probably surpasses that which women encounter in any other area of American society. As Marie Hart, a woman physical educator, recently told me, "Our society cuts the penis off the male who decides to be a dancer and puts it on the female who participates in competitive athletics." The woman athlete, no matter how high her level of athletic skill may be, is never fully accepted in this milieu with all its male mythology. Nothing could be more devastating for a male athlete than to be defeated by a woman; at the same time, the aggression and strength required for athletic success often result in women athletes being ostracized by other women. Because she is perceived as a threat by both men and women, the woman athlete is often a lonely, marginal person, never fully accepted by either group.

Mildred "Babe" Didrikson Zaharias, described by Paul Gallico, one of America's most distinguished sports writers, as "probably the most talented athlete, male or female, ever developed in our country," encountered the difficulties suggested by Dr. Hart on an almost daily basis throughout her athletic career that lasted from the early 1930s to shortly before her death from cancer in 1955. Mrs. Zaharias won national and international titles in nearly every sport open to women during her 25-year career as a competitive athlete. Before turning to golf during the later years of her career, when she won every amateur and professional title available to a woman, she was a star in track and field at the 1932 Olympic Games and was a perennial All-American in basketball. Though she stood only 5 feet, 6½ inches and weighed no more than 125 pounds, she was constantly portrayed by the male sportswriters of the time as having a boyish appearance. She wore her hair short for convenience, but she was an extremely attractive woman. Despite this, she was always referred to as a tomboy, and according to Gallico, one of the favorite jokes of the male sportswriters was that athletic promoters never knew whether to assign her to the men's or women's locker room when she showed up for a competition.

It is of course true that there are some women athletes whose size and appearance qualify them as being "unfeminine" according to traditional Western standards, but, as was the case with Mrs. Zaharias, most women athletes are treated the same regardless of their actual physical appearance or behavior. Exceptions occur in sports characterized by graceful, rhythmical movement, such as ice skating, diving, gymnastics, and skiing, the handful of sports in which a woman can participate without being called "masculine."

Not surprisingly, most women who participate in competitive athletics are extremely conscious about looking feminine. Vicki Foltz, as a 27-year-old married woman probably one of America's finest women long distance runners, was asked in an interview whether she had any "feminine hang-ups about running." She responded, "Yes, I have lots of hang-ups. You wouldn't believe it. I always worry about looking nice in a race. I worry about my calf muscles getting big. But mostly I worry about my hair. The morning before my last big race it was hailing and blowing, but there I was in the hotel with rollers in my hair. I knew the rain would ruin my hair-do, but I fixed it anyway. I suppose it's because so many people have said women athletes look masculine. So a lot of us try, subconsciously maybe, to look as feminine as possible in a race. There's always lots of hair ribbons in the races!"

If an attractive, mature, married woman with children like Vicki Foltz feels this pressure, one can only imagine what it must be like for younger women athletes such as the female swimmers who often participate in the Olympics while still in their early teens. Marion Lay, for instance, participated in the Tokyo Olympic Games when she was only 14 years old. By 1967 she had developed into one of the finest female swimmers in the

Men and women in sport:
the "manhood" myth
Jack Scott

world, winning four silver medals at the Pan American Games that year. She won a medal at the 1968 Olympic Games and also at the age of 18 served as captain of the Canadian Olympic women's swimming team. But in many ways her career was frustrated. The only coaches available to her were men, since in swimming, as in nearly all other sports, it is next to impossible for a woman to advance in the coaching profession. Marion found that nearly all the male coaches and officials she met refused to accept the fact that she was as dedicated to swimming as any of the male athletes. The attitude of male coaches and officials seems to be that women are somehow incapable of being as dedicated to sports as men, whereas in reality the opposite is often true. Treated as a marginal person, as I pointed out earlier, the female athlete often dedicates herself to sport with a fervor unmatched by male athletes since athletic success is one of the few satisfactions available to her. Unlike the case for male athletes, athletic prowess does not assure a woman of social status. The Catch 22 of women's sports is that those women athletes who do totally dedicate themselves to sport are invariably labeled as being masculine by the male-controlled sports establishment.

In fact, all the desirable qualities athletes must possess if they want to achieve a high level of success have been made synonymous with our cardboard concept of masculinity. This point was brought home to me when in a recent *Sports Illustrated* article the male diving coach of Micki King, America's and perhaps the world's finest woman diver, attempted to compliment Miss King by saying he knew early in her career that she was going to be great because, "She dives like a man." My immediate reaction on reading that statement was that she certainly doesn't dive like me or any other man I ever met. In fact, she doesn't dive like 99 percent of the men in America. What she obviously does do is dive *correctly*.

Another myth that the male-dominated athletic world works to perpetuate about women, especially the female teenage swimming sensations who began their careers at the age of 12 or so, is that they invariably retire when they get to be about 17, because they become interested in boys and no longer have time for competitive athletics. Conveniently ignored is the fact that most male athletes are not known for their sexual abstinence. If male athletes have time for girl friends, there is no reason why female athletes could not also continue to participate in sports while dating. The shortness of their careers is due to other circumstances: the tremendous 167 social pressures I have mentioned, and also the fact that only a handful of colleges in the entire United States give even partial athletic scholarships to women. Compared to men, the opportunities for women to be supported while competing in athletics after high school are almost non-existent. Additionally, most women college physical educators attempt to steer women students away from highly competitive athletics.

If a woman does survive all this, she faces a double standard even after achieving sufficient skill to participate in national or international competition. This past track season the AAU barred one of our most prominent female track stars from international competition because of "unladylike" behavior on a foreign tour the previous summer. Her "unladylike" behavior involved a member of the U.S. men's international team that was touring along with the women's team, but he was not even reprimanded.

Because of the limited opportunities for women to participate in sport at any level, a New York State court recently ruled that girls can participate against boys in high school in non-contact sports. Some women and many men hailed this ruling as a major breakthrough in the attempt to end the discrimination against women in sport. However, since only a very few girls will be able to make the "boys' team," this ruling could exacerbate rather than attenuate the discrimination against women if people see this as the end of the struggle. Women do not so much want to compete against men—although there is of course no reason they should not have that opportunity if they want it—as they want to have the same opportunity to participate in sports that men have. This means providing women with the same facilities and trained coaches that men enjoy.

The frustration of the woman athlete is further compounded by her inability, because of basic differences in speed and strength, to ever achieve success according to male standards. Hopefully, our society will come to the point where women will not only be given equal opportunity to participate in sport, but will not be made to feel that they are somehow inferior athletes because they run 100 yards in 10.5 rather than 9.5. Simone de Beauvior best expresses this view in *The Second Sex*, where she writes, "In sports the end in view is not success independent of physical equipment; it is rather the attainment of perfection within the limitations of each physical type: the featherweight boxing champion is as much of a champion as is the heavyweight; the women skiing champion is not the inferior of the faster male champion; they belong to two different classes."

168

Existentialism, education and sport

Neil T. Laughlin
University of San Francisco

*What true education requires of us is faith and courage—
faith that children want to make sense out of life and
will work hard at it, courage to let them do it without
continually poking, prying, prodding, and meddling.*

John Holt

In some ways writing a paper about Existentialism is not very Existential. For one thing, it is inconsistent with those aspects of Existential philosophy which question the ability of man to acquire knowledge which authentically represents the reality of experience. If men cannot really know the reality of something, if they cannot really know what is in another's mind, then why attempt to publish one's ideas? Even at its best, trying to transmit thoughts to others is a bit absurd.

Whatever absurdity exists in attempting to discuss Existentialism as a philosophy is compounded when one attempts to define what existentialists might say about education. However, this author still believes that writing about existentialism and education can be worthwhile because what we do as educators is determined to some degree by what we believe, and what we believe is an essential concern of philosophy. Speculating about the impact of philosophy on education can help to make education more logical, meaningful and moral. More specifically, speculating about existentialism, physical education, and sport may provoke questioning of those beliefs which guide physical educators and coaches in their decisions, suggest new ways of looking at previous practices, and inspire innovation in areas where it is needed.*

In the *Myth of Sisyphus*, Albert Camus, one of the best known existential writers and philosophers, compared man to Sisyphus, the character in Greek mythology who was punished by the gods for his impudence toward them and his passion for life. Sisyphus was doomed to roll the same rock up the same hill for all eternity—only to have the stone roll back to the bottom each time he reached the top. Camus argued that this supposedly hopeless, apparently absurd task was similar to the situation that man faces by the mere fact of his existence: he is born into a silent, irrational world, a world which yields no definitive answers, a world which, by itself, is absurd, a world which is meaningless without man. It is only the individual who gives value to life. Thus life need not be absurd if man revolts and refuses to accept this absurdity, if he chooses to give life meaning. Similarly, Sisyphus is not doomed to an absurd fate. If he is happy in what he does, his punishment is not punishment. *He* can make his task meaningful. He knows it is *his* rock, he knows *he* will begin again, he knows he can *choose* to begin again.

If, as Camus argues, the world is silent and irrational, if it yields no answers to man in his quest to know, then knowledge is a personal thing. A song, a poem, a victory, a defeat mean what you think they do. Neither faith, nor reason can yield definitive answers for man. Thus a person *is* as old as he feels. Thus vanilla ice cream tastes different to every man. Thus every basehit is unique to every individual.

If each individual alone knows what something means for him, then what of IQ tests, aptitude tests, any kind of test? For the existentialist they are often absurd. In fact, the teacher who gives a test may be demonstrating a lack of faith in his own ability to teach and in his students' ability to learn. John Holt indicated how testing can imply a lack of faith in the learning process when he wrote: "There are two main reasons that we test students: the first is to threaten them into doing what we want done, and the second is to give us a basis for handing out the rewards and penalties on which the

---

*An outstanding treatment of this area is in Howard Slusher's *Man, Sport and Existence: A Critical Analysis* (Philadelphia: Lea and Febiger, 1967).

Existentialism, education and sport
Neil T. Laughlin

educational system—like all coercive systems—must operate." (1969, 55).

Psychologist Carl Rogers probed another aspect of the absurdity which many existentialists would attribute to testing when he stated, "You cannot teach anyone anything (1952). If you cannot teach anyone anything, how much more absurd is it to test students on what you think you have taught? After Rogers uttered his provocative statement he elaborated on its meaning. He argued that those ideas of real importance to the individual, those concepts which are of consequence to each man, he himself must decide to learn. Thus teachers are, first and foremost, provocateurs. Students will really learn only what they want to. A teacher is like someone who lays down the concrete for a runway. That is about all we do. *Students* must decide whether they will pilot a plane and in what directions they will fly. The kind of knowledge a teacher can impart to a student can be compared to a highway. It is limited. It goes in few directions. The kind of knowledge a student decides to acquire for himself can be compared to a skyway. A new dimension has been added. It is capable of much greater expansion; there are many more aspects, many more directions it can take.

For the existentialist, the teacher or coach should strive to be more a resource aid than an authority figure. His ultimate goal should be to render himself obsolete, to make his students or players free of him, able to make their own decisions, self-reliant, responsible to themselves. Only by giving students the opportunity to make decisions about their education—in choice of subjects, in criteria which determine success, in standards of behavior, in every aspect of their schooling—will they be best educated to be able to make their own lives meaningful. If, as many existentialists argue, choice is one of the most fundamental facts of man's existence, then children must be given the opportunity to develop their ability to choose. They cannot be expected to choose wisely as adults if we make their choices for them.

Many existentialists would tend to agree with those who argue that formal schooling often hinders rather than enhances learning. Unfortunately, much too often sham smothers substance, "form triumphs over spirit," (Gardner, 1964, 17), and schools seem to serve everyone except their clients. It is the child, of course, who suffers most, who loses his potentiality, his capacity for maturity, his spontaneity, his naturalness, his *humanity*.

A sad illustration of how schooling sometimes interferes with the development of physical potential is the fact that many adults and adolescents 171 have to be *taught* to use their body efficiently in the bench press when almost all of them once possessed this ability when they were little children. In this exercise the individual lies supine on a bench with both arms extended and attempts to lower and lift up again a barbell that has been placed in his hands. Most six-year-old boys naturally arch their backs when they experience difficulty executing this movement. But by the time they reach adolescence, many will not know what to do when they can't quite lift the weight. They will have lost a good deal of the spontaneity and efficiency of movement that they possessed as children—They have to be taught to arch.*

And wouldn't you know?

Even though arching allows one to lift the greatest amount of weight in the bench press, it is not permitted in competitive bench pressing. The rules of the event seem to restrict success, to hold back potentiality, to limit movement, to curtail human endeavor.**

Existentialists would probably look with distaste at every example where the bureaucracy of schools encroaches upon a student's individuality. Indeed, it is the individual who should be the focal point of education. For the existentialist the curriculum should be child-centered, instruction should be individualized, and the subject matter should be that of choice. In other words, the individual in his function as a choice-maker should be a primary concern of the entire educative process. Wherever the individual judgments of students receive the greatest attention in the total school experience is where existentialists would probably manifest great interest.

What of measurements, records, scores, and all the other symbols of victory and defeat? What do they tell us? Little or nothing, says the existentialist. Only the individual participant has any real idea about what he derived from the experience of movement. Only *he* knows the quality of his experience, how much effort went into it, what he felt, what he learned. Existentialists might be disposed to argue that measurement engenders exploitation. Measurement compares people, sets limits, creates boundaries. With its means, standards, norms, it focuses upon predictability, emphasizes homogeneity, destroys individuality. For existentialists each man is an individual and those things which impede the development of his individ-

---

*At least if efficiency is defined in terms of one's ability to lift what for him would be a maximum load or to be successful in completing a lift when extreme difficulty is encountered.

**While safety may be enhanced by prohibiting arching, there are many examples of much more dangerous practices which are permitted in various forms of competitive lifting (*e.g.*, the dead lift in power lifting).

uality, his uniqueness, are bad for him. Thus, the existentialist would look for the exception to the rule, the instance where the experts were wrong, the underdog who achieved victory. The Jets and the Mets of 1969 might make existentialists happy because they show that any team can win, that we really can't predict who will be the world's champion or, more importantly, how "good" a team is.

Many existentialists would probably react with extreme distaste toward the determinism that has evolved from an overemphasis on measurement in professional sport. For example, they would not like the fact that even to try out for professional football, a prospect has to be a certain height, a certain weight, and able to run at a certain speed.* Even less would they favor the achievement motivation tests that many teams are now giving to athletes to try to predict their performance. How can we measure the motivation of an individual in any area? How can we know what is on his mind or in his heart, when we can't even authentically define the capabilities of his body? Some women *can* lift cars if their children are trapped under them! John Holt cogently commented on the difficulty of trying to measure the minds of others when he said; "To learn even a part of the contents of our minds is a most slow, subtle, difficult, often painful task. How then can we be so sure of our ability to discover the contents of the minds of others?" (1969, 62).

I am reminded of a story which illustrates the absurdity of attempting to evaluate or predict physical performance. Like many young men who participate in sport, I was eager to learn about athletes who were stars in the sport I played. The sport was football, and I remember asking about Tommie McCormick, who played professionally from 1953 to 1958. When I met a teammate of his on the Los Angeles Rams, I asked: "What was McCormick like? Was he fast?" The answer was, "No, actually he might have been the slowest back in pro ball." "Was he big?" "No, he only weighed about 172 pounds." "Was he shifty?" "No, not really." "Oh . . . Was he the kind of guy who breaks the tackles, who could slide for a yard or two more?" "No." "Well, what the hell was he? How did he make the pro's?"

"He was the meanest son-of-a-bitch who ever put on pads. He was a 'psycho' when he played."

---

*It is interesting to note that the prospective player's speed is measured by a stopwatch. Is running against a clock the same as running when you are trying to catch or elude other players in a game?

I think that many existentialists would see the above story as illustrative of the belief that man can't truly measure the quality of any human experience. The experience of movement is no exception. What do clockings in the forty-yard dash, measurements of height and weight, scores on motivation tests tell us about each athlete's experience in sport? What can we really say about Tommie McCormick's career as a football player? Little when compared with what *he* can say about it. It was *his* experience and only he can define to any degree what it meant for him.

What of getting to know one's students or players? Obviously, for the existentialist, it is a *sine qua non*. Learning the names of each student, coaching each player differently is essential. If the class is large, the teacher can take pictures of each student to help him learn their names. If the coach cannot show interest in every player, he should not coach. In short, both teacher and coach must *care* about each and every student. This seems obvious, but anyone who has seen the almost frenzied, avalanche-like exodus of cars from the faculty parking lot of a high school when the last bell has rung may sometimes wonder if some teachers really care. Similarly, those who have seen players struck, or cajoled into playing with injuries that can result in lifetime debilitation, or ignored if they weren't starting, or forgotten about after they graduated, might wonder whether some coaches really care.

Taking roll is another practice that an existentialist might find disturbing. All too often students in physical education classes fall in on numbers, line up at attention, move in some formation, or wear the same uniform. Wouldn't many of these practices be much more appropriate for military training? What they do to the individuality of each student should be evident. The world of sport is also replete with examples of military-type practices that do little for the development of the individual. Unfortunately, for some coaches, players are little more than a number or an investment. I am hard pressed to cite examples of coaches whose approach is existential. It would almost seem as if inherent in the nature of highly competitive sport is a spirit that sometimes stifles individualism. Thus the more popular, the more professional, the more competitive the sport, the less the chance for the individual development of the participant. To my knowledge, the best example of existentialism in coaching a popular sport like football is that of George Davis. After several winning seasons at Willits High School in Northern California, Davis began to question the value of what he was doing. What was he teaching his players of victory and defeat? What was he teaching them of life? As long as he made all the decisions for them, they were not really able to evaluate their own experience. So Davis drastically changed his style of coaching. Players were allowed to decide if they wanted to practice or not. They were allowed to pick their own starting lineup. They didn't "win" as many games, but Davis feels that for the first time in their athletic experience they were able to see the consequences of *their* decisions. Perhaps they learned something different about what the value of practice is, what it really means. Perhaps they learned something new about what it is to select a team. Perhaps they gained new insight into the meaning of "victory" and "defeat."

I think that some teachers and coaches can learn a lot from George Davis' experience. Maybe football coaches don't want to go as far as he did, but what about those who call every play, engineer every defense? Don't we have enough faith in our players to let them make some of their own decisions? If, as many coaches claim, sport is a place where "kids build character," then why not let players begin to become involved in making their own choices? Ultimately, each person must learn how to choose. Even if one rejects much of existentialism, I think he must agree that choice is an important part of man's life. If coaches make all the decisions, they are curtailing character development, not enhancing it. We learn to choose by choosing. In a sense, character is composed of the choices one makes.

What of ability grouping? It is not difficult to ascertain the existentialist's view of this practice. How can we group by ability when we can't really define or determine ability, when only each individual can give any real clue to the quality of his experiences? Perhaps the only kind of grouping which is justified is that which occurs by choice. The existentialist might argue that physical education is fortunate because the athletic program provides an opportunity for students to group themselves by choice. They can decide which sport they want to go out for or not to go out at all. Many subject matter areas do not provide such choices. Since the athletic program allows students to group themselves and since ability is probably an important factor in how this grouping occurs, then there seems to be almost no justification for ability grouping in the regular physical education programs except for individualized programs of instruction. As the existentialist might argue, why do something that has a *prima facie* potential for harm when it is already provided for in the only area where it makes sense?

Discipline is another area in which the Existentialist tends to dissent from the more traditional philosophies. Van Cleve Morris suggests two questions which are useful in differentiating educational philosophies with 175 respect to discipline (1961, 424). The first question is; How should the student be controlled? Morris argues that existentialists would probably rephrase the question and ask: How should the child be taught to control himself? The Existential educator or coach would probably contend that students or players learn to control themselves by being given opportunities to make their own rules, by being allowed to make decisions concerning how to control themselves. Self-discipline should be an important goal of the existential educator or coach, and it comes from practice in disciplining oneself. The second question is: Is there a bad student? Morris contends that the existentialists would disagree with the Progressivist educators, who would say "no." (428-30). If existence precedes essence, if choice is a fundamental fact of existence and man shapes his life by the kinds of choices he makes, then he is responsible for his choices. Neither environment nor heredity, nor a combination of the two can be blamed for our failure. Like Sisyphus we can transcend any destiny decreed by fate. Our life is our own. We are free to choose its course.

On this issue the existentialist looks with some skepticism on the research in sociology and psychology which views behavior as the result of heredity and environment. If, as progressivist educators tend to claim, misbehavior is merely a symptom of underlying causes, if heredity or environment determine man's destiny, if the student is not really to blame for his actions, then, argues the existentialist, responsibility, morality, virtue, vice do not really exist. If man is not ultimately answerable for his acts, freedom is dead, morality becomes moot, man is not really man.

Finally, what subjects in the curriculum would the existentialist tend to favor? What sports would he like most? What practices in physical education would he praise or condemn? Existentialists would probably show a greater interest in the fine arts than in the sciences, because the arts tend to be more open-ended. They provide more opportunity for creative expression, choice, aesthetic development. An artist can choose anything for a subject. A play can be presented or interpreted in a thousand different ways. The law of gravity, the Pythagorian Theorem probably do not possess the same freedom of interpretation.

In physical education Existentialists would probably like those sports which have more aesthetic aspects, such as gymnastics, dance, and movement exploration. These activities would be liked not only for their fine arts emphasis, but also because they probably provide more opportunity for creative expression and individual choice than many other sports. In floor exercise, after the compulsory requirements of the event are met, a gymnast can design his own routine; in modern dance one can develop his own interpretation. As the phrase indicates, "movement exploration" allows one to explore different kinds of movement. Granted opportunity for creativity, for variety of choice exists in all sports, there seem to be fewer ways to catch a pass, or throw a baseball than there are ways to move in gymnastics, dance, or movement exploration.

Existentialists would also probably favor individual rather than team sports. Since existentialists emphasize the uniqueness of each individual, and the importance of his role in defining the quality of his experiences, they would probably argue that there is a greater opportunity for individual development in individual sports. Here he has less responsibility to a team, and its ideals; he is more free to set his own standards, create his own criteria for success or failure. Thus jogging might be preferable to track because the individual is freer to run at different speeds, to set different goals, to choose his own course. He can enjoy the beauty of a beach or a park or a sunrise or a sunset and take his time about it. He need not try to run as fast as possible unless he chooses to. No team will be harmed if he only runs as fast as he wants to.

Related to the issue of responsibility to a team versus responsibility to oneself is the issue of the rewards that are emphasized in a sport. Existentialists would probably favor sports where the motivation is more intrinsic than extrinsic. Surfing, sky diving, ballet are examples of activities where the individual is competing more with himself or against some independent standard rather than against others.

Similarly, existentialists would probably favor sports which de-emphasize officiating, scoring, competition and coaching. If men must learn to make their own decisions, if man is an axiological animal (and existentialists emphasize that he is), he must be given the opportunity to make moral choices. For the existentialist, providing officials can remove responsibility from the participants, encourage cheating, and thus curtail character development. George Leonard expresses an existential position on this issue in the following passage:

> Baseball characterizes much that has passed away. Its rigid rules, its fixed angles and distances shape players to repetitive, stereotyped behaviors. Its complete reliance on officials to enforce rules and decide close plays removes the players from all moral and personal decisions, and encourages them, in fact, to get away with whatever they can. Its preoccupation with statistics reveals its view of human worth: players are valued for

177

how many percentage points, hits, home runs, runs batted in and the like they can accumulate. Everything is acquisitive, comparative, competitive, limiting.

As for present 21st century games, many are improvised by the children themselves, then revised day by day. Refinement generally runs toward simplicity, elegance and an absolute minimum of rules. With no officials to intervene, the players themselves are repeatedly up against moral decisions (1968, 168-69).

Physical education and sport have been subjected to a good deal of criticism in recent years because of their emphasis on competition and the dehumanizing practices advocated by some teachers or coaches. Existentialists would probably agree with much of this criticism. Many examples could be cited to illustrate some of the horrendous practices of teachers and coaches which sometimes result when competition is unduly emphasized. One of the worst this author witnessed was perpetrated by an elementary school teacher and coach who told a player of his on third base to get ready to run home because the opposing pitcher was about to throw the ball toward the coach without calling time out. Then armed with the rhetoric that an authority figure in sport often possesses, he asked the opposing pitcher to throw the ball to him for examination. Manifesting faith in the opposing coach, trusting him as a human being, the pitcher threw the ball to the coach, who stepped aside and yelled the runner home. The winning run scored on this "play." The author does not wish to belabor the kinds of problems which arise when "winning at all costs" is an accepted philosophy. There are many examples of coaches who do not follow such a philosophy; indeed, few probably do. However, the existentialist would be concerned with the less blatant, but nevertheless harmful, examples of coaches who—knowingly and unknowingly—teach players to bend or beat the rules in order to achieve victory.

Concomitant with an overemphasis on officiating, scoring, and competition is a growing tendency toward "overcoaching"—whether defined in terms of degree or number. Existentialists would obviously look with disfavor not only on the degree to which coaches make decisions for players, but also on the growing bureaucracy which seems an almost necessary accoutrement to increasing the number of coaches. The game is supposed to be for the players, not the coaches, though sometimes it's difficult to realize this.

Existentialists would probably prefer rugby to football, at least in regard to the way the two games are played in America. There are fewer coaches, and the players have a greater voice in deciding who plays, in scheduling opponents, and in establishing training rules. Diversity in hair length and other types of personal behavior is probably a good deal greater in rugby than football. Moreover, the participants play because they want to, not because they are on a scholarship or are getting paid to. They are perhaps freer in choosing why they play. The temptation of extrinsic rewards is not as powerful a constraint on the participant's choice as it is in football.

To some degree existentialists' probable preference for rugby rather than football can also be used to illustrate another aspect of sports of which existentialists would approve. Existentialists would tend to like sports which provide for lifetime participation. Granted there are many sports which are better examples of lifetime activities than rugby. But when compared with football, rugby allows more people to play for a longer period of their lives. Almost any individual can join a rugby team and keep playing until he chooses to quit. In football, the opportunities to play on a team gradually diminish as one moves from grade school, to high school, to college, to professional. Indeed, few play on a team after high school and even fewer after college.

Participation is a key word for the existentialists. They would probably argue that the individual has a more authentic experience when he plays than when he watches. The player can feel the joy and the agony, the pleasure and the pain more deeply than the spectator. Thus existentialists would applaud those who criticize the kind of "spectatoritis" which is often characteristic of professional sport.

In short, an existential athlete is more concerned with being involved in a movement rather than outcome. His opponents are his teammates, and they enjoy the game together. Perhpas Kurt Vonnegut portrayed an existential attitude toward sport as well as any man when he wrote:

> A friend of mine was a superjock at Yale, but in his senior year he quit the varsity ice-hockey team. He organized a hockey team where you had to have a beard to play.* He challenged Rhode Island School of Design to a game, and the two teams skated to the middle of the hockey rink carrying their jerseys. They made a big pile of them, then chose up sides. That was beautiful. These were friendly, cheerful people and they were doing amusing things. Their goal was to delight themselves, not to defeat each other.

---

*This sentence is existential in the sense that it portrays the importance of revolt in making life meaningful. It is not existential in that it sets forth rules of exclusion.

REFERENCES

Camus, Albert. As quoted in *Existentialism from Dostoevsky to Sartre*. New York: Meridian Books, 1956.

Holt, John. *The Underachieving School*. New York: Pitman, 1969.

Rogers, Carl. From remarks presented at the Harvard Conference on Classroom Approaches to Influencing Human Behavior, April 4, 1952.

Gardner, John. *Self Renewal: The Innovator and the Innovative Society*. New York: Harper and Row, 1964.

Morris, Van Cleve. *Philosophy and the American School*. Boston: Houghton Mifflin, 1961.

Leonard, George. *Education and Ecstasy*. New York: Dell, 1968.

Slusher, Howard. *Man, Sport and Existence: A Critical Analysis*. Philadelphia: Lea and Febiger, 1967.

Physical education and sports: business as usual vs. by any means necessary

Mal Andrews
California State University, Hayward

INTRODUCTION

In the past, the few black physical educators could not tell their true Black story for worrying how white to say it. Most American people have never learned what is *Black* for being so busy being white. Most of America's whiteness is the indoctrination of a false sense of being superior to non-whites. The white man is a super-ego of himself and so I must, unfortunately, militantly keep him from ripping off my id.

I am an African, born in America, moving in Black culture, and feeling my body, soul and mind dig the rhythms and flow of beautiful Black physical development. Then I carry this orgiastic knowledge out into all sports as art for any man or woman. Finally, I think that the only possible way a white man could change or revolutionize his racist attitude would be to step into his senses and

181

listen to what the Black man in sports is saying. Maybe then he could begin to understand his Black brother's sensitive world and learn without being afraid to see himself. Power to verbal Blackness!

Physical Education in America and its co-author Sports glorify the past, pat custom and tradition on the ass and attempt to systematically embrace a castoff of thought processes related to kinetics that has been stabilized once and for ALL?

Black people who want to create an authentic Black culture in movement in America—and a few whites trying to stay alive in sports—are realizing the realities of the nation first, which got us in a trick, then keeping on with Truth and Soul. Out of Truth and Soul the learnings of a new future in Mind and Body will emerge.

The study of Truth and Soul does not exclude or alienate any race. Truth is preached and Soul is exalted BY ANY MEANS NECESSARY.

From an African tongue and organic aesthetic kinetics, chained psychologically by racism, to Black language and physical style and grace, the Black man and woman survived a distinct personality related to movement which is unlimited in Black cultural identity.

Black physical education is language and movement going on at the same time. Sound is triggered by the "Soul" in action from a collage of cultural and individual expressions made from a creative energy that extends life into various kinetic styling possibilities.

We *live* in our movements and *style* in our actions in a performing sense. Movement does not control us. We cause what happens to it, and, the way we express it makes it Black.

In all sports activities, individual or team, we come styling and leaning to see how bad our opponents gonna be. But no matter what the results, our "Movement" carries with it an underlying sense of Black, a sense which grows out of a bunch of experiences that have expanded the being of what Black is.

The action becomes Art, Poetry, for a people open to forming new ways, soulfully and mentally, of expressing Body Magic. This is a contrast to general white motion and motor development, which is really not close to white kids even though they got it down pat.

TESTIFYING

Sometimes we look at life and see nothing;
Sometimes we look at life and see everything.
It's Everything or Nothing to most people.
But to Black people who thrive on creativity

**Physical education and sports: business as usual vs.
by any means necessary**

Mal Andrews

It's Nothing to Everything
'Cause, everything is you.
"TURNING ON" (motivation) SHORE IS FUNKY, YEA.

You can dream impossible dreams when you're Turned On. You can beat unbeatable foes too. Only when you're turned on can Black and White athletes do their "thang" together. Otherwise, we go our separate ways. Because we are Turned On at the university, some of my best friends are white. Only because we are Turned On, we can face each other with separate truths about where we are coming from, Blacks, Chicanos, Asians, Whites. Our P.E. Department gets hot, but fire don't bother us as much as others 'cause *we are already Turned On.*

Soul before the truth, so we can be ready to handle what is real compared to what.
Track and Field—the purest form of Sports,
　　The roots of organic survival.
Flash happenings—smoking, skying.
An escape from a bounceless
　　quickless world—from Limits.
Escaping deeper into the nths of seconds.
Higher and farther than Measures.
Surer than sure. Beyond races of people.
Sexless. Stronger than muscles in
　　Rhythms of Forces. Cheers flushing
　　your body into Frantics, matching your
　　Escape.
Crash ounceless—fall breathless—now
　　endless, less, you fall into Escapelessness.
Truth and Soul Track
　　starts *now* but never ends.
A Legend of Truth and Soul.
To be a pioneer is to be in a frantic mood
　　to move with Soul, Mind, Body, and
　　Spirit daily into *new* experiences, hopes,
　　achievements—Tireless.

To know the Truth . . . and IT shall set us free, for SOUL.
And SOUL . . . What it is? IT is IT. Money can't buy IT—YOU got to *get* IT—but you got to be where IT'S AT, or you can't get IT. ONCE YOU GET IT, then, when you have IT, "YOU GOT IT."

183

You don't know what IT is,
You just know IT IS.
You can't describe IT,
All you can do is feel that
"I GOT IT," "HE GOT IT," "SHE GOT IT,"
"WE GOT IT," "WE GON' DO IT," "HE AIN'T GOT IT,"
or "THEY AIN'T GOT IT."

There is no explanation of how we feel IT, we jus' do. And, by feeling IT, one becomes IT.

IT is an overpowering force that pervades the soul of those who give and get IT. "Telling IT like IT is," is speaking of the true conditions of how things are. That's what IT is . . . Truth and Soul.

Black or White we got to make IT right. *By any means necessary.*

Once you have Truth and Soul as a track man
    you are constant
But your spirit as a Track performer
    alternates between TOTAL VISION
    and ABSOLUTE BLINDNESS.
Somebody will have soul spirit Saturday
    and WE will all feel "IT."

The athlete's Body is a fantastic organism. With your Soul the manager—your Mind the engineer—tripping on spirit, energy, work, and having a communication between the Body parts, you can turn on any time—if you be cool.

Now you could be swooped on, go through goo-gobs of changes, but you still have movements that feel beautiful and relaxed.

Muscle is the spice of power, psychoblackology is the glory, elastic communication adds a touch of variety to exploding movement, forever, forever, RIGHT ON!

Physical Education and Sports—a creative fine Art. Any literal interpretation we read into our action, or any story, score, or result we connect with it is secondary to its real meaning.

Organic physical movement and what the body is really doing in sports is animalistic and a silent experience. What's the score, what place did she take, etc., has become too important in modern times. It is also an indication that people do not allow their feelings to respond to the real beauty of movement and body happenings before they try to comprehend it. They expect to be able to get its meaning through words; they seem to think that all that "super bad action" out there on the field can be explained to them, and are generally impotent to deal with the essence of it all.

**Physical education and sports: business as usual vs.
by any means necessary**

Mal Andrews

We ain't gonna lie and pretend that we love all the sports all the time, in exactly the same way, and from moment to moment, and that all sports all the time are creative. The veritable life of our athletic emotions and relationships are intermittent like other fine arts. But there are many people, including physical educators, that see most movement and physical activities only as a collection of related or unrelated rules, as business.

We want our bodies to move, to provoke, stimulate, and excite us. Ain't really no purposes of nothing unless they get down with our immediate passions.

Because we go through continual changes in athletics we seldom come upon a perfect performance, but the moving was good, and we all have glimpses of perfection in our own lives and these brief experiences of motion and energy give us perpetual insights into what a new beautiful world of physical sports might be.

The Men of my team turn to each other—in the hope of being in creative movement with each other. You, Truth and Soul leaders, are invested with the power of enchantment and would be guilty if you failed to exercise that power on the uncreative. Complacency can rip off the Big Time Soul moving in you.

We must remember that a track team is not operating in an atmosphere of fear but in an atmosphere of innovation and exciting change to make Us what's happening in Soul Sports life.

Don't be half-ass;
Be *Soul*
Fear accompanies the part while calmness
accompanies the *Whole.*

*In the beginning of truth and soul was cold duck time—on the seventh year he rested
— and the coach said "it was good."*

You know? They said that if I comes here talking all that Black stuff that I won't have no white cats on my team after a while. Funny, they been talking lily since I don't know when and they keep a bunch of Black cats on *their* teams. What do THEY mean, "some of my best friends are white"?

The Coach is a resource man,
a place to go for help
if an individual wants it.

185

All athletes, even *team* Sports,
     must see their "individual Self" first
     and then the event or position becoming
     a part of their daily life.
Let me be ME, I'll let you be you.
I won't mess with your mind—please don't jive me.
You come to the track 'cause it's YOU,
I'm just here too.
Don't do me no favors, take care of yourself.
I'm already ME.

I, the Coach, want to be *with* people, not over them. I want to look *at* people, not down to them. No, I don't like everybody, and I don't treat everybody the same. That's a trick to keep you from being you. It ain't really that important what others think of our approach to track or how we appear to a lot of people. We just want to develop from within, not from without. I just hang loose with administrators and colleagues. No, I don't hate them. I deal with them, confront them. But only a few see the Light.

There are no limits to what the body can do. But you gotta have fire. There are two kinds of fire. A sort of PG&E type (Business) which is regulated by the individual or coach, or a wild forest fire type which just burns, Baby, burns, and only you can prevent it once you know how good it feels. The wild fire is what makes a man or woman jump from 21 feet to 25 feet over-night. You don't know who it's gonna hit or when it's gonna hit. It has no respect of person. But at every track meet it hits *somebody*. We all see it and feel IT.

Rapping with athletes as people is my type of daily therapy, the Match. A coach has to combat all of the people's past. We have been led by a lot of different forces.

It can drain the coach—but one meaningful rap could be the thing that freed the Mind. I run, jump, play, bullshit, and shuck and jive too. We have a good time—especially with rookies. We take a rookie's crutches (inhibitions) away from him or her, quick.

P.E. must be a Jubilee—a great rejoicing, a complete unselfish willingness to relate in some way on all social, academic and sports levels. Soul can be tied down and generally is. I develop freedom in the cats—release them. "Do your own thing" is the first attitude. "Hang loose, Bro."

I did not come to the university to build a winning team. I came to promote a School of Thought. I reject written-down rules. One man's Soul is often another man's hang-up. Indoctrination builds fear—education builds

Physical education and sports: business as usual vs. by any means necessary

Mal Andrews

Freedom. A lot of coaches *train*—I would rather *Teach* (rap). They can take it or let it be. I'm dealing with people's lives while I deal with my life. I don't force my "thang" on others. I will not be a part of tradition in college coaching. I'm not interested in Power and Glory—you lose humanity, vision, getting hung up in that. That's what happened to the 1972 Olympics. White Power, Business As Usual.

My function as "coach" is to act as a resource man. I'm a library. My men and women want something, they come to me and ask for my help, I go from there—from the top of my head, triggered by Soul, rapping what I know. I know what I know. Maybe I can help, maybe I can't. Ask somebody else too. It don't make no difference *who* helped you jump 7′5″ as long as you "DO."

But I refuse to stand out on the field, yelling, with a bull horn, controlling my people in jumping jacks. Hell! You make them nervous with all of that hollering. That's a control game—release them from that program—they already had too much of that.

I try to develop individual responsibility, and then pray like hell that they can. If not, then *we* get together and "pull their coat" some more. But, it's up to them. I must relax too. I must practice freedom too. *By any means necessary.*

At a time when young athletes are rebelling, trying to be themselves, to shape a new, more exciting life—I permit it. Scared? Uh, hon. But I feel that codes deprive an individual of his right to express himself, his life, his "meaning." You can discipline a man to discipline himself without being some kind of iron god.

The worst thing a coach can do is to "use" an athlete for his own purposes and welfare just to build himself a record. I don't have a record, I have an idea. My athletes will keep their own personal record in their souls. And how do I keep a job? I don't worry too much about it. I do what I gotta do, stop for the red light—AND MOVE ON. Just stay in rhythm with Myself.

Because I promote Freedom, it don't mean I don't call some shots when things get uncool. But I call the shots from my soul, my immediate passion, emotionally, not from some list of rules and procedures. We don't put people out—but sometimes they just leave. There are a lot of rookies and chumps on the team who take advantage of academic and athletic freedom in going to class and working out. But it shows up in the meets and in the grades. When it happens, the whole team get a good laugh, like standing on the corner, tell it like it is. The chump knows, he knows what's happening with 187 himself. Our track program is a family affair—generally a close-knit group—'cause we got Soul.

White people in sports become happy slaves content to deal with things rather than meaning, happy to live on the surface of sports, gladly casting the human soul into an external trip and becoming systematic educational junkies.

The System has ripped off white soul and mental potency to get down into activities. Jealousy of the non-white Soul movement has sterilized whites' ability to realistically confront their racism. This dried-up humanity in whites is the main cause for their inhumanity to themselves and to non-whites, and their total injustice in today's sport society.

Black people are especially convicted daily in athletic departments, physical education departments, Olympic Games, and professional sports by a white court of superiority. White coaches and officials never really listen to any of the relevant evidence about Black life. America consistently creates an atmosphere in the athletic environment where Black and non-Black sports people have a suffocating sense of being enclosed in white business by racist attitudes which are absurd and inexorable. An example is the NCAA's 1.6 rule which excludes many non-whites from sports in college; and racist decisions in the 1972 Olympic trials heat seeding and Munich Olympic victory stand as white over-reactions to Black expression.

So it is obvious that Black athletes must dissociate themselves from assimilating into super-ego reason to "make it" in sports in America. White reason cannot turn on the Black super id or deal with the depths of why Black life in sports is Truth and Soul. Black studies in the symbolism of Black reason, rite and art of Truth and Soul Physical Education and Sports entails the prior creation or acceptance of a new picture of the world. Black athletes who have thrown off the shackles of oppression ain't impressed by the dominating culture to the point of self-subjugation no more. We are recalling that feeling that makes us want to shout Revolution! We are making all of our brothers and sisters more overtly aware of their unique and different cultural abilities to MOVE—without the threat of being overwhelmed by White Power. Revolutionary people must tear away from those values that have been corrupted in Sports and Physical Education if we are to escape serious psycho-affective injuries to our minds and culture. Control of how we speak and move affords us liberation in that it allows for an accurate as possible expression of the "form of life" which is most soulful to US. To establish our own context is to *make* physical education and sports function in a way congruent with our level of self-determination. *By any means*
188 *necessary.*

Physical education and sports: business as usual vs. by any means necessary

Mal Andrews

THE TRICKS

The existing culture—hits the fan. Physical Education and Sports in its present design is like a science fiction that ain't fiction at all. The tricks of racism in Sports is like Big Brother in 1984 with P.E. in a Godfather role. Many people, including radicals and revolutionists, don't even know that most athletic departments over America have been used to perpetuate racism in America. Racist Business as Usual.

I don't care what kind of a mind you have to tell your body to move—if you don't have a superior body your ass is grass. Only a superior body can physically get done what a superior mind has expressed.

There is evidence to indicate that the Black physique is genetically superior. Many educators will go along with these findings. But what I have

TRICK GRAPH

(Face of P.E. and Sports)

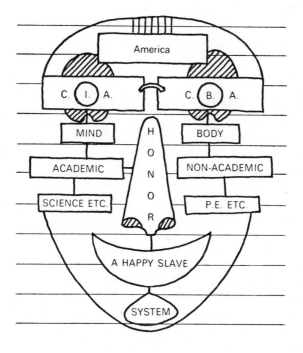

189

to hip you to is the fact that the System (Those at the Top) secretly knows that with a genetically superior body there generally accompanies a genetically superior mind—this, of course, giving allowance for birth damage, etc.

The System, with the Black cat coming on the scene as organically superior, had to systematically protect a weaker white society. And the only thing left was a PSYCHOLOGY.

In the name of a God whose genesis was white, racism became a national phenomenon in process and practice. Physical Education, placed in a military and perpetuation role, could not get an academic birthright and was thus doomed to busywork, non-academic and turned-off to creating. Kept ROTC right in or near the Gym, even substituted it for P.E. credit. Anytime the nation's students are raising hell and most of the other departments are going through changes, the Military and Physical Education departments are "Business as Usual."

Most people recognize that the gang bang is Economics and Political Power, but since from about three years old we have been in a MELODY OF TRICKS and now the White Mind is regulated.

At almost any time
You can see Big Brother President
On the sports pages
Glorifying the White Sports idea,
Keeping Sports people feeling superior,
Buying them off in the name of the *Star Spangled Banner*.
Sports people stand up more times,
Many times a week—more than any other subject.
White repetition affects white behavior,
Lulls coaches into a sense of pimps and hustlers.
Athletes turn to prostitute behavior,
You can always buy them off,
Make them heroes—make them think they going to be rich
Business As Usual.
When they get drained from trying to overcome
Their loss of individuality, they stop
Trying to go up—they come down,
Down to be "just" Physical Education teachers.
They turn into gluttons of insensitivity
Like Business and Political people.
They run home and drink all night.
They got to get drunk to relax

Physical education and sports: business as usual vs.
by any means necessary
Mal Andrews

From telling everybody all day
Not to drink.

It becomes a requirement for all children to be sent to a loser. These losers aren't thinking about Love, Poetry, Art. Some of them come to school and take out on the children the aggression they feel like doing to their wives or even the System. But, they are caught in the go-along already. They love to holler at children, yelling like crazy—keeping MINDS nervous.

When a child does something "Systematically" wrong, the principals don't send them to the Philosophy Department for discipline, do they? Nor to the Science, Art, etc. No, no! HEE, HEE, THEY GO TO P.E. Physical educators can't teach really meaningful P.E. for being babysitters to the school system's business:

PICK UP TRASH (for sitting wrong in English class); *bag for trash picked up in the Gym.*

RUN SOME LAPS (for speaking up too loud in Science); *makes running seem ugly.*

TAKE A SHOWER (to stay lily for the Math teacher).

GET A P.E. HAIRCUT (this coming from their own P.E., who will even cut it).

The cycle continues—the System continues. Merrily, merrily, life of P.E. is but a dream. Business As Usual. Healthy children, Black and non-Black, are sent to a nervous department or system. None can escape it, even Brave White Athletes who want to liberate their minds from the Man's control of Sports and live with all people. The System promptly swoops in to suffocate them, labeling them long-haired troublemakers even when they don't have long hair. Actually, if you don't know it, the System will give a white radical P.E. or Sports man or woman more pressure to discourage them from individual thought and action than a Black man or woman. They feel that a strong creative and free white mind and body will eventually "see" their Game of Inhumanity and become white allies with Black Liberation. The trick to eliminate these true, few, superior white people is to suffocate them, then re-channel them to Philosophy of something deep, superglorify that Mind and let the Body dissipate. The mind alone is unable to physically defend an Idea. The Body alone is unable to create or implement an Idea. 191

So everything is "groovy" and all, as long as what's white in this world is flourishing. White people don't fight white tricks. Systematic sex becomes part of their normal psychological school.

But when the Superior Black Man and Woman came on the scene, as (mythically) free, you should have seen the Government Gamers go to work. All hell broke out. P.E. departments all over America called time out from custom. They *officially* became the brawns department in a defensive predicament 'cause they knew they couldn't hold the superior Black physique back. The Black man just *standing* there looking at white people—free—was enough to scare the doo-doo out of them, let alone *moving*.

"Call the Physical (Body) Education (Mind) Department. Hurry up you bleeding bloats, get to stepping ya'll bloody fools, tell them to super-concentrate on a genetic white superior mind renaissance. . . . White-Mindedness, single-mindedness, hell! White Mind Power. Reserve "thinking" positions in Football, Basketball, Track and Field, Baseball and other whole sports. To hell with the Body for awhile, let the Nigger have it, he's Animal anyway. Hurry, we ain't got too much time 'cause *they* got both Mind *and* Body and you know they gon' be smoking and they ain't joking. We messed their mind up in Slavery a little bit but it was too strong to die. Hurry, fuck 'em up in a new sense of development within the context of a white democracy. At least until we find some more tricks."

So a social evil confrontation between the Wit and the Grit set up some mean shit that raped the beauty in physical development and sports in America.

The Man sent the "master plan" of all the tricks, to give little white kids a false sense of superiority, down to the Safe—the P.E. Department. And a copy to the military. In the Safe was a game, in the name of Peace, that shows American white people with a passionate desire to stay on the top, and non-white people *must* stay on the bottom. A set plan to keep the two competing groups—white and non-white—mutually exclusive, but confused in an "Assimilation Game." A special note attached—please rush the assimilation of the Blacks into white values, delay them from identifying their culture. We may be in trouble if they do.

If white physical educators and coaches are going to relate to all people they got some dues to pay. They got to recognize and accept differences between Black and White people and they can start *now* by studying and living the real Physical Education, the psychoblackological experience. Then maybe we can get on with what's PEOPLE in this world.

Time is the space between Love . . .

Love records all time in space.

**Physical education and sports: business as usual vs.
by any means necessary**

Mal Andrews

Truth and Soul is part of that space.
Only when Truth and Soul is
Recorded and can be Business As Usual,
Can all races of people have Love
In space in time with People
By any means necessary.

Authoritarianism in physical education and sports

William Paul

University of San Francisco and
California State University, San Francisco

The 1972 Olympic Games, in which numerous athletes who were disqualified, banned, recalled, and otherwise cheated by the world's leading sports politicians, are a painfully vivid example of authoritarianism in sport. The ugly authoritarianism which allowed petty sports officials to treat this planet's most dedicated athletes as if they were inmates in a reform school was shockingly evident. The games also illustrate the ultimate effects of militarization in physical education—the exercise of power over others by controlling that which they love.

The physical educator should rightfully object to the linking of sport with physical education, since it is precisely this connection of competitive athletics with education which has often served to create authoritarian ten-

Authoritarianism in physical
education and sports
William Paul

dencies in the gymnasium. The traditional goal has been to train for victory, to produce winners (and implicitly losers), and allegedly to improve all participants through the demands of the competitive process. The objective is clear: to win for the cause, be it the team, school, or nation. The similarity to military psychology is apparent.

The influence of militarism on organized athletic training can be traced throughout history. In classical China, martial arts (*wu shu*, training with or without weapons) was the major form of serious athletics (Smith, 1969); in the ancient Olympiad, all the games were explicitly military events; resistance training (isometric and isotonic) began in ancient Persia as a military discipline in the *zur khaneh* ("house of strength"); the appropriate sports for English yeoman were wrestling, quarterstaff, and longbow. Indeed, the European prototypes to modern physical education were military and political—the German Turnverieien (gymnastic societies) and the Eastern European Sokol gymnastics groups. In these examples we see actual military effectiveness as an immediate goal, since until recently warfare was largely athletic in substance. The larger objective, however, has been to develop military attitudes and nationalist values based upon loyal obedience to authority. Pete Dawkins, former West Point football great, in an A.P. interview in Vietnam during 1967, analyzed the war in these terms: "This is the big stadium and I'm on the varsity; this is where I want to be." Similarly, Mao Tse Tung has said, "The ultimate purpose of athletics is military heroism on the battlefield" (Smith, 1969). The ultimate goal has been to create a model human who would fit the needs of the state, movement, or ideology which directs the physical education program.

There are several reasons why physical education in particular has been used for political indoctrination. First, there is an *immediate payoff*. The participant is visibly improved by his physical activity. Improved cardiovascular efficiency produces feelings of increased energy and health, as does the sense of muscular strength and well-being produced by resistance training. These well-known benefits of physical training are especially important to a person who has had a relatively poor level of physical condition. When the physical improvements occur within the framework of a group which promotes a particular cause, the association of benefit with the cause seems quite natural. Thus, widely disparate evangelistic ideological systems have made physical education a vital component of their conversion program. Highly successful Black Muslim recruiting programs in jails and prisons 195 that used physical training as a medium for self-discipline were broadened to include personal hygiene and intellectual development, just as the Hitler Youth took working class boys into the mountains and guided them to personal improvement through physical education. In both cases the new self image, the health and general sense of wholesomeness, is naturally linked to the cause which made it all possible. It's a rewarding cause indeed that can actually make one *feel* good.

Second, physical activity promotes Collective identity. Well-organized physical education can effectively integrate a lonely individual into a group, thus providing acceptance and perhaps friendship. In a modern urban context of isolation, a lonely person is likely to welcome any invitation to some condition of belonging. The shared experience of intense effort in sport seems to create solid social bonding. Individual anxieties and insecurities are often submerged within the collective identity; conversion to this identity is usually easy, since it occurs within the familiar group context of the game.

Third, there are few ambiguities in sport. Goals are usually clear; merit and achievement measurable. This aspect of sport is especially relevant, since the inability to accept ambiguity is one of the major dimensions of the authoritarian personality as measured by the F scale (Adorno et al, 1950).

Established authoritarian governments have developed pervasive and sophisticated physical indoctrination programs. Japanese history was deeply influenced by the warrior class (*samurai*) and the martial arts (*bugei*) which they practiced, to the extent, in fact, that the language is permeated by martial terms and concepts. At the beginning of the modern era the ancient concept of art or discipline as a vehicle for truth was adapted to physical education and athletics. The highest goal of sport was the development of *yamatodamashii* ("fighting spirit of the Japanese race") and *bushido* ("way of the warrior"). A "Greater Japan Military Virtue Society" (*Dai Nippon Buto-kukai*) was established and connected to the Education Ministry (which governed all martial arts). Its duty was to inculcate in all physical disciplines a martial, patriotic spirit.

The impact of this organization on Japanese athletics over a fifty-year period was very deep and is still apparent long after the society's official demise. The influence of militarism was so vast in fact that nearly every competitive sport is now a vehicle for martial arts (*budo*) tradition. This traditional conditioning is characterized by rigid hierarchies of authority among the students based upon vertical senior/junior (*sempai/kohai*) roles. The central themes of Japanese sport are subjection of the individual to the group, total loyalty and obedience, and dedication to victory. More than this, the athlete often lives with his teammates in a training quarters (*gass-hukujo*) in a highly integrated life which is perfectly described by the Japanese

Authoritarianism in physical
education and sports
William Paul

social principle of "total envelopment" (*marugakae*), an important concept to remember, perhaps, when discussing American athletic social phenomena. The influence of athletic group identity is so overwhelming that broken noses and especially cauliflowered ears are viewed as badges of honor to be cultivated and nurtured. In top-level judo, sumo, wrestling, rugby, and other teams, the seniors deliberately strike the injured ears of juniors and aggravate the wound so as to permanently disfigure the boy. This is done, so they say, in order to develop "guts" and a manly image in the lucky recipient of this brotherly attention.

The large Japanese corporations which function as the modern sociopolitical equivalents of the ruling feudal clans practice a sophisticated paternalism comprising social envelopment of employees in a familial identity. Sport and physical fitness programs are important media for group cohesion. Many corporations hold mass exercises on company time and most large companies sponsor semi-professional "industrial league" teams in a variety of sports. The old virtue of martial spirit is so admired in the big conglomorates that several of these corporations made direct employment appeals to the very same *Zengakuren* rebels mentioned earlier. Job opportunity advertisements read, "We want to hire aggressive competitive men who have *konjo* ("guts") and aren't afraid of a fight." (This must represent new heights in the psychology of cooptation.)

Germany has traditionally seen military heroism as a normal act. This view is deeply embedded in Nordic myth and the heritage of the Teutonic knights. Frederick Jahn (1778-1852) used physical fitness as a form of military training, combining it with patriotism defined as allegiance to the Germanic Volk. The infamous German university dueling societies are another example. These societies were the forerunners of the modern fraternities, in which facial wounds were grisly marks of honor and manhood, and became repositories of militarist and ruling class values. These social and athletic institutions played a significant role in the construction of German racial and nationalist mythology, which Hitler used to gain support for Nazism.

Most totalitarian systems provide a central position for physical fitness and athletics in education. The use of physical conditioning as a form of indoctrination is quite apparent in such modern fascist states as Franco's Spain, the Greek military dictatorship, and the Brazilian junta, all of which possess sound physical education programs and splendid athletes.

More recently, a wide variety of militant ideological movements have **197** mobilized physical education as a medium for indoctrination including Black liberation groups, women's liberation groups, the Jewish Defense League, and the Palestinian guerrillas. A few years ago certain militant, radical groups viewed violence and physical confrontation as an act of personal self-definition, in other words, as a moral action. They sometimes carried out group tactical drilling and unarmed combat practice, although these training sessions seem to have been primarily for morale and media consumption. Nevertheless, the objectives remained the same—ideological reinforcement and group cohesion.

In Japan from 1966 to 1969, organized physical political action reached a kind of saturation point just short of armed insurrection. The various factions of *Zengakuren* (Student Self Government Associations) trained and drilled with great dedication for the revolutionary ideal of Gewalt ("violence," a transplanted German word). Physical training was done with a *gebabo*, a stick similar to a quarterstaff. Other group training methods included the famous snake dance, a kind of mass roadwork. The snake dance is a persuasive example of the dynamic potential of organized physical activity for political groups. Since firearms and explosives are acknowledged as taboo by all sides in Japanese riots, the scene often resembles a medieval battle. The student factions wear brightly colored helmets, *kabuto*, which incidentally are traditional symbols of manhood (Nakanishi, 1970); the riot police (*kidotai*), most of whom are ex-athletes, wear armor and carry shields. The result is a vast physical collision of ideology, lifestyle, and generations which seems to take on gamelike qualities. Clearly, radical political action, although seemingly a world apart from athletics, does have characteristics in common with sport. In fact, militant activities seem to embody some of the old athletic goals: teamwork, lots of competition, demanding physical activity (for cardiovascular overload there's nothing quite like running from the police), a capacity to "take it" (if you can't run fast enough), and, of course, the enthusiastic fans. One major difference is that in this game the referees all have clubs. Moreover, after battles, front line participants, having "put it on the line" and taken the risk, seemed to gain social stature; the fighters tended to gain authority. Thus the physically violent groups became the spokesmen for all radical groups and were implicitly acknowledged as such by legal authorities, who often brushed aside nonviolent groups even when they truly represented a majority of all radicals. Both sides recognized *physical* authority and showed a tendency to perceive hesitation or equivocation as weakness.

The fundamental philosophical parallel between the athletics and militant use of physical activity lies in the assumption that in physical achievement, competition, valor, daring, or combat there resides some special moral virtue,

Authoritarianism in physical
education and sports
William Paul

and that this virtue accrues to the cause or ideal. The unstated premise of all this conflict is that physical action, by definition an expression of power, somehow vindicates and exalts "our side." Judeo-Christian mythology has it that Jehovah will bless the righteous with victory and smite the wicked. Thus the bloody, gruesome outcome of a knightly trial by arms was adjudged God's handiwork and therefore sanctified by the Church. This may be the reason the public expects such unrealistically high moral standards from their sports heroes. The tremendous sacrifice, the self discipline, the enduring effort of the will—all personal qualities of athletes—are quite naturally identified with truth and virtue. Strength, self-mastery, and physical excellence tend to identify the athlete as the good guy.

The identification of military or athletic strength with virtue is also rooted in the Social Darwinists' contention that survival of the fittest is the essence of human existence. "Fittest" is defined as the capacity for victory in the ruthless and never-ending struggle for existence. The theory holds that an inexorable and universal process of violent selection brings forth not only superior species but stronger social groups and systems. Unfortunately, although condemned by both Darwin and his colleague Wallace, Social Darwinism has been used as a rationale for imperialism, fascism, and Stalinism (Nasmyth, 1971).

The much maligned "old coach" often, if not always, felt that by developing in his players tenacity, aggressiveness, and a will to win, he was providing them with the psychological armor that would sustain them against the assaults of a competitive, hostile world. It usually did not occur to this archetypical coach and his collective counterparts in nations like Germany, Japan, and the Soviet Union that their well intentioned programs of mental and physical conditioning might serve to *perpetuate* competition and hostility. In any case the tradition of preparation for struggle with others was integral to sport and physical education. The relevance of Social Darwinist "kill or be killed" theories to Physical Education becomes clear when we remember that psychological measures reveal a tendency in authoritarian personalities to ascribe aggressive motives to others (Adorno et al, 1950). If for generations we have been brought up to expect conflict from others, and this belief is constantly reinforced in every game we play, then eventually aggression is called "human nature" (Stagner, 1965). Thus for much of human history the great conquerers and generalissimos have been copping a plea behind "only doing what comes naturally."

In recent decades, however, definitions of fitness and strength have be- 199 come broader and more refined. Whatever evolutionary selections have occurred in the human species, the variation and combination of genetic advantages is simply enormous; many DNA survived no doubt because of a seductive eye and a cute wiggle. It is simplistic and unscientific to view human development solely from the perspective of the predatory naked ape, as if the adrenocortical fight-or-flight responses were our central physiopsychological function. This lurid view of the human experience is a convenient rationalization for the social aggressor, and perhaps has within it a certain swagger, an arrogant pride in primitive origins, a final justification for modern savagery.

In fact, it is the human capacity for cooperation and mutual understanding that makes societies possible. It is remarkable that one should find it necessary to defend such a self-evident proposition, yet many people believe that the U.S.A. will remain great only by maintaining its capacity to obliterate weaker nations—almost as if it must remain the toughest team in the league. It is precisely such warlike tendencies which helps to destroy higher civilizations. For example, it is popularly thought that Rome fell because of a general weakness characterized by excessive sexuality, poor physical fitness, and a lack of the will to win. The painfully relevant truth (for us) is that Rome suffered from chronic social violence arising from the insensitivity of a system based upon war. Small counterinsurgency and pacification operations, while liquidating a regular quota of the youth and also serving to destroy faith and social conscience, affected that empire like a bleeding wound. Other civilizations have died a similar death from the same disease.

The philosophy of a universal human drive for dominance produced by genetic imperatives is based essentially upon a very low opinion of mankind and ultimately forms the basis for Nazism, if not social paranoia (Stazner, 1965). Nazism, fascism, or Stalinism, however, is not restricted to those bad guys with the uniforms and heavy accents; rather, authoritarianism is a mode of behavior which is culturally induced. And substantial evidence indicates that an authoritarian view of life is more likely to occur among physical educators than among teachers from other disciplines (Feldman and Newcomb, 1969; Locke, 1961).*

---

*With respect to the personality of coaches, it is interesting to note Ogilvie and Tutko's findings (1968) that successful coaches tended to exhibit most of the personality traits and career motivations associated with professionals in other fields. However, they also found a general inability to change and to adapt to new ideas, and an incapacity to relate to the personal needs of their players and students. I am inclined to scepticism at this last finding. It has always seemed to me that male coaches more than other faculty members maintain a capacity to operate within the frame of reference of American boyhood and to communicate within that system of values. Perhaps boyhood has changed.

Authoritarianism in physical education and sports

William Paul

Many traditional American physical education programs, however, have expected teachers and coaches to condition youth to exhibit the conventional values and behavior of society. This goal of conditioning provided the role which we affectionately call the "old coach." Once a heroic figure in America, he has been rejected by the counterculture and probably received more abuse than he deserves. He was cast as the disciplinarian; a role which helped build a negative image, especially among victims of official wrath. He is not unlike the policeman who, by carrying out orders, becomes the villian. In a sense, the coach was often the school cop, since it was he who would be cast as the chief villian during the battles over hair length, when American doctrines of personal liberty were put to the test. His considerable arsenal contains weapons such as group ridicule directed at those who were unmanly or hoodlums (often meaning "lower class"), or had failed in some other way to conform to the socio-cultural standards which it was his duty to enforce.*

The traditional educational priorities in physical education are such that the average instructor was also a coach and that this role was his paramount concern. Physical educators tend to relate to the general student population in the same terms as in coaching. In view of the pressures put upon the coach/teacher it was inevitable that he should often come to look upon the student body as a talent pool and the individuals as potential recruits. Thus the physically inadequate are seen as "weak" and the less skillful or the noncompetitive are often seen as "losers." The coach often invests his real energy and attention in his prize athletes, while ignoring standard gym classes save for role call and dismissal. Considering the situation, this neglect, is occasionally a blessing for the kids involved, who, when not supervised, are sometimes able to develop a love of sport in spite of the system.

It would be unjust, however, to attribute these motivations to all coaches, for coaches and players have indeed often enjoyed mutually rewarding personal contact. Many coaching colleagues will doubtless resent the negative image of the "old coach" presented above, and so they should. Yet the casual unfairness serves perhaps to demonstrate a truth. For years physical

---

*It is quite appropriate, therefore, that coaches have often gone into educational administration. As embodiments of American cultural values, these men and women were considered ideologically safe. Moreover, the stresses and conflicting interests of the athletic system were such that a successful coach or athletic director tended to be necessarily an able and resourceful practitioner of bureaucratic school politics.

education has been in the business of attempting to produce an acceptable model youth. The discipline dealt in archetypes, paragons, and heroes—the image was all. The social system smiled upon this handsome athletic ideal and awarded appropriate recognition, opportunity, and position, often to the detriment of the antitype, the kid who didn't fit the image and who never would. Now from some quarters, notably the counterculture, the entertainment world, and the intelligentsia, come avenging bigotries about "stupid jocks," "brutal athletes," "sadistic coaches," and so on. The athlete is cast as a brutal buffoon. The creative children's television program, "Lidsville," features a distorted football helmet with legs, called "Rah Rah," who is the subject of clever ridicule, some of it vicious. It seems tragic that athletes as a whole should be stereotyped as stupid, aggressive brutes. What kind of resentment and pain could have produced this kind of cultural vengeance?

Quite a few kids come to athletics in search of comfortable authority, perhaps even a needed father/son role missed at home. Authoritarianism after all requires followers who desire security and freedom from ambiguity and doubt, who need situations where goals are clear and value measured in touchdowns, points, and time. But group identity in athletics often becomes a powerful force in youth culture, to the point where it overshadows all other values. Gary Shaw, now a psychologist, played under the famous Darrell Royal, who said of his players that he trained them to be "like trained pigs who'll grin and jump right in the slop." This is how Shaw describes football:

> To me what people don't know about college football . . . is the way coaches use a player's fears as a weapon to keep him obedient and what all this does to the player, what it eventually makes him as a person.
>
> You hate it. You're miserable. You want to quit. Why don't you? Well, one thing you'll have to give up is your friends, since nearly all the people you've ever closely associated with are football players. The common link all of you have is football and 'never say die.'
>
> So you know that your best friends will probably lose all respect for you.
>
> What I was caught up in was the extreme of what most American men are caught up in. . . . Football was not just an activity for me. It had become my way of dealing with life—playing the game. I played to win at everything, which meant I could never let down my defense for a moment for fear an opponent would score against me and as a result, like most American men, I was basically without real human contact—alone and scared.
>
> Many never leave football . . .
>
> Threat of punishment reinforced our total dedication and tacitly de-

ISSUES IN PHYSICAL EDUCATION / CULTURAL
**Authoritarianism in physical
education and sports**
William Paul

manded that we should never question our coaches' authority. Like a
good soldier, our job was to follow orders—not think about them.

Admittedly the above is an extreme example, but it is still representative of the internal mechanisms of social enforcement that often exist within
a team. It is not unlikely that successful methods of enforcing social norms
in athletics should be applied by a socially dominant athletic group to the
other kids in physical education, to the "weaklings" and the "losers." Beyond the masculinity games and associated cruelties which tend to emerge
from this traditional sports atmosphere, there are the attitudes and habits
of hostility towards misfits and social deviants of any kind. These attitudes
are especially brutal in those communities where the athletic life style is
still dominant. It is a sad commentary on our traditions of fair play and
sportsmanship that during the past few years peace activists and "hippies"
sometimes had to fear actual physical attack from athletes in some parts
of middle America.

In a sense the athletic existence is a valiant attempt to create an eternal
childhood wherein the game is all. Naturally, the happy faithful resent the
intrusion of the realities and contradictions of modern life. In my experience
as an athlete and instructor I have known many fine and intelligent athletes
who violently rejected any serious conversation on social issues or fundamental ideas. Such rejection is a psychic defense mechanism against ideas
which might challenge a secure, uncomplicated life. Big time athletics,
whether high school, college, A.A.U., Olympic, or professional requires an
insulated social setting to nourish and reinforce the high levels of motivation and sacrifice necessary for meeting the demands of top flight competition. The dedicated athletic existence is really a different dimension of
consciousness in which the nonathletic world is perceived as self-indulgent,
and morally ambivalent. Again, I feel this stems from the belief that athletic
performance is a measure of human merit and moral value, the belief that if
we (athletes) are stronger, we are then superior to others.

The high moral values of sportsmanship and fair play which we traditionally attribute to sport seem to suffer quite a mauling in big time competition. McAfee (1968) found that athletes tend to sacrifice moral standards
as early as junior high school. Kistler (1958) and Richardson (1962) both
found a correlation between high levels of competition and decreasing
levels of sportsmanship. Kistler found significant numbers of varsity

203

athletes who approve of cheating in order to win—if there is a low risk of getting caught. Varsity level competitors also tended to exhibit a lesser degree of sportsmanship.

Competition is not a purely American invention nor are totalitarian tendencies in sport. To return again to the unhappy example of the Munich Olympics we see the athletic ideal mobilized by some as an instrument of national policy and a vehicle for propaganda. Whole youth populations become talent pools for those nations who choose to allocate resources and offer financial and political incentives for athletic victory in the international arena, quite overshadowing the performance of the champion as an individual. The unhappy fact emerges that any modern industrial society can produce medal winners with enough investment. The outcome, as in other more explicit forms of warfare, is not usually decided by individual valor nor sacrifice. The role and power of international sports politicians as high priests of nationalism is a glaring contradiction to the Olympic ideal. These power brokers have an exact image of how the proper patriotic model should behave. Thus Mitchell and Collett, members of the U.S. track team at the Munich Olympics, are banned forever for not standing at attention during the American national anthem.

In the face of increasingly critical demands to justify physical education's share of educational resources, perhaps our most worthy goal is to recreate student enthusiasm and participation. To this end we should develop a new emphasis upon the intrinsic benefits of physical activity to the participants and a recognition that a basic goal is to serve the students, not merely to recruit students who will serve athletics. The trend toward physical education as an elective, clearly, indicates that old habits of regimentation and external discipline must give way to the creation of a positive learning atmosphere if we are to maintain student support. Our discipline should probably respond to the demand for innovative programs involving such previously alien subjects as Yoga and Tai Chi Chuan. Asian martial arts of all kinds show huge registration and attendance. Furthermore, there is a vast potential in traditional Western sports for increased motivation through study of areas such as self-discipline, respiratory dynamics, and sensory awareness. A recent encouraging development is the recognition of physical education's potential for social contribution, reflected for example in the NCAA summer sports program. Other community programs have successfully used physical education in such areas as drug education, interracial communication, and the redirection of violence.

Physical education also has tremendous potential as a medium for
psychotherapy. The rapidly developing field of sports psychology may be

ISSUES IN PHYSICAL EDUCATION / CULTURAL
Authoritarianism in physical
education and sports
William Paul

expanded to include clinical physical education. Moreover, there must be an increased recognition of the substantial scientific contributions made by physical educators to exercise physiology and the positive function of athletics as a laboratory of human performance. Also emerging is the study of the sociology of sport and physical training, which seeks to examine the socio-cultural impact of various kinds of physical movement. Just as physiologists have found their way onto various physical education faculties, so social scientists should be able to contribute through teaching and research. More than anything else our field must be open to all people who would benefit and contribute, regardless of lifestyle or belief or background. The Olympic ideal is that sport should serve as a moral substitute for war. Considering the warlike character of competitive athletics, perhaps physical education can serve as a moral substitute for sport.

REFERENCES

Adorno, Frenkel-Brunswik, *et al. Authoritarian Personality*. New York: Harper and Row, 1950.

Feldman, Kenneth A., and Newcomb, Theodore M. *The Impact of College on Students*, Vol. 1. San Francisco, Calif.: Jossey-Bass, 1969.

Kistler, Joy A. "Attitudes Expressed about Behavior in Certain Sports Situations." *Coll. Phys. Educ. Assoc. Proc.* 60(1958):55–58.

Locke, Lawrence F. *The Performance of Administration Oriented Physical Educators on Selected Psychological Tests*. Ph.D. dissertation, Stanford University, 1961.

McAfee, Robert. "Sportsmanship Attitudes in Sixth, Seventh, and Eighth Grade Boys." *Research Quarterly* 24(1955):120.

Mosse, George L. *Nazi Culture*. New York: Grossett and Dunlap, 1966.

Nakanishi, Masahiro. *Kakumaru: Analysis of Ultra-Left Group*. In *Zengakuren Japanese Student Left*, edited by Dowsey. Berkeley, Calif.: Ishi Press, 1970.

Nasmyth, George. "Social Progress and Darwinian Theory: A Study of Force as a Factor in Human Relations." In *Science as Metaphor*, edited by Olson, p. 132. Belmont, Calif.: Wadsworth, 1971.

Ogilvie, Bruce, and Tutko, Thomas. *Problem Athletes and How to Handle Them*. London: Pelham Books, 1968.

Richardson, Deane. "Ethical Conduct in Sports Situations." *Coll. Phys. Educ. Assoc. Proc.* 66(1962):98–103.

Rohm, Ernst. *Die Geschichte eines Hochverraters*. Munich: Verlag Eher Nachf., 1928.

Shaw, Gary. *Meat on the Hoof—the Hidden World of Texas Football*. St. Martins Press, 1972.

Smith, R. W. *Asian Fighting Arts*. Tokyo: Kodansha, 1969.

Stagner, Ross. "Psychology of Human Conflict." In *The Nature of Human Conflict*, edited by McNeil, p. 53. Englewood Cliffs, N. J.: Prentice-Hall, 1965.

Psychology
of the woman
who competes*

Ruth Berkey
Occidental College

How much do you know about your own athletes? How will they react in a rough game situation? Will their reaction be any different than the one you see every day during practice? If it is, why is it, and how can you predict what the reaction will be? How much thinking have women done about women athletes? Do they differ from male athletes, and if so, why?

Beisser (1967) did many studies on differing types of athletes in his book *Madness in Sports*, showing how people demonstrate their behavioral patterns in sports activities. However, there were no examples of women

---

*Portions of this article are adapted from an article that appeared in CAHPER JOURNAL, January/February 1972. CAHPER has kindly granted permission for using those portions.

Psychology of the woman
who competes

Ruth Berkey

athletes. Why? Even Tutko, who has published material on the varying types of athletes, has seldom mentioned women as athletes. Do the tender-minded athletes, as he refers to them, include women? Should we expect women athletes to be tough-minded? Is it possible to be a psyched-out athlete as a woman or does this phenomenon only apply to men? As a coach, can I use Tutko's and Richards' book, *Psychology of Coaching*, with any confidence that it will work with my women athletes?

Numerous studies have investigated the effects of high-level athletic competition upon personality. However, with respect to the female competitor, little literature is available which asks or answers the most important questions. There is a serious lag in the opportunities offered to the American female to pursue physical excellence. This may be less true for the European female athlete. Metheny (1965) has written an extensive review of the historical roots of the problem of the feminine image. Summarizing the attitudinal changes since the Greek civilization, with its ideal of the masculine, athletic Greek gods, through the Western shift from muscle to intellect, she says nothing at this time which indicates that sport harms female personality structure.

However, all audiences seem to show a perceptual preference for physical grace and movement that conforms to some cultural norm. Metheny has stated that some forms of international competition are "categorically unacceptable" as feminine activities, including wrestling, judo, boxing, weightlifting, hammerthrow, pole vault, longer foot races, high hurdles and all team sports with the exception of volleyball. Sports in which an opponent is subdued by force, where there is bodily contact, are also considered unfeminine. Traditionally, competing with men in athletics is acceptable for a woman, unless she plays to win. The male finds it tolerable when she plays the game without pursuing personal victory—as long as she is a non-competitor, without any potential threat of becoming deeply involved, she is in perfect compliance with cultural expectations and is therefore feminine.

Masculinity and femininity, as culturally defined, have been extremely resistant to modification, particularly where sport is concerned. Even in this age of radical feminism there have been few, if any, changes in the traditional sport activities for women. The male, consistent with his traditional role, determines what range of behavior he will condone as being feminine for the average woman. Evidence from studies of motor skill development indicates a lack of sex differences in skill acquisition, except in terms of   207 social rewards extended on the basis of sex. Early in the life of the female, our culture begins to extinguish high motor activity where aggression and physical contact are important for success. Middle class standards are so constraining that males measure significant increments in physical skill with age, while females measure a significant loss of skill with age. Our culture, in general, is much more inclined to reward the motor activity of the male, while extinguishing that of the female. The psychosocial rewards for each sex parallel each other into the onset of puberty, but from then on find that physical competition on the part of the female is devalued.

Vanek and Cratty (1970) suggest different stages in the development of an athlete, with different motives corresponding to different stages. The first state is "generalization," which occurs in the early years of life. The athlete is probably drawn to sport because of the rewards of participating in movement activities. Categories usually include team games, individual activities, or track and field events. The second state is "differentiation," in which the athlete becomes selective of the sports he engages in. As his selection continues, he rejects activities in which he experiences unpleasant outcomes and retains interest in those which give him pleasure. A number of secondary social motives impinge upon his performance and selection of activities at this stage.

The third state is that of "specialized preferences," in which the choice of activity becomes more specific. Although the primary motives persist, secondary social motives gain increasing influence. Anxiety and apprehension may increase as the athlete reaches the top levels of competition. In the fourth category, the "involution" stage, performance is still at a high level, and the athlete continues to be motivated by secondary motives, but at times he regresses to dependency upon the basic motives encountered at the initial stages.

Vanek does not make any reference to the sex of the performer in his scheme. But in many respects his basic ideas go along with the evidence that motor skill acquisition in the female and male are different due to the secondary social motives which take place at the specialized preferences stage. He also contends that the athlete must be subjected to careful guidance. How many women receive this guidance and are prevented from underestimating their potential during early stages?

Ogilvie and Tutko (1967) studied a group of twenty San Jose State women competitive swimmers. The women had established an outstanding winning record within the California state college system. They were victorious in all meets and had set time standards for nearly all swimming events for college women. They were tested on the *Cattell 16 Personality*

Factors Test and the *Jackson Personality Research Form B*. Although statistical tests were not applied, the results are interesting in light of cultural differences between male and female personality structure. These women's test profiles were compared with the test profiles of twenty-seven Tokyo Olympic male swimmers, with the women's scores differing from the men's on the traits of impulsiveness, dominance, aggression, nurturance, succorance, and harm-avoidance. Thus those traits which our culture defines as feminine —low dominance, low aggression, high nurturance, high succorance, impulsiveness, self-abasement, and a sensitive awareness of danger—seem well supported for this small sample. But there is also a degree of profile similarity for both samples that indicates the existence of one basic competitive swimmer personality, rather than one for males and another for females. Although a more representative sample is needed to validate this conclusion, this is the only study I know of that compares male and female competitors.

Kane and Callaghan (1965), in a study of world class women tennis players and tournament class women, reported significant differences favoring the former. Such traits as emotional stability, ego-strength, self-confidence and low frustration were much more characteristic of world class players. In both these studies we find no loss of the feminine traits most valued within the culture. In fact, there was strong evidence that at least this small sample of women had markedly feminine personalities in the presence of outstanding success as competitors. Can one then say that participation in athletic competition is unfeminine? Or are swimming and tennis merely exceptions?

Anyone who has reviewed any of the literature on personality differences among athletes knows that there is a great deal of research on the male athlete and his personality. In reviewing literature for a pilot study I conducted two years ago, I was overwhelmed with the amount of material there was available on male athletes. In fact, athletes in different sports have been shown to possess different personality characteristics. The team athlete versus the individual athlete has also been studied extensively. However, when I tried to find some information about women athletes, I unearthed very little, and most of it was unpublished.

My study was designed to test the hypothesis, first, that women who participate in intercollegiate basketball have a higher expression of dominance over their peers than a group of non-participants, and second, that 209 these participants would score higher on aggression than the non-participant. The *Edwards Personal Preference Schedule* (Edwards, 1954) and the *Ascendance-Submission Reaction Study* were used for this study.

The *Edwards Personal Preference Schedule* is designed to measure "a number of relatively independent normal personal variables" in a list of needs as proposed as a part of a theory of personality. I was looking mostly at aggression. However, five other subscales were interesting to watch: deference, succorance, nurturance, abasement, and aggression. The *Ascendance-Submission Reaction Study* purports to measure the disposition of an individual to dominate his fellows or be dominated by them. Not all items measure an invariable ascendance or submission, for most people show both types of behavior. My study attempted to detect whether one of these reactions is more characteristic.

The basketball team, whom I shall refer to as athletes, had successfully completed a season with a 12 and 3 record, in competition with other four-year colleges in southern California. The nonathletes were students from a beginning contemporary dance course, none of whom had had prior experiences in competition. Both groups were students at Occidental College. In analyzing the data, I found that the results of the *Ascendance-Submission Study* showed a significant difference (at the one percent level) between the athletes and nonathletes. However, the nonathletes scored higher on the ascendance side of the scale, while the athletes scored higher on the submission side of the scale. Thus, the test showed 1) that the nonathletes had a higher expression of dominance over their peers; 2) that the athlete group had significantly higher scores on the abasement need of the Edwards scale, indicating a greater abasement need on the part of the athlete group; and 3) that no significant differences emerged between the athlete and nonathlete groups with respect to aggression, deference, dominance, nurturance and succorance needs as measured by the Edwards scale. These results were somewhat different from many results in the review of the literature for men athletes. Almost every study on aggression shows the male athlete as more aggressive than the nonathlete. Does this indicate that aggression is a masculine quality even in athletes?

Mushler (1970) has done a cross sectional study of personality factors of girls and women in competitive lacrosse. She was attempting to show 1) that there would be a significant difference on one or more personality factors between each sample and the applied norm; 2) that fewer differences would be found between the sample and the norm as age level and experience decrease; 3) that each sample group would tend to differ from its norm on the same factors as other sample groups; and 4) that there would be signi-

Psychology of the woman
who competes
Ruth Berkey

ficant differences between sample groups on those factors where samples have common differences from the norm.

Mushler tested junior high, senior high, college and national team levels. The junior high group tested more intelligent, assertive, happy-go-lucky, and circumspect than the norm. The senior high group were more reserved, intelligent, assertive, happy-go-lucky, expedient, tough minded, suspicious, forthright, experimenting, undisciplined, and tense than the norm. The college group, were more intelligent, assertive, happy-go-lucky, expedient, tough-minded, suspicious, forthright, and experimenting than the norm, and the national team were more reserved, intelligent, happy-go-lucky, shy, tough minded, and experimenting than the norm. Her first hypothesis was supported: there were significant differences on one or more personality factors between the sample and the norm. The second hypothesis, that the lower age levels would show fewer differences between the sample and the norm, was not supported. And the third hypothesis, that each sample group would tend to differ from the norm on the same factors as other sample groups, was supported. Mushler also suggests that personality development may be independent of competitive sports, that self-selection of the individual into competitive sports may be determined by personality factors that the individual already possesses. This has been a belief of mine for several years, that the individual, because of certain personality factors, will choose one sport over another. My experience in coaching volleyball and basketball over the past ten years, has added to this belief, and I began to draw some conclusions about the type of women who play each of these sports. There are always some who play both, but even then they usually prefer one over the other. I have felt that there is a basic difference between women who choose to play volleyball and those who choose to play basketball, because of the difference in the nature of the two sports.

To test this hypothesis, I began searching for a personality test which I felt would measure differences in degrees of personality. I decided to use the *California Personality Inventory.* This inventory is intended primarily for use with normal subjects, and its scales are addressed principally to personality characteristics important for social living and social interaction. Subjects were students at Occidental College and California State University, Los Angeles, and were grouped according to whether they preferred basketball to volleyball, or preferred volleyball to basketball, or played only one of the two sports.

211

The CPI scales are broken into four categories: 1) measures of poise, ascendancy, and self-assurance; 2) measures of socialization, maturity and responsibility; 3) measures of achievement potential and intellectual efficiency; and 4) measures of intellectual and interest modes. From the results of the small sample at this date, the results of the CPI concluded that basketball players are more dominant and have greater social presence, meaning that they are more clever, enthusiastic, imaginative, and have greater self-acceptance than the basketball-volleyball players. The volleyball players on the other hand are more mature, forceful, demanding, and foresighted than the basketball players.

Why is it important for a coach to be aware of personality differences among competitors? Will such differences affect their play, especially during the important contest? I believe it will. It is also important to realize that just as women are different from men as people, they will be different from men as athletes, because of the nature of our culture. So I do not think it is possible to pick up one of the latest books on the psychology of coaching and apply the material to female athletes. Obviously some generalizations may be made, but in the last analysis, we who are concerned about competition for the female must begin to do some studying of the female competitor. I am not sure the psychologists are going to do these studies for us. The Eastern Europeans have done some excellent studies, some on women, but the majority of the studies have not been done with statistical information to validate the findings. Tutko (1971) has developed personality tests for the male athlete. When will we begin to develop similar tests for the female competitor, tests that do not decide masculinity or feminity on the basis of whether a woman wants someone to open the car door for her? It is my opinion that the time has come for women coaches to become more curious about personality differences that are involved in athletic competition for women. Their support is vital to insure a valid and responsible analysis of the woman competitor.

BIBLIOGRAPHY

Beisser, Arnold R. *The Madness in Sports.* New York: Appleton-Century-Crofts, 1967.

Edwards, Allen L. *Edwards Personal Preference Schedule Manual.* New York: The Psychological Corp., 1954.

Kane, J. E., and Callaghan, "Personality Traits in Tennis Players." *British Lawn Tennis,* July 1965.

Metheny, Eleanor. *Connotations of Movement in Sport and Dance.* Dubuque, Io.: Wm. C. Brown, 1965.

Mushler, Carole, "A Cross Sectional Study of the Personality Factors of Girls and Women in Competitive Lacrosse." Ph.D. dissertation, University of South Carolina, 1970.

**Psychology of the woman
who competes
Ruth Berkey**

Ogilvie, Bruce C. "The Unanswered Question: Competition, Its Effect Upon Femininity."
Address for the Olympic Development Committee, at Santa Barbara, Calif., in June, 1967.

Tutko, Thomas A., and Richards, Jack W. *Psychology of Coaching.* Boston: Allyn and Bacon, 1971.

Vanek, Miroslav, and Cratty, Bryant. *Psychology and the Superior Athlete.* New York: Macmillan, 1970.

Stigma or prestige: the all-american choice

Marie Hart
California State University, Hayward

gnorance about, and lack of investigation concerning human social relationships in physical activity is due largely to preoccupation with numbers. Many students and faculty members have become increasingly disenchanted with the recitations of statistical measures as a means of understanding social behavior. It has become a professional and personal requirement in America to view life through numerical abstractions. The importance of facts as a basis for action, for knowledge about people in social relationships now and in the past, is undeniable. However, many researchers and scholars appear satisfied to stop when the statistics suggest that the hypothesis is, indeed, proven to be true.

However, we need to know more than correlations, standard deviations, insurance

Stigma or prestige:
the all-american choice
Marie Hart

rate increases, and the statistics on incoming athletes. We need to know what social conditions, taboos, norms, superstitions, expected roles, and rewards make people behave as they do. In physical education, why do people group, regroup, divide, alienate, subdivide, collect and subcollect in such great diversity? The tension and conflict engendered by the archaic social rules and roles which govern physical education are no longer tenable, and furthermore, they are the cause of the divisions within physical education.

I propose that a social situation, heavy in prestige for some and laden with stigma for others, has been created and is perpetuated by the archaic male and female role expectations. Due to these role expectations, female athletes and male dancers live a stigmatized life much of the time. The male cultural environment of sport sets up this difficult social situation.

Beisser (1967) and Fiske (1972) have suggested that sport acts as a rite of passage into the male adult role in American society. The male is expected to be, or to act biologically superior, and sport is the only remaining testing ground. Sport gives the young male an opportunity to learn and practice the attributes still held and valued by his elders. Dance exposes the young female to accepted attributes of grace, poise, and beauty but dance is not nearly so pervasive and regulated as the sport system is for the male. Physical education is largely conducted according to male needs and expected role behavior, thereby creating the problems for female students and teachers.

Women's roles in society are in conflict with those perpetuated in physical education. In an investigation of women's roles, Griffin stated: "Being involved in sport and education, she combines the roles of woman athlete and woman professor and accordingly, is perceived as possessing all the "unsavory" characteristics of the active and potent woman. She is seen as intelligent, competitive, aggressive, strong, and experimental. These characteristics, while desirable for success in realms of sport and academia, appear to be of much less value to a woman in the social world. Physical educators must be aware of the conflict of the traits expected of women in the social world and women in athletics and the professions" (1973, 98). These traits may not only be of less value in the social world, they may, indeed, bring stigma to a woman.

Goffman's (1963) ideas on stigma and social identity may add insight to American social behavior in sport and dance. He defines stigma as "an   215 attribute that is deeply discrediting, but it should be seen that a language of relationships, not attributes, is really needed. An attribute that stigmatizes one type of possessor can confirm the usualness of another, and therefore is neither creditable nor discreditable as a thing in itself" (p. 3). If this definition seems too harsh, he offers another: "the situation of the individual who is disqualified from full social acceptance" (preface). In Goffman's terms, attributes in certain situations and relationships create positive social identity (normalize an individual). Those same attributes in a different context may create negative social identity, and cause the individual to acquire stigma. In contrast with the stigmatized person, Goffman states: ". . . in an important sense there is only one complete unblushing male in America: a young, married, white, urban, northern, heterosexual Protestant father of college education, fully employed, of good complexion, weight, and height, and a recent record in sports." (p. 128) It is suggested here that the only one complete unblushing American female is married to this unblushing male.

If this is the definition of the most normal and accepted people in America, what is the result for those individuals who do not measure up to this list of all-American attributes? They are "disqualified from full social acceptance." The female athlete and the male dancer, in particular, do not measure up to this unblushing individual.

The model which follows may help to illustrate the relationships between female and male roles, and the cultural forms of sport and dance. It is suggested that these relationships can result in negative social identity, and cause the formation of groups, based on stigma.

The acquisition of stigma appears to be the natural result, since women athletes are in male cultural territory and male dancers are in female cultural territory. Goffman (1963) suggests several behavior patterns engaged in by the stigmatized person. Three seem especially appropriate to physical education and sex roles: 1) the stigmatized individual may use his disadvantage as a basis for organizing his life; 2) he may control carefully the stigmatizing information; and 3) he may develop tension management activities.

Organizing life in terms of one's social disadvantage becomes apparent in the half-world of women's sport and dance, which largely take place in sexually segregated groups. Physical education and athletic organization for women are often organized around the recognition that women are not welcome in male sport groups. These groups were well established as all-male before women became involved in sport, and that tradition is often tenaciously maintained. Women are misrepresented, underrepresented, underbudgeted, and often not well trained as athletes because of the tradi-

Stigma or prestige:
the all-american choice
Marie Hart

tion male dominance of sport in American institutions. But organizing into a half-world is only a reaction; it does not answer the needs of the woman in sports.

Separatism in sport in contemporary American society is basically perpetuated by the middle class, which traditionally supports educational sport and dance. Such separatism does not provide for shared social experiences; it cannot form a basis for common interests, experiences, and conversation. Instead of providing a basis for interchange, sport tends to isolate and alienate people. In physical education male-designed architecture and separatist organizations contribute to isolation and alienation. Some sexual privacy may be necessary, but the present situation leads to exceedingly limited communication and little if any shared experience.

One important result of the stigmatizing process is how information is handled and controlled. When asked what he does, or what he teaches, a person may formulate the information carefully. Typical reactions from outsiders are often clumsy or, worse yet, insulting. Remarks like "I never would

FIGURE 1
THE AMERICAN SPORT EXPERIENCE AND SOCIAL IDENTITY

I. *Through sport:*

  A. The Male Achieves, Derives, Pursues and Accepts:

      Prestige and Positive Social Identity

                                            +

  +   +

  least (aesthetic and noncontact)   most (strength and contact)

  B. The Female usually Acquires but can Avoid:

      Stigma and Negative Social Identity

                                            −

  −   −

  least (aesthetic and rhythmical)   most (strength and contact)

II. *Through dance:*

  A. The Female Achieves, Derives, Pursues and Accepts:

      Prestige and Positive Social Identity

  B. The Male Acquires and rarely Avoids:

      Stigma and Negative Social Identity

217

have guessed you were a dancer (to a male);" or "I wish there were more women athletes with your looks" are loaded with double meaning. Consequently, they set up tension within the recipient.

The media control information about women athletes in much the same way as individuals do. Either the media gives no information, or dresses up the message to be pretty, to be acceptable. Newspapers and magazines cover only selected sports for women, and most often show how attractive the woman is in her costume, rather than how skillful she is in action. *Women's Track and Field World Yearbook* (1968) is an extreme case in point. It emphasizes, through pictures and descriptions, the eyes, measurements, legs, and figures of the athletes as much as it does their athletic achievement. The captions read: "a woman athlete doesn't have to look like a horse to run like a thoroughbred;" "the lady with the alluring lips," "Diamond Lil is a darned attractive babe", and "the two sweetest dimples we've ever seen." The oversell of the femininity of these world class athletes is demeaning. They are presented as "super attractive" females as if they were competing in a beauty contest rather than competing in world class track and field. It is a way of protesting the masculine image and promoting the feminine one. There is never a need to sell male athletes in this way.

Finally, much effort is directed toward diminishing the tension created by the masculine attributes associated with women in sport, and the feminine attributes associated with male dancers. As meaningless, futile, and unnecessary as such behavior may seem to outsiders, it nevertheless continues endlessly. Women coaches often ask or require sports teams to wear dresses when travelling. Orientation meetings are held in many institutions, for the sole purpose of instructing women physical education majors in a special dress code. College women in history, drama, or sociology would not tolerate such humiliation. Men taking courses in dance may find wearing a leotard personally difficult, if not impossible. The stigma is heavy.

One woman college student illustrates the intensity of the conflict in the following statement: "The female athlete feels very unfeminine when she enters the male-dominated sports world. If she shows any athletic ability or correct technique, she is not praised because of ability or technique but because she can "move like a man." Our student then asks, "What does this do to the woman in sport? I can only answer that from my own feelings and those of my friends. It makes me question my own femininity—the very roots of my being. If I am a woman, why do I enjoy sport? Why do I participate?"

Women have not been publishing or writing about their sport experiences long enough for educators and the public to realize what meaning

the experiences carry for the woman athlete. Current writing is often elo-
quent in its expression of the inner struggle for identity. There is also a
drive to resolve the conflict, a drive reflected in a group of verses from the
poem "First Peace," by Barbara Lamblin:

> i was the all american girl, the winner, the champion,
> the swell kid, good gal, national swimmer,
> model of the prize daughter bringing it home for dad
> i even got the father's trophy
> i was also a jock, dyke, stupid dumb blond
> frigid, castrating, domineering bitch,
> called all these names in silence,
> the double standard wearing me down
> inside
> on the victory stand winning my medals
> for father and coach
> and perhaps a me deep down somewhere
> who couldn't fail because of all the hours
> and training and tears
> wrapped into an identity of muscle and power
> and physical strength
> a champion,
> not softness and grace
> now at 31, still suffering from the overheard
> locker room talk, from the bragging and swaggering
> the stares past my tank suit
> insults about my muscles
> the fears, the nameless fears
> about my undiscovered womanhood
> disturbing unknown femininity,
> femaleness
> feminine power.

The masculine-feminine game as now played needs careful and expert
study. It also needs to be called off in departments of physical education
and athletics.

In the preface to their book, *Masculine/Feminine: Readings in Sexual Mythology and the Liberation of Women* (1969), the Roszaks state with eloquence
and force:

He is playing the kind of man that he thinks the kind of woman she is playing ought to admire. She is playing the kind of woman that he thinks the kind of man he is playing ought to desire.

If he were not playing masculine, he might well be more feminine than she is—except when she is playing very feminine, she might well be more masculine than he is—except when he is playing very masculine. So he plays harder. And she plays . . . softer.

But the female athlete does not always play softer. She does not always lose on purpose. She may not always see it as a compliment to have her athletic endeavors compared with male records and then disregarded. The final result of role playing is emphasized by the Roszaks when they state: "He is becoming less and less what he wants to be. She is becoming less and less what she wants to be. But now he is more manly than ever, and she is more womanly than ever. Examples of this phenomenon in sport and dance populate gymnasiums and dance studios in American schools. The inflated male athlete, girl cheer leaders, song leaders, "major and minor" sports, women in approved sports and dance acting superior to women in "masculine" sports are only a few examples of the roles played. The Roszaks draw a conclusion and make a final plea to a society caught up in these social roles: "She is stifling under the triviality of her femininity. The world is groaning beneath the terrors of his masculinity. He is playing masculine. She is playing feminine. How do we call off the game?"

REFERENCES

Beisser, Arnold. *The Madness of Sport.* New York: Appleton-Century-Crofts, 1967.

Cevasco, Rose. "Femininity and the Woman Athlete." Unpublished student paper. California State University, Hayward, 1972.

Fiske, Shirley. "Pigskin Review: An American Initiation." In *Sport in the Socio-cultural Process,* edited by M. M. Hart. Dubuque, Iowa: Wm. C. Brown, 1972.

Goffman, Erving. *Stigma.* Englewood Cliffs, N.J.: Prentice-Hall, 1963.

Griffin, Patricia. "What's a Nice Girl Like You Doing in a Profession Like This?" *Quest* 14(1973):96–101.

Lamblin, Barbara. "First Peace." Unpublished poem. Hayward, California, 1973.

Roszak, Betty, and Roszak, Theodore. *Masculine/Feminine: Readings in Sexual Mythology and the Liberation of Women.* New York: Harper Colophon, 1969.

Women's Track and Field World Yearbook. Claremont, Calif.: Women's Track and Field World, 1968.

Contributors

MAL ANDREWS received his bachelor's and master's degrees from the University of Arizona at Tucson and, following some high school coaching experience, became head track coach at California State University, Hayward. He is well-known for his unusual approach to teaching track, with emphasis on the beauty of movement as expressed by the involvement of the whole body, soul, mind, and spirit. Now an Associate Professor in the department of Kinesiology and Physical Education, Cal. State University at Hayward, his major areas of development are the psychoblackology theory (the cultural identification of Black movement in physical education and sports), racism in sports, and sports as art.

221

RUTH BERKEY, Assistant Professor of Physical Education at Occidental College, obtained her bachelor's degree from Pepperdine College and her master's from the University of Southern California. From 1964-67 Mrs. Berkey served as Dean of Women to Occidental students. Currently she serves on the College Admission Committee. She was selected to Outstanding Young Women of America in 1970. Her outside interests include membership in the California Association of Health, P.E. and Recreation, the Western Society of College Physical Education for Women, and the American Association of Health, P.E. and Recreation. She is presently serving as Chairman of the Department of Physical Education at Occidental.

JOHN E. BILLING is Assistant Professor of Physical Education at the University of Connecticut. He received his Ph.D. from the University of New Mexico, where he was the recipient of a National Teaching Fellowship. Before taking his present position he served for six years as Chairman of the Department of Health, Physical Education and Recreation at the College of Santa Fe. Dr. Billing's research has been concerned with body composition and applied oxygen debt concepts.

GEORGE A. BROOKS. While studying for a Ph.D. at the University of Michigan, George Brooks became interested in problems of metabolic adjustments to exercise and other problems of metabolic regulation. At Michigan, and later at the Muscle Biology Research Laboratory at the University of Wisconsin, Dr. Brooks worked to elucidate the mitochondrial basis of post-exercise O_2 consumption (the O_2 debt) and the pathways of lactic acid metabolism after exercise. Now at the University of California, Berkeley, Dr. Brooks is looking forward to developing a high quality exercise physiology laboratory.

DORCAS SUSAN BUTT, Canadian-born, received her Ph.D. in clinical and research psychology from the University of Chicago. Since 1967 she has been an Assistant Professor in the Department of Psychology at the University of British Columbia. She is also Clinical Consultant in psychology at Riverview Hospital, Vancouver. Dr. Butt is the author of many publications in the area of personality measurement, delinquency, village structure, values and socialization. Currently Vice-President of the Canadian Lawn Tennis Association, she captained Canada's national women's tennis team in 1970, 1971, and 1972. As Canada's number one ranked woman player, she toured the international tennis circuit extensively between the ages of 19 and 23; from that time, she has observed and been concerned with the negative relationship between much competitive sports participation and constructive personal and social development, in addition to the social values which support that relationship.

GAY CHENEY is a dancer and choreographer who received her Ph. D. from the University of Southern California. She is now an Associate Professor of Physical Education at the California State University, Hayward, and, with Janet Strader, was co-author of *Modern Dance*. Her work in dance, influenced by D'Houbler, Ellfeldt, Slusher, Metheny, and Whitehouse, is based on the premise that the experience of an expressive, articulate body in intelligent and creative movement is the educational right of every human being.

BRYANT J. CRATTY is currently Professor of Kinesiology and Director of the Perceptual-Motor Learning Laboratory at the University of California at Los Angeles. His teaching has been chiefly concerned with motor learning, the psychology of athletics, and perceptual-motor education dealing with the movement problems of atypical children. Dr. Cratty has published between thirty and forty books and monographs, including *Movement and Spatial Awareness in Blind Children and Youth*, which has been translated into braille. Additionally, he has authored the "sensory-motor learning" section of the *Encyclopedia Britannica* and is an editor of the *Research Quarterly* and the *Journal of Motor Behavior*. Dr. Cratty has conducted workshops and symposia in 32 states of the Union as well as in eight foreign countries.

PAUL A. DANIELS graduated from the University of California in Berkeley in 1961 with a major in physical education and received his master's degree from San Francisco State College in 1964. He now holds both a general secondary teaching credential and an administrative credential. Mr. Daniels has been teaching physical education for the past eight years in the Berkeley, California, Unified School District, and is currently department chairman, athletic director, and varsity basketball coach at Berkeley High School.

DONALD B. DAVIES did his undergraduate work in physical education, health and biology at Springfield College and his graduate work in educational administration and physical education at the University of New Mexico, University of California and the University of Oregon. He has taught in the areas of physical education and health in the elementary, junior high, and high schools. He was the district coordinator of physical education at Berkeley and now has an administrative position at Los Altos

High School, California. Mr. Davies has managed a summer family camp and published articles on handball.

BLANCHE JESSEN DRURY, Professor Emeritus, retired in September 1972 from California State University, San Francisco, where she taught physical education for 27 years and developed the pre-physical therapy program. Dr. Drury is co-author with Dr. Andrea Schmid of *Gymnastics for Women* and of a new volume to be released in January 1973 entitled *Introduction to Gymnastics for Women*. She assisted in the development of the film, "Beauty in Motion," for the Olympic Development Committee, and has authored teaching phonograph recordings through the Hoctor Recording Company, in addition to several other publications. In 1963, Dr. Drury was one of the California representatives to the first National Conference on Girls and Women's Sports; in 1966 she was one of the California representatives to the Joseph P. Kennedy Physical Fitness Workshop for the Mentally Retarded, at Brigham Young University. She has served on the Advisory Board for the Recreation Center for the Handicapped in San Francisco. In 1968 Dr. Drury received the Bay District CAHPER Distinguished Service Award, and in 1972 was given the State CAHPER Verne S. Landreth Honorary Life Membership Award.

HOLLIS F. FAIT has been professor of Physical Education at the University of Connecticut, Storrs, since 1954, having received his Ph.D. from the University of Iowa in 1951. Among his many affiliations is membership in the Task Force on Programs for the Handicapped; he is also a Fellow of the American College of Sports Medicine, and of AAHPER. Dr. Fait has a large number of publications to his credit, including *Curriculum Guide for Teaching Physical Education to the Profoundly and Severely Mentally Retarded* (1969), and *Teachers Guide for Teaching Physical Education to the Elementary School Child* (1970). He has conducted considerable research into the problems of mentally and physically handicapped children and adults.

JAN FELSHIN is a professor and Coordinator of Graduate Studies in Professional Physical Education at East Stroudsburg State College, Pennsylvania. Her new work, *MORE THAN MOVEMENT: An Introduction to Physical Education,* is a significant contribution to the profession. She is also well known for her work in sport theory, with particular attention to the relationship of sport and society.

KATHILEEN A. GALLAGHER is currently an Assistant Professor of Physical Education at the University of San Francisco. She received her master's degree from California State University, San Francisco, where her emphasis was in dance. She is presently Vice President-Dance for the San Francisco unit of CAHPER. Her most recent workshops have been in yoga and in the use of videotape for choreography and the teaching of dance. For the past four summers she has directed gymnastics and dance for girls in the NCAA-sponsored National Summer Youth Sports Program held at the University of San Francisco. Recently, her interest in yoga and other relaxation techniques has led her to research in biofeedback and its potential for physical education.

MARIE HART, an Associate Professor in the Department of Kinesiology and Physical Education at California State University, Hayward, has written many articles on women in sport. In 1972 she edited an anthology entitled *Sport in the Socio-Cultural Process.* Dr. Hart has enjoyed wide teaching experience in public and private schools, junior college, and private and state universities. She spent a year traveling and teaching in the South Pacific and New Zealand early in her career, and received her Ph.D. from the University of Southern California in 1967.

FRED W. KASCH developed a three-minute step test in Chicago at La Rabida Cardiac Hospital for use in evaluating the effects of rheumatic fever in children. After moving to San Diego in 1948, he was primarily responsible for the development of the gymnastics program in the public schools and received the Breitbard Foundation Award for achievement in physical education. Working with several investigators, he developed foot and postural evaluations and therapeutic exercise techniques for asthmatics and the mentally retarded. Studies followed on congenital heart disease in children and the use of therapeutic exercise in controlling hypertension in adults. With Ira H. Wilson, M.D., Dr. Kasch developed therapeutic swimming methods for use in a variety of diseases; with John L. Boyer, M.D., he initiated a coronary heart disease rehabilitation unit in San Diego. Having founded the Adult Fitness Program in 1958, he then published a book entitled *Adult Fitness,* in collaboration with Dr. Boyer. In 1968 Dr. Kasch received the President's Council fitness award, which was presented to him by President Johnson in Washington, D.C. His wide research has resulted in many publications delineating the use of exercise to combat disease.

NEIL T. LAUGHLIN is Assistant Professor of Health and Physical Education at the University of San Francisco. He is presently doing research on drug   225 usage among athletes, the effect of teacher beliefs on student performance, and sensitivity training. He is also interested in the implications of existential philosophy for physical education and sport. A fourth degree black belt, he still actively competes in judo. Dr. Laughlin received his Ed.D. from Stanford University.

PAUL A. METZGER has taught physical education at all grade levels from kindergarten through graduate school. He spent several years directing the elementary physical education program in Audubon, New Jersey, one year at Kansas State Teachers college and two years at the University of North Carolina before assuming his present position as chairman of the department of health and physical education at John F. Kennedy High School in Willingboro, New Jersey. He is the author of a book of readings entitled *Elementary Physical Education*. While teaching in Kansas, Dr. Metzger developed a program for the Emporia elementary schools in which physical education majors did the actual teaching.

MUSKA MOSSTON relinquished the post of Chairman of the Department of Kinesiology at Rutgers University in order to direct the Teaching Behavior Institute in Somerville, New Jersey. His major crusade is for innovative instruction, "new ways of looking at ourselves and our relationships with students"; to this purpose he has given 300 workshops and seminars in over thirty states and in five provinces of Canada, covering physical education, special education and educational psychology. The author of several books on movement education and teaching, Dr. Mosston's latest publication is *Teaching: From Command to Discovery* (Wadsworth, 1972). In 1967 he received the Author Award from the New Jersey Association of English Teachers, and the following year, the Honor Award from the New Jersey Association of Health, Physical Education and Recreation. Dr. Mosston is the creator of the "Spectrum of Teaching Styles."

RUDOLF MUELLER, presently a faculty member at East Stroudsburg State College in Pennsylvania and formerly of the College of Arts and Science at Rutgers University, has been involved with teacher education for the past twelve years. Previous to this he was a public school teacher, coach, director of Athletics, chairman of the Health and Physical Education Department, director of education for handicapped children and consultant to a number of educational projects. He is currently completing his doctoral degree in the area of Educational Leadership with a concentration in Human Development.

Professor Mueller has published a number of works, including *Developmental Movement and Basketball—Phase 1, Phase 2 and Phase 3; Looking at Movement Education;* Introduction chapter to *Thinking and Moving; An Educational Climate for Children Who Cannot; Mom, Dad and the B.I. Child.* He is also president of the Teaching Behavior Institute, Inc., a company dedicated to the improvement of instruction. Their concern is to make teaching a more conscious act where the teacher's behavior is both prescriptive and descriptive; where teachers realize that what they do is directly responsible for the kind of process and the resulting outcomes.

BRUCE C. OGILVIE is a Professor of Psychology at California State University, San Jose, and is also psychological consultant for twelve NFL teams, fourteen National Baseball teams and six NBA teams. A Fellow of several prestigious organizations, Dr. Ogilvie is also co-director of the Institute for the Study of Athletic Motivation, and was psychological consultant for the 1964, 1968 and 1972 Olympic teams. He was a recipient of the Distinguished Teaching Award, California State Colleges, in 1966. Ogilvie has published forty articles in the area of sport and sport motivations. One of his more recent articles, written in collaboration with Thomas Tutko, was "Success Phobia," published in the October 1971 issue of *Swimming Techniques.*

WILLIAM PAUL graduated in social science from San Francisco State University. His serious interest in sport-judo, and Asian disciplines such as Chinese *chuan fa* led him to study for two years in Japan. In Tokyo he attended Tokyo University and the Kodokan judo college, where he was a member of the International Research Group or *Kenshusei.* While in Tokyo he was employed as an English instructor and free-lance journalist. As an athlete, Mr. Paul has represented the United States in judo several times, and in 1967 was named A.A.U. All-American. For the past two years, Mr. Paul has directed a summer youth program involving sports as a medium for drug education, interracial communciation, and the redirection of violence. He is currently teaching physical education at the University of San Francisco and at San Francisco State University.

BENJAMIN RICCI is the author of three books on physiology, including *Experiments in the Physiology of Human Performance* (Lea & Febiger, 1970), and   227 numerous articles published in American and European scientific journals, in addition to presenting papers at international scientific meetings. His professional affiliations include Sigma Xi, Phi Kappa Phi, and the American College of Sports Medicine. Dr. Ricci has conducted post-doctoral study in physiology in the School of Medicine at the University of Milan, Italy (1963) and at the Institute of Work Physiology, Oslo, Norway (1971). He was the recipient of a Fulbright award in 1971.

RICHARD S. RIVENES serves as the Coordinator of Graduate Studies, Department of Kinesiology and Physical Education, California State University, Hayward. His academic specialty is learning and performance variables affecting motor skill, and his research in the fields of retention of skill, transfer, and kinesthetic performance may be found in various journals concerned with these topics. Dr. Rivenes received his Ph.D. from Pennsylvania State University in 1964.

JACK SCOTT is Chairman and Athletic Director at Oberlin College in Ohio. He received his Ph.D. from the University of California at Berkeley, and prior to his move to Oberlin he was director of the Institute for the Study of Sport and Society in Berkeley. In addition to many articles, Dr. Scott has recently published two books; *Athletics for Athletes* and *The Athletic Revolution*, and is an editor of the widely read magazine *Ramparts.*

DARYL L. SIEDENTOP is an Associate Professor of Physical Education at Ohio State University and the author of five books and several articles on sports and physical education. One of his most recent publications is "On Tilting at Windmills while Rome Burns: The Mixed Metaphor of Teacher Training in Contemporary physical education," published in *Quest,* June 1972. Currently, Dr. Siedentop's chief areas of research are the applications of behavioral psychology to physical education, sport, and play theory. He is a member of several national societies of physical and health education, and of sports psychology. In 1971 he received an *Outstanding Young Men of America* citation.

CHRISTOPHER L. STEVENSON received his doctorate in the School of Education, Stanford University, California. He obtained an undergraduate degree in biology at the University of London, England, and a master's degree in physical education at the University of British Columbia, Vancouver, Canada. His interests and publications lie in the area of the sociology of sport, and especially in socialization and its consequences for institutions He is presently Assistant Professor of Physical Education at the University of California, Berkeley.

228